ATHLETICS
OF THE ANCIENT
WORLD

SPECIAL DIRECTIONS FOR THE USE
OF THIS EDITION

All the plates of the original edition are now grouped together at the end of this book. The majority of the captions, however, remain on their original pages. Use of the following sigla will enable the reader to locate a particular plate in the back.

1) In the *List of Illustrations* (pp xvi-xviii) a small circle° indicates that the illustration has been moved to the plate section at the end of the volume, eg. °*facing page 10.*

   A small square ▢ following the page number indicates that the descriptive caption belonging to the plate remains on its original page.

2) In the text two special symbols have been employed to to indicate that a particular illustration, whose caption alone appears on a page, must be searched for in the plate section at the end.

   ☛= All illustrations whose captions appear on this page will be found in the plate section.

   ◀= This particular illustration will be found in the plate section.

ATHLETICS
OF THE
ANCIENT WORLD

By

E. NORMAN GARDINER, D.LITT.

With a Preface to the American Edition
By
PROF. STEPHEN G. MILLER

ARES PUBLISHERS, INC.
CHICAGO MCMLXXXVII

First American Edition 1978
Reprinted 1980
Reprinted 1982
Reprinted 1987

Enlarged Reprint of the Edition:
Oxford 1930
ARES PUBLISHERS INC.
7020 N. Western Ave.
Chicago, IL 60645-3416

Printed in the U.S.A.
International Standard Book Number
0-89005-257-3

PREFACE TO THE AMERICAN EDITION

Nearly half a century has passed since the original appearance of E. Norman Gardiner's *Athletics of the Ancient World.* In the interval many discoveries have been made which ought to have rendered Gardiner's work obsolete; many books have been written on the subject which ought to have replaced *Athletics of the Ancient World.* It has, however, not been replaced as is shown not only by this, but also by previous reprints in 1955, 1965, 1967, and 1971, all of which have sold out making the book once more unavailable. The principal reason for the continued usefulness of *AAW* lies with its author. E. Norman Gardiner was recognized during his own lifetime as the unrivaled authority on Greek Athletics. Between 1903 and 1924 he wrote nearly a dozen articles (mostly in the *Journal of Hellenic Studies*) dealing with a variety of specific problems in ancient athletics. In 1910 he brought forth his *Greek Athletic Sports and Festivals* which, like *AAW*, remains today a very useful book, although it too might be thought of as hopelessly outdated. Gardiner's *Olympia: Its History and Remains* (1925) is still the best book in English upon that topic despite the more recent appearance of other books such as *Olympia* by Ludwig Drees (1968). The timelessness of Gardiner's work lies, then, partly in his enormous learning. It lies even more, however, in his ability to write intelligibly for both the interested layman and the specialized scholar. The status of our knowledge is made clear, the source of information obvious, problems well defined, but never to the confusion of the reader. His learning sits gracefully upon his lucid prose, and one recognizes that Gardiner knew his subject matter intimately, cared for it tremendously, and wanted to share it generously.

Nonetheless, Gardiner did occasionally err and more recent discoveries bring near the time when *AAW* must be redone. Indeed, several books have appeared since 1960 which might be thought to rectify the situation. First among these may be placed the monumental work of Julius Jüthner, a near contemporary of Gardiner, whose work, originally planned for six volumes, was only published posthumously in two volumes: *Die athletischen Leibesübungen der Griechen* (Vienna 1965 and 1968). Despite the efforts of the editor, F. Brein, this work all too frequently reveals its incomplete state at the time of its author's death. Furthermore, the illustrative material, although copious, is of indifferent quality and often random in both selection and effect.

In certain respects, the successor to Gardiner has been another English scholar, H.A. Harris. Yet Harris himself admits in his *Greek Athletes and Athletics* (1964) that his work did not supersede Gardiner's monumental works. Harris' opinion was quite correct due, at least in part, to his admitted aim toward a readership other than "those who know a great deal about ancient Greece but nothing about its athletics." As so often, lowered targets produced lowered scores. Nonetheless, Harris did make a significant contribution in that he examined the evidence for many individual ancient athletes and their careers, although more could be done even in this respect. Harris' sequel, *Sport in Greece and Rome* (1972), is concerned largely with Rome and with activities other than athletics. In other words, Harris kept the torch aflame but did not advance it far.

In 1972, another general book appeared, this by R. Patrucco, *Lo Sport nella Grecia Antica*. Produced in limited quantities, this large and lavishly published book is little known outside Italy. The author's treatment of the material is uneven, showing good insight in some cases and great superficiality in others. There are also a few outright mistakes, although the ideas advanced seem, on balance, to offset them.

As has tended to be the case in modern Olympic years, two more general books appeared in 1976. One of these, *The Olympic Games* by M.I. Finley and H.W. Pleket, is aimed exclusively at a popular audience and has virtually no references to ancient and modern evidence. Indeed, much evidence is ignored, although significant new "demythologizing" theories are advanced, largely due to Pleket's interest in and work upon the sociology and ideology of ancient athletics. However, the arguments on behalf of, and the evidence for, these theories are presented in articles published elsewhere by Pleket (see further below).

The other book of 1976 was *The Olympic Games through the Ages* (ed. N. Yialouris). This is a large "coffeetable" book with many splendid color photographs of ancient material and a useful summary of the history of the modern Olympics. The text, although written by several different scholars, is well done, but again there are virtually no references to the evidence. Furthermore, the price of this book makes it prohibitively expensive to all save the fortunately wealthy or the desperately interested.

Thus *Athletics of the Ancient World* remains the most useful text on the subject for the serious student and the English speaking layman alike. But there is much new evidence since Gardiner's time thanks largely to archaeological excavations, and especially those at the four panhellenic sanctuaries. This evidence can only be superficially indicated here, but it will hopefully serve to guide the student to the appropriate bibliographic starting points.

Even though most of the major excavation at Olympia was done by the end of the last century, certain details were unknown to Gardiner. The most significant of these were in the stadium where the excavations were not completed until the 1950's. Thus, although Gardiner knew and could make use of the starting lines at either end of the track (fig. 84), he did not know of the judges' stand and the significance of its location.[1] In addition, more recent scholarship has been able to establish certain details about the Olympic Games. For example, the statement on page 223 about the time of the games must now be changed to read: "The festival took place every four years, on the second full moon after the summer solstice, in the months of July or August."[2]

The excavations at Delphi were completed by Gardiner's time, but the formal publication has been very slow to appear. Thus, the Palaestra-Gymnasium complex (figs. 39, 40) was published only in 1953[3] and the formal publication of the stadium has yet to be seen although recent work augurs well for this.[4] This meant that many details of construction and chronology were obscure for Gardiner. This was an obvious handicap as was the lack of a full publication of the important third century inscription which records preparations for the Pythian Games. Working from a preliminary publication of 1899, Gardiner was able to include several significant facts (pp. 132-133), but a recent study and full publication has revealed several more facts from the inscription as well as necessitating corrections in some of Gardiner's conclusions.[5] Again, certain aspects of the Pythian Games and their history have been scrutinized with results relevant for Gardiner's work. For example, Gardiner used the generally accepted date of 582 B.C. for the beginning of the Pythian era (p. 36), but that date is surely incorrect and must be replaced by 586.[6] This means that several victories by athletes must be updated by four years.

For Isthmia, Gardiner was almost completely without physical evidence since the excavations there began only in 1952 under the guidance of Professor Oscar Broneer of the University of Chicago. Those excavations have produced results of great importance for our understanding of ancient athletics and their development. First and foremost, Broneer's discovery of the earlier Isthmian stadium revealed several significant facts.[7] The location of that early stadium is very close to the Temple of Poseidon which shows a physical tie between ancient religion and athletics. This tie had long been noted, but the graphic situation

---

[1] A. Mallwitz, *Olympia und seine Bauten* (Munich 1972) 180-193.
[2] S.G. Miller, "The Date of Olympic Festivals," *Ath. Mitt.* 90 (1975) 215-231.
[3] J. Jannory, *Fouilles de Delphes II, Le Gymnase* (Paris 1953).
[4] P. Aupert, *BCH* 98 (1974) 783 .
[5] J. Pouilloux, "Travaux à Delphes à l'occasion des Pythia," *BCH Suppl. IV. Études Delphiques* (1977) 103-123.
[6] S.G. Miller, "The Date of the First Pythiad," *CSCA* forthcoming.
[7] O. Broneer, *Isthmia II* (Princeton 1973) 46-66.

at Isthmia makes us realize the strength of the bond. The early stadium at Isthmia also provides evidence for an informal and relatively small seating area for spectators throughout the fifth century B.C. The point that athletics in the Classical period were less of a spectator sport than later was again thus driven home. Later stadia with elaborate seating arrangements reveal the evolution of the relationship of athletics and society away from one of relatively full participation toward one of specialization and professionalism.

Most important of all Broneer's discoveries, in an athletic sense at least, was that of the starting arrangements for the foot race in his early stadium. This is a unique example consisting of a triangular paved area with the running lanes marked out by sockets for vertical wooden posts along the long side of the triangle. At the peak of the triangle is a circular "manhole". Radiating from this hole back toward the long side in the surface of the paving are a series of grooves, one to each post socket, with a bronze staple at each end of each groove. The interpretation of this discovery by Broneer, surely correct in general outline, is that of arrangements for a starting mechanism for the footraces with a hinged bar from each vertical post across each lane. The bars are dropped, and the race started, by a judge in the "manhole" either releasing or pulling upon the strings which ran through the grooves and staples to each post. This arrangement is unique and is the earliest physical evidence for mechanisms for starting the races. It sheds important light upon such mechanisms and their functioning although there is some controversy about whether it is to be identified with the *hysplex* or the *balbis*;[8] indeed, the confusion of these two terms was current already in antiquity and we are not yet in a position to apply either label with security.

The work at Isthmia led Broneer to re-examine another problem regarding the Isthmian crown of victory. As known by Gardiner and long before, the victory crown at Isthmia was of pine (p. 36), although there were some ancient references to a crown of dry parsley in imitation of the fresh parsley crown at Nemea. Broneer has been able to show that the crown at Isthmia actually did change from pine to parsley early in the fifth century B.C., and back to pine again in, probably, the second century B.C.[9] This curious change in the victory crown almost certainly has a bearing upon the political background of the ancient games, even though its exact cause and significance are not yet clear.

The final major contribution of the Isthmian excavations to our understanding of ancient athletics came with Broneer's discovery of another, later stadium located at some distance from the Temple of Poseidon. It is most unfortunate

---

[8] Broneer, *op. cit.* 137-142.
[9] O. Broneer, "The Isthmian Victory Crown," *AJA* 66 (1962) 259-263.

that Broneer was unable to acquire the privately owned property where this stadium is located. Thus, Broneer was restricted to a series of test trenches which revealed the general outline of the stadium, but few of its details. It is clear that this stadium was constructed in the second half of the fourth century B.C., and that it provided a significant increase in seating facilities for spectators at the Isthmian Games. Once again, a change in the relationship between athletics and society is indicated. As the analogies between Isthmia and Nemea are increasingly revealed, the inability to study the later stadium at Isthmia becomes more frustrating. To walk through the fields at Isthmia today and to know that a few feet of earth lie between one's own feet and the floor of the ancient stadium, to know that significant details of the athletic facility are so near, is an intolerable situation. Every student of ancient athletics must hope that the situation will change.

As at Isthmia, the information available to Gardiner from Nemea was virtually non-existent. That situation is now changing as the University of California at Berkeley carries on its excavations at Nemea under the direction of this writer. Those excavations are not yet complete, but several discoveries have already increased the evidence for several aspects of ancient athletics.[10] First of all, it appears that the situation at Nemea was quite similar to that at Isthmia with the earlier stadium near the Temple of Zeus.[11] The precise location of that stadium has not been uncovered as of this writing, but it can be anticipated within the next few years. Again, as at Isthmia, Nemea saw a new stadium constructed at some distance from the Temple of Zeus in the second half of the fourth century B.C. This stadium also, as at Isthmia, provided an expanded seating capacity, although not on a level of formality comparable to, for example, the Roman seats in the stadium at Delphi. That is, the seats at Nemea were formed by carving out a series of ledges in the soft bedrock of the hill around the stadium, and only the lowest of these were covered with cut stone seats.

Along the sides of the race track at Nemea run stone channels, characteristic of nearly all stadia, which brought fresh drinking water to athlete and spectator. At intervals of 100 ancient feet (29.63 m. at Nemea) along both sides of the race track are set markers, similar to those noted by Gardiner at Epidauros (p. 129), which were visual aids for runner, judge, and spectator. Along one side of the track there have appeared the foundations for the judges' stand in a position similar to that at Olympia. The starting line at Nemea is similar to most others in ancient stadia; it has the typical double groove for the athlete's feet and sockets for vertical posts, but it has an additional feature in a later

---

[10] See the annual preliminary reports in *Hesperia* beginning in 1975.
[11] D.G. Romano, "The Early Stadium at Nemea," *Hesperia* 46 (1977) 27-31.

added projecting stone at either end of the line. Similar projections have been found in the later stadium at Isthmia, in the Forum at Corinth, and in the stadium at Epidauros.[12] All of these are clearly beddings for a mechanism for starting the race although the precise working of these mechanisms is not yet clear.

For the student of ancient athletics, the most significant discovery at Nemea to date has been the stone base for a single turning post or *kampter*. This base is located near the south end of the track, level with the track's surface, about 5.30 m. north of the starting line and 3.40 m. west of the center of the track. Although the northern end of the Nemea stadium appears to be eroded, the mate for the southern base may still be found there. This single turning post thus forces a modification in our understanding of the turns in the foot races. While Gardiner's conclusion (p. 137) seems still correct that the runners in the *diaulos* each turned individual posts, those in the long distance *dolichos* must all have turned a single post. This conclusion has been argued at greater length elsewhere,[13] and it accords well with a variety of ancient evidence including vase paintings such as one presented by Gardiner (fig. 92). In other words, we can now understand that the different lengths of ancient foot races, as of modern, required variations in their performances.

One more discovery at Nemea should be mentioned, although it may be slightly premature. In 1977 the entrance to the Nemea stadium was discovered, but only a part of it has been excavated at this writing. Nonetheless, several dozen fragments of bronze sculpture have already been found in the entrance, and more will almost certainly appear during the excavations of 1978. These remind us of the Zanes, or statues of Zeus, set up at Olympia from the fines imposed upon athletes who had been involved with bribery (p. 103). Nemea may thus provide additional evidence of ancient corruption and its penalties.

In addition to the new discoveries from the four panhellenic centers, excavations elsewhere have revealed evidence for athletic practices. Halieis, in the extreme eastern Argolid, has revealed a stadium with an extremely short track of 168 m.[14] It is not clear, however, whether this is a formal competition athletic track, a practice track, or one to be associated with religious ceremonies. The formal publication is awaited.

Four other running tracks must also be studied and added to those discussed by Gardiner. These are at Didyma, Miletus, and Priene in Asia Minor[15] and in

---

[12] Broneer, *Isthmia* II, plates 96-98.

[13] S.G. Miller, "Lanes and Turns in the Ancient Stadium" *AJA* forthcoming.

[14] M.H. Jameson, "The Excavation of a Drowned Greek Temple," *Scientific American* (October 1974) 111-119.

[15] G.E. Bean, *Aegean Turkey* (London 1966) 242-243, 229, 207-210, respectively.

the Athenian Agora.[16] These four tracks are particularly significant because they all lack, in their original phases, the characteristic continuous stone starting line. Rather, all four of these have a row of separate stone bases for individual posts. Do these represent an ethnic (in this case Ionic) variation in athletic practices? Are these strictly athletic facilities or are they perhaps to be understood as ritual in character as for torch races (pp. 142-143)? Whatever the answer, it must be incorporated in Gardiner's framework.

In addition to these discoveries, other more specific work by different scholars must also be recognized. In the realm of the lists of Olympic victors, the work of L. Moretti, *Olympionikai* (1957), has been most important.[17] Unfortunately, no similar work has been done on updating the lists of victors at the other three panhellenic sites despite very considerable new evidence since the collection of J.H. Krause, *Die Pythien, Nemeen, und Isthmien* (1841).

Gardiner's section on the palaestra and gymnasium (pp. 72-85) needs to be updated due partly to discoveries and partly to publications since his time. Most notable is the study by J. Delorme, *Gymnasion* (1960), although this work too now needs some revision. It is also within the context of the palaestra that more account must be taken of baths and bathing, and here the work of Rene Ginouvès, *Balaneutikè* (1962), is of help.

So too, Gardiner's section on the method of deciding the victory in the pentathlon (pp. 178-180) needs to be updated. This difficult problem, about which Gardiner clearly felt less than secure, remains unanswered today although it has been extensively argued. There has been some new, but inconclusive, evidence upon the problem, and thus, even though the issue is far from settled, the more recent evidence and arguments will have to be incorporated into Gardiner's account.[18]

Finally, recent work by H.W. Pleket on the sociology and ideology of ancient athletics must be recognized.[19] In this respect, Gardiner may be fairly said to reflect those attitudes which gave rise to the modern Olympics with their (original?) emphasis on idealism and amateurism. One can best see this on pages 66-71, but Gardiner had to admit (pp. 99-106) that, long before professionalism took away the idea of competition for its own sake, the potential for abuses, and real abuses, existed. Within the seeds of professionalism were also to be found the seeds of corruption. Pleket has taken us a step further and has shown

---

[16] T.L. Shear, Jr., "The Athenian Agora: Excavations of 1973-1974," *Hesperia* 44 (1975) 363-364.

[17] See also L. Moretti, "Supplemento al catalogo degli Olympionikai," *Klio* 52 (1970) 295-303.

[18] For the most recent debate and references to earlier arguments, see R. Merkelbach, "Der Sieg im Pentathlon," *ZPE* 11 (1973) 261-269, and J. Ebert, "Noch einmal zum Sieg im Pentathlon," *ZPE* 13 (1974) 257-262.

[19] H.W. Pleket, "Games, Prizes, Athletics and Ideology," *Arena* I, 1 (1975) 48-89.

that, even though there was no professionalism *per se* in Archaic and Classical Greece, there was no true amateurism either. Most of the victors at the panhellenic games at that time clearly came from wealthy families and thus had the leisure to practice their athletic specialties. They were also free to travel to the Games, and they had enjoyed a superior diet from infancy which provided a subtle advantage to them. Furthermore, at least at Athens, the practice of giving free meals for life to an athlete victorious at any of the four penhellenic festivals meant, in effect, that the athlete was state-supported for any subsequent victories he might win. We must also remember that the sculptors Myron and Polykleitos (pp. 64-65), through whose statues we see an ideal of ancient athletes, did not carve their sculpture for free; neither did Pindar (pp. 68-71) compose his victory odes without pay. The reader with a natural idealistic tendency and hope may be reluctant to accept such a verdict, but it seems to be correct and we must realize that amateurism is a modern concept. Anyone who knows the tragic history of Jim Thorpe will agree. On the base of Thorpe's posthumous statue in a small town in Pennsylvania are inscribed the words, first spoken by the Swedish King Gustav when he presented Thorpe with his medals at the 1912 Olympics: "Sir, you are the most wonderful athlete in the world." We should add: "Sir, you were the victim of an ancient ideal which never existed."

There must be a new *Athletics of the Ancient World* which will make use of the material outlined above, but until the excavations at Nemea are complete such a book would be premature. In the meantime we can be grateful that the old *Athletics of the Ancient World* is once again available to us, and I can hope that the references provided above will aid the student of antiquity.

University of California
   at Berkeley, March 22, 1978   Stephen G. Miller

PREFACE

IN the following pages I have attempted to give a short and simple account of the history and practice of athletics in the ancient world which will appeal to all who are interested in athletics and be of use too to students of the past. As far as Greece is concerned the book is based on my *Greek Athletic Sports and Festivals*, published in 1910. But the present work is both shorter and simpler. Much matter of purely historical or archaeological interest has been omitted. In particular I have not tried to give the details and history of the various athletic festivals of Greece, nor in a book dealing with athletics have I thought it necessary to devote a special chapter to chariot- and horse-racing. But the work is no mere abridgement of my earlier book. New material has been incorporated throughout. I have endeavoured to deal more fully with the traces of athletics to be found among other peoples of the ancient world, and I have included a chapter upon Ball-play. For the benefit of those who are not classical scholars I have given in the Index explanations of the commonest Greek technical terms. For students, I hope I have provided sufficient guidance in the notes and bibliography.

The illustrations are a special feature of this work. Our knowledge of Greek athletics is largely derived from the representations of athletes and athletic scenes in Greek Art, especially in vase-paintings. The greatest pains have been taken to select the most suitable monuments and only those that are authentic and to ensure that they are faithfully reproduced in the illustrations. For this purpose photography has been employed as far as possible, and many photographs have been taken expressly for this work. The grouping of the illustrations will, it is hoped, prove helpful to the general reader, and also be of value to the student. For the latter, full notes are provided giving dates, references, and other details, and also a special Index of Museum references.

The interest of ancient athletics to us lies largely in the

numerous parallels that we find in them to the athletics of our own day. We can still perhaps learn something from the Greek athletic ideal; we can certainly learn much from the history of Greek athletics and the causes that led to their decline. Many of the evils that led to that decline are but too apparent in some forms of sport to-day. Attempts are frequently made to compare the performances of ancient and modern athletes. All such attempts are futile: the evidence does not exist. But the drawings on Greek vases do enable us to form some idea of the style of Greek athletes, and for purposes of comparison I have placed beside these drawings photographs of modern runners and jumpers. I have also included illustrations of the athletic bronzes of my friend, Dr. R. Tait McKenzie. They are the nearest modern parallel to the athletic art of Greece.

My obligations to the many archaeologists at home and abroad who have furnished me with illustrations are acknowledged in the notes. Above all I am indebted to Professor Beazley, not only for providing me with many photographs, but for his constant help in selecting my illustrations and for revising my notes upon them. My thanks are also due to my friend, Mr. Ernest I. Robson, for the care that he has taken in reading my proofs.

E. N. G.

OXFORD,
June 1930.

CONTENTS

LIST OF ILLUSTRATIONS

The figure on the title-page represents a winged runner, probably one of the sons of Boreas. It is taken from a Nolan Amphora recently acquired by the British Museum, published in *B.C.H.* xxiii, p. 160.

I

INTRODUCTION

THE MEANING OF ATHLETICS

THE story of ancient athletics is the story of Greek athletics. The Greeks, as far as we know, were the only truly athletic nation of antiquity. To them we owe the word 'athlete' and the ideal that it expresses. This does not mean that the Greeks were the inventors of the various sports and games that we describe as athletic. The love of play is universal in all young things. Running, jumping, throwing various objects, fighting are common to children of all races and all times. But play is not athletics, though the instinct of play is undoubtedly one of their motives, and recreation is an important element therein. The child plays till he is tired and then leaves off. The competitor in a race goes on after he is tired, goes on to the point of absolute exhaustion; he even trains himself painfully in order to be capable of greater and more prolonged effort and of exhausting himself more completely. Why does he do this? Why does he take pleasure in what is naturally painful?

The idea of effort is the very essence of athletics as the Greeks understood the term and as we understand it; it is indeed inherent in the word itself. For the Greek word from which athlete is derived has two forms, a masculine form (ἆθλος) usually meaning a contest, and a neuter form (ἆθλον), usually denoting the prize of the contest. Of these two meanings there can be no doubt that the idea of contest is the earlier and root-meaning, for it determines the meaning of the words derived from it. The word is used by Homer to describe the ten years' struggle of the Trojan War; it is used of the labours of Heracles. This meaning of the word is clearest in the adjective (ἄθλιος) formed from it, which from meaning 'struggling', 'contesting' comes to mean 'miserable', 'wretched'. We find this same feeling in Homer when he describes boxing and wrestling as 'grievous' (ἀλεγεινός), an epithet which he also uses of war and battle. Yet the Homeric warrior delights in these grievous contests, and Pindar describes the athlete as one 'who delights in the toil and the cost'.[1] We too have the same feelings. The game that appeals to every true athlete,

---

[1] *I.* v. 10.

the game that he delights in, one that he remembers when his playing days are over, is 'the hard game', the game that puts to the utmost test all his physical powers and all his skill.

But why does the athlete delight in the grievous contest? Why do we enjoy a hard game? The athlete is one who competes for something, but it is certainly not the material value of the prize that attracts him. The prize may be an ox, or a woman skilled in fair handicraft, a tripod, or a cup, but the most coveted prize in the Greek world was the wreath of wild olive which was the only prize at the Olympic Games. The real prize is the honour of victory. The motive that turns his effort into joy is the desire to put to the test his physical powers, the desire to excel. It is not every people any more than every individual that feels this joy in the contest, in the effort. The athletic spirit cannot exist where conditions of life are too soft and luxurious; it cannot exist where conditions are too hard and where all the physical energies are exhausted in a constant struggle with the forces of man or nature. It is found only in physically vigorous and virile nations that put a high value on physical excellence: it arises naturally in those societies where the power is in the hands of an aristocracy which depends on military skill and physical strength to maintain itself. Here are developed the love of fighting and the love of glory, and here we find the beginnings of athletics in wrestling, boxing, and other forms of combat which are the training of the young and the recreation of the warriors. Such were the conditions among the Homeric Achaeans, and probably among many of the tribes of central Europe. But for the tradition which the Greeks inherited from the Achaeans the later development of Greek athletics would have been impossible. And we may doubt whether the modern athletic movement would ever have taken place but for the spirit handed down to us by our Anglo-Saxon ancestors.

In the following chapters we shall trace the causes that led to the astonishing development of athletics among the Greeks. Chief among these was the desire to excel. No people has ever been dominated to such an extent by this desire as the Greeks were; no people has ever been so fond of competition. Competition entered into every department of their life. They had competitions in music, drama, poetry, art, even beauty competitions. But stimulating as was the spirit of competition and wonderful as were the results that it produced, it was and is a dangerous motive when uncontrolled. It was akin to that spirit of individualism which was the bane of Greek politics. We may doubt if team games could ever have acquired the same popularity among the Greeks as individual contests. Nor was the worship of success always compatible with the feeling of generosity towards the defeated, or scrupulousness as to the means of obtaining victory. Over-competition, as we shall see, led only too soon to specialization and professionalism with its attendant evils: it proved fatal to the true amateur spirit.

Before we proceed to the story of Greek athletics, let us briefly see what traces we can find of athletics in the great civilizations of the East.

II

SPORTS OF THE ANCIENT EAST

EGYPT

O F the popularity of games among the Egyptians from the earliest times we have abundant evidence in the paintings of their tombs. The walls of Beni-Hassan in particular present us with a truly marvellous display of games and sports.

With the sedentary games we are not here concerned except so far as they illustrate the antiquity of the games which have been popular at all times in the Mediterranean, especially of games of chance. It does not follow that we must look for the origin of these games to Egypt; rather it seems that they are the common property of the whole Mediterranean world, and possibly, if we had fuller knowledge of the Sumerians, we should find the same games among them. Here a few examples must suffice. One of the oldest and most widespread games is draughts. We have the draughtboard and draughtsmen that the Egyptians used, and Cnossos has yielded up a beautifully inlaid draught-board. We have a picture of Rameses III seated on a throne and playing draughts with a lady, perhaps his queen, who is standing opposite. He is in the act of moving one of the men. We remember too how in the *Odyssey* Athena found the suitors seated before the palace, taking their pleasure in draughts. A late terra-cotta group from Athens shows us a young Athenian and a woman quarrelling over a game of draughts, while an aged dame expostulates with them. In the Via dell' Abondanza at Pompeii an inscription on the walls tells us of the existence of a draughts or chess club (Latruncularii). Yet a more striking example of the persistence of a game is the Italian game of Morra, known to every visitor to Italy though forbidden by the Italian law. It was especially common among the ladies of fourth-century Athens, and two thousand years earlier the Egyptian artist depicted it on the walls of Beni-Hassan.

With acrobatic performances we come somewhat nearer to athletics, for they imply physical agility and strength and require long and strenuous training. The Egyptians, like all orientals, loved shows of every sort. Acrobats were introduced at their feasts to amuse the guests just as they were at Xenophon's Sym-

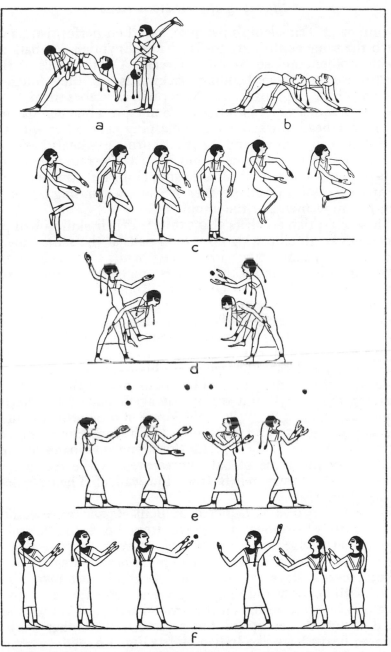

1. Egyptian games. Wall-paintings from tombs of Beni-Hassan. *a*, *b*, acrobats; *c*, hop and jump; *d*, *e*, *f*, ball games. *Archaeological Survey of Egypt, Beni-Hassan*, ii, pls. V, VIII, XIII, XV; Wilkinson, *Ancient Egyptians*, ii, p. 54 *sq.*

posium or at Trimalchio's banquet, and their performances were much the same as they are to-day. The Egyptian acrobats were mostly women, and so were the Greek. On the walls of Beni-Hassan we see them bending backwards till they touch the ground (Fig. 1 *b*), preparing, as Xenophon describes them, to turn a series of somersaults backwards. Sometimes one acrobat picks up another head downwards, and clasping each other with their heads between each other's legs they turn cartwheels backwards (Fig. 1 *a*). In one curious group we have a representation of 'hop-skip-and-jump' without the jump (Fig. 1 *c*); the hop is seen in three successive positions, then we have a standing figure, and then two movements of the jump.

These Egyptian acrobats also exhibited their skill in ball play, sometimes singly, throwing up several balls at the same time and catching them sometimes with crossed hands (Fig. 1 *e*), or again throwing balls to one another. These ball-playing scenes recur with strange persistence in Greek and Roman art. For example, at Beni-Hassan we see girls mounted pick-a-back on one another, in one case seated side-saddle, and tossing balls to each other to catch (Fig. 1 *d*). It is perhaps the game that the Greeks called *ephedrismos*, in which any player who dropped a catch had to be the ass (ὄνος) and carry his fellow on his back. On Greek vases we see it played in the palaestra by young men with an instructor presiding (Fig. 209), and we find it again played by the little Cupids depicted on the walls of the house of the Vettii at Pompeii. It is stranger still to find what looks like a team game with three players on each side (Fig. 1 *f*), for this scene anticipates in a most curious way the game of ball represented in the recently discovered sixth-century reliefs from the wall of Themistocles at Athens (Fig. 212).

These ball games as depicted at Beni-Hassan were confined almost entirely to women and, as their dress shows, they are mostly professional performers. Yet we can hardly suppose that the games thus represented were not popular also among the young of both sexes. Boys certainly had games of their own. They played with hoops as did the young Greeks and Romans. In one scene two boys are seated on the ground back to back with arms linked trying to get up off the ground. In another they are swinging heavy bags like Indian clubs (Fig. 2 *b*, *d*).

The only truly athletic exercise is wrestling. At Beni-Hassan there is a wonderful variety of wrestling scenes (Fig. 2 *a*). On one wall alone there are two hundred and twenty wrestling groups.

They look like illustrations of the wrestling school. Some of the groups show consecutive positions, but it is difficult to discover any definite system or arrangement. The wrestlers are naked save for a loin-cloth. Every conceivable grip and throw is repre-

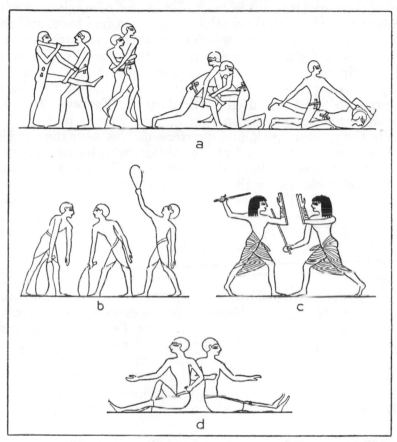

2. Egyptian games. *a*, wrestling; *b*, swinging weights; *c*, single-stick; *d*, lifting game. *Beni-Hassan, l.c.*

sented. All holds seem to be allowable, and the wrestling is continued on the ground. It looks as if it were necessary to get an opponent on his back with his shoulders down. There is, however, no indication of hitting as in the Greek pankration.

These wrestling groups must represent part of the training of the soldiery; they are always associated with other military exercises, such as shooting with the bow or sham fights. In the latter we see men fighting with bucklers and short sticks in a manner

that reminds one of some of the medieval fights in Italy. Herodotus particularly remarks on the hardness of the Egyptian
skulls, which he attributes to their habit of shaving the head.[1]
Certainly there must have been many broken heads in Egypt.
One of their sports seems very similar to that of single-sticks; the
combatants fight with short sticks about two feet long, and their
left arms are protected by wooden armguards strapped on (Fig.
2 c). A more formidable weapon was the *neboot*, which is still
used in Egypt and still used to decide quarrels. It is a stout
pole, six to eight feet long, grasped in both hands like the old
'quarterstaff', and was used particularly by Egyptian boatmen,
who must have given one another many a 'bloody pate'.

Wrestling, single-stick, and quarterstaff-play were the exercises
of the common people, and of the soldiery who formed a distinct
class. There is no evidence that they were ever the amusements
of the upper classes, or that there were ever organized competitions in them. The absence of such competitions is certainly
implied by Herodotus,[2] who was surprised to find gymnastic
contests of a Greek type held by the people of Chemmis at the
festival of Perseus. The upper classes seem to have preferred
sedentary games and watching the performances of professional
acrobats.

Among the popular shows in Egypt were also bull-fights, sometimes fights between two bulls, sometimes between a man and
a bull. Both types are represented in the Beni-Hassan pictures,
and Strabo[3] tells us of bull-fights held before the temple of
Hephaestus at Memphis. The popularity of bull-fighting at an
early date in Egypt is interesting in view of the importance given
to it in Crete, but the scenes of the Egyptian bull-ring are singularly tame compared with the wonderful performances of the
Minoans.

From this account of the games of the Egyptians it is clear that
they had no claim to be an athletic people though there may have
been plenty of athletic material among the poorer classes. For
thousands of years the upper classes lived a life of luxurious ease
and security in the fertile Nile valley. They were not a military
people, their army was recruited chiefly from the warlike tribes
of the Sudan. Among such a people athletics are not likely to
flourish, and whatever else Greece owed to Egypt it is certain
that she did not owe to them the athletic impulse. Let us turn
now to that other great Mediterranean civilization in Crete.

[1] iii. 12.   [2] ii. 91.   [3] xvii. 31, p. 807.

CRETE

M. Glotz [1] tells us that the Greeks were indebted to Crete for their athletic system and their athletic festivals. He calls attention particularly to the slim athletic type of figure represented in Cretan art, and describes the Cretan athlete as using a gymnastic belt. The figures represented are certainly of an athletic type, but the slimness that M. Glotz notes is characteristic of much early art, and the wasp-like waist is equally noticeable among the Egyptians. Moreover, the heavy belt which he describes as a gymnastic belt is part of the ordinary Minoan dress worn by women as well as men. Let us see what we can learn from the monuments.

The key to Cretan sports is furnished by the well-known Boxer vase from Hagia Triada (Fig. 3).[2] It is a steatite filler, eighteen inches high and was originally gilt. Round it run four bands in relief representing various sports. The topmost band is much damaged, and it is difficult to understand its meaning. Under the handle are two men fighting, possibly wrestling. They are naked save for loin-cloths and a sort of high boots. Beyond them is a pillar with a curious oblong capital, then two men advancing to the right with outstretched arms, and a third figure stooping down; the rest of the figures are lost. All three men wear high crested helmets. What are they doing? They are generally supposed to be fighting, but their attitude seems inappropriate. It has been suggested that the first two may be engaged in a foot-race, and that the third is jumping; or the first two may be taking their run for a jump. There does seem to be some sort of gradation in the three figures. But without the rest of the group, or the discovery of similar scenes no certainty is possible.

The second band represents a scene from the bull-ring. Two magnificent bulls are careering in full gallop, and the second of them is tossing a cowboy; the rest of the scene is lost.

The two remaining bands represent boxing scenes. The upper band is divided into three panels by pillars similar to that in the topmost band. Between the first two pillars stands a victorious boxer, while his opponent has fallen on the ground. In the next panel only the victor's figure is left, in the third only that of the fallen. The boxers wear close-fitting helmets, possibly of

[1] Glotz, *Aegean Civilization*, pp. 289, 293.
[2] Hall, *Aegean Archaeology*, p. 61; Evans, *Palace of Minos*, i, pp. 688 ff.; *Jahrb.* 1915, p. 248.

leather like the later wrestling caps; their hands seem to be padded, and the forearm also protected by some sort of guard. The attitude of the victors is very vigorous. They have the right arm drawn back for hitting and the left advanced. We may notice that the left arm is always bent, a position far superior to the stiff straight guard shown on some Greek vases.

In the lowest band the fighters are apparently boys, if we may judge from the thick masses of hair and the short curls on the forehead. Their hands are bare. Two of them have fallen; one sitting on the ground supports himself with his left arm while he holds his right arm above his head to ward off further blows. The other seems to have been knocked head over heels. Mosso sees in this position traces of the *savate*. Dr. Hall thinks he has been swung by the legs and dashed to the ground, but the attitude of the three standing figures is precisely the same as that of the boxers in the zone above and there is nothing in them to suggest wrestling.

The bull-ring and boxing are, with the doubtful exception mentioned above, the only sports known to Minoan art, and their spectacular character is clearly indicated on our vase. The bands are divided by triple lines and the panels separated by pillars with curious capitals. Both the pillars and the triple lines are, as Sir Arthur Evans shows,[1] characteristic features of Minoan architecture, and by them the artist is indicating the façade and tiers of seats of some grand stand from which the Minoan lords and ladies watch the sports. Moreover, in some of the frescoes connected with these sports we see the actual spectators, elegantly dressed ladies watching from an upper box, or dense crowds represented by a sea of heads.[2] Such scenes are almost unknown in Greek art; for a parallel we must go to the tombs of Etruria, and Etruscan games, as we shall see, have more in common with the Roman amphitheatre than with Greek sports.

The scene from the bull-ring represents the Minoan sport of bull-leaping which was a favourite subject of Minoan artists as early as 2000 B.C. It was depicted in frescoes at Cnossus and at Tiryns; it is engraved on seals of Crete and of the mainland. In the Ashmolean Museum at Oxford there is a solid bronze group of a bull and a bull-leaper, and to the same context must belong the well-known ivory figure of a leaper.[3] The scene obviously belongs to the acrobatic performances in the circus. The acrobats are sometimes youths, sometimes girls, the latter being

[1] *Palace of Minos*, i, pp. 687 ff.   [2] Ib. pp. 444, 527.   [3] *B.S.A.* viii, pl. II.

distinguished by their white skin. The scene is most clearly depicted in the great fresco of the palace of Cnossus, a copy of which is in the Ashmolean Museum (Fig. 4). The acrobat leaps at the bull as it charges, seizes it by the horns, throws himself up at arm's length as the bull tosses its head, and making a somersault lands on the bull's back, and then leaps off into the arms of a fellow acrobat waiting to receive him. It was a dangerous feat requiring skill and courage, and we can imagine the enthusiasm of the Minoan ladies as they leant over the balconies to watch the feats of their favourite performers.

Another scene is represented on a gem said to have been found at Priene.[1] A great bull with lashing tail is drinking at a tank, while from some place above an acrobat leaps upon him and grasps his horns. Whether he is going to grapple with him and throw him to the ground we do not know, but here too we are witnessing a performance in the circus.

These circus performances, as Sir Arthur Evans points out, had their origin in the feats of huntsmen or cowboys capturing or mastering the wild bulls in the open country. This is the subject represented on the well-known Gold Cups found at Vaphio.[2] The character of the landscape is shown by rocks and trees. On one cup the bulls are being stampeded into nets. In the centre a bull is struggling in the net, two others bulls have broken away, one of them is tossing a cowboy who has tried to grapple with him while another who has jumped on the creature's back is falling to the ground. The scene on the other cup is more peaceful, in appearance at least. It is the capture of the bull by a decoy cow. We see the bull first following the cow, then dallying with her, then striding off with uplifted head bellowing with indignation, as he feels the lasso with which the cowboy has fettered his hind leg.

The hunting of the wild bull was a dangerous sport, but in many cases it was a necessity. The wild bull must have been a danger to the country and towns, and many a story was told of the feats of heroes who rid the country of him. One of the labours imposed by Eurystheus on Heracles was to capture the Cretan bull, while the Athenian hero Theseus freed the land from the ravages of the bull of Marathon. These were favourite themes with the Greek artists. From the rodeo of the cowboys of the West we know how man by skill and daring can master the wildest animal, even without weapons. The Cretan cowboy had the same skill. On many a Cretan seal we see him grappling with the bull.

[1] Ib. p. 376, Fig. 274.   [2] *Jahrb.* xxx. 1915, pls. IX–XII.

We see him with one hand grasping the bull's horn and with the other his lower jaw and twisting his head round so as to force him to the ground. In historical times there were no wild bulls in most of Greece, but the sport survived in Thrace and Thessaly where they hunted the bull on horseback, chasing the animal till he was

5. Boxer, on fragment of steatite Pyxis from Cnossus (about 1600 B. C.). Candia Museum. *B.S.A.*, vii, p. 95, Fig. 31.

exhausted and then leaping on to his back and forcing him to the ground. Thence the sport passed to the Roman amphitheatre and it still survives to-day in the Spanish bull-fight, and in Provence.

In the boxing scenes the chief point to notice is the covering of the hand. This is most clearly seen in a fragment of a relief from Cnossus (Fig. 5). The hand is clenched and the guard of the arm extends above the elbow. It resembles, therefore, the late Roman caestus, not the straps of oxhide with which the Homeric boxers bound their hands, and which are always represented in vases of the sixth and fifth centuries. Now the development of the caestus from these thongs can be clearly traced. Here a thousand years earlier we find apparently a regular caestus in use. How did it originate? Boxing of the Greek type is a highly specialized form of fighting. It is not natural for the untrained man or the child to use the clenched fist. I will hazard the suggestion that the fist when first used was not empty but held a stone. The Homeric soldiers in battle still hurled stones from a distance. What more natural than that at close quarters stones should be used for striking an opponent? For thousands of years stones were used as hammers, and the use of the stone for crushing the victim's head survived in Roman ritual.

Here then, I suggest, we have the origin of the use of the clenched fist for fighting. If I am right, we can understand why the Minoan boxer has his arm protected. His hand is not padded, but holds some hard object, perhaps also has some hard covering. The Greeks of the fifth century with their hands bound with soft thongs had no need of such protection, but when a sharp ring of hard leather was fastened round the knuckles it became necessary to protect the forearm.

6. Boxers of late Minoan period. Fragment of Mycenean krater from Cyprus: about 1100 B.C. In British Museum, C. 334.

But whatever truth there may be in this conjecture, the fact that some of the performers wear helmets is clear proof of the military character of these contests. They have their origin in the experiences of actual warfare just as the bull-leaping in the experiences of hunting. In the same way we saw that in Egypt wrestling was part of the training of the common soldiery. It is in these contests that the athletic spirit first finds its opportunity. And perhaps it is to the tradition of such combats that boxing owed its early popularity in Eastern lands. The earliest picture of a true boxing-match is on a vase from Cyprus in the British Museum which may be dated about 1100 B.C. (Fig. 6). We also find boxing represented on a Babylonian relief in the British Museum. But the relief belongs to the ninth century, and long before this date, as we know from Homer, boxing had developed as a true sport.

The combats represented by the Minoan artists however are, we feel, not real athletics, however vigorous they are. They are not proper boxing but a sort of free fight like the fights of those common pugilists, *pugiles catervarii*, who fought in companies in the Roman amphitheatre. There is no indication of any competition any more than there is in the scenes from the bull-ring. It does not even seem clear that they are fighting in pairs. Boxers and cowboys alike are performing not for their own joy in the contest but for the pleasure of the spectators. They are professional performers, slaves, possibly, or captives, or mercenaries. They have nothing in common with the Homeric warriors who take their delight in the grievous boxing. Nor can we infer from such scenes that the Cretans were themselves athletic any more than we can infer that the spectators in the Roman amphitheatre were all athletes. It was not from Crete that the Achaeans derived their love of sport, nor is Crete the home of Greek athletics. Moreover, even if it be admitted that bull-leaping had a ritual signification and that these shows took place at religious festivals, there is not a particle of evidence to connect with Crete the origin of the great athletic festivals of Greece.

It may be, of course, that these shows of the Minoan amphitheatre had their origin in a yet earlier age of genuine athletics, perhaps on the mainland. Excavations are constantly revealing to us the existence of highly developed civilizations in the third millennium or earlier in Asia Minor, Mesopotamia, the highlands of Persia, and even north-west India. But so far they have not revealed to us the sports of those lands. In the luxurious civilization of Mesopotamia we should hardly expect sport to flourish, but further north in Asia Minor or Persia there were hardier races. Those old Persians who learnt to ride, to shoot, and to speak the truth, must surely have been fond of sport. When did they first learn to play polo? Wrestling and ball-games are widely popular in India, but we have no early records of them. For any record of sports in ancient times we must go yet farther east to China.

CHINA AND JAPAN

We do not usually associate the Chinese with athletics. And yet it seems certain that in the Age of Chivalry 600 years before Christ, the Chinese were not only devoted to sports, but that they had something at least of the athletic spirit. Indeed it was from them that the Japanese learnt the 'gentle art' of jiu-jitzu. It is stranger still that the most popular Chinese sports were boxing and football. There is another early sport in China known as 'butting'. In 'butting' the opponents put over their heads ox-skins, horns and all, and proceeded to butt one another. We are

not surprised to learn that in these fights 'there were smashed
heads, broken arms and blood running in the palace yard'.
But 'butting' was not introduced into China until 221 B.C., and
polo seems not to have been played before A.D. 600, though the
Tartars, from whom the Chinese learnt the game, must have
practised it centuries earlier.   Boxing and football were far older
sports.

Chinese boxing was more like the Greek pankration than our
boxing. No gloves were worn and it included wrestling, *la savate*,
and even the use of the quarter-staff or the spear.   It was an
aristocratic sport.   In a campaign in 631 B.C. we are told that
the Marquis of Chin 'dreamt that he was boxing with the Viscount
of Ch'u who knocked him down and kneeling over him sucked
his blood'. Boxing was regarded more as a business than a sport
owing to its practical value in military training. Some of the
most famous exponents of the art were Buddhist priests who
practised it for the defence of their monasteries, and marvellous
feats were related of them.   In later times text-books of boxing
were compiled. Here is an interesting passage from a late text-book
written when boxing was evidently degenerate: ' The art of self-
defence is twofold, exoteric and esoteric. The exoteric style consists in striking an opponent and then by an acrobatic bound
placing oneself out of reach. The esoteric style consists in
opposing the adversary but not letting fly unless compelled by
force of circumstances.' So Dio Chrysostom describes a boxer
of his own day who defeated his opponent without striking
a blow.

Boxing was evidently an aristocratic and military sport. Football was also encouraged as a military training but was more
popular. An old Chinese writer, speaking of the town of Lin-tzü
in the third century B.C., says: 'There were none among its inhabitants who did not perform with the pipes or some string
instrument, fight cocks, race dogs or play football.' There is
something strangely modern about the passage, and so too when
we are told that during a campaign when his army was running
short of provisions Ho Ch'ü-ping hollowed out a place for them
to play football in. It was not, however, considered a suitable
game for emperors, and when one of them persisted in playing
one of his councillors sent in a protest against it as too exhausting
and undignified for an emperor.

The ball was round, formed of eight pointed strips of leather,
and stuffed with hair, but in the fifth century A. D. an air-filled ball

was introduced. It is difficult to form any clear idea of the game, of which there seem to have been several varieties, but apart from kicking the ball and the use of a goal there seems to be little in common with our own game which, as we shall see, bears a much closer resemblance to the Greek game of *Episkyros* and the medieval Florentine game of Calzio, though its origin is undoubtedly independent of either. The Chinese had apparently only one goal, formed of two bamboo poles, thirty or more feet high, joined by a silk cord over which the ball had to be kicked. In another form of game a net was stretched across the goal in which was a hole a foot in diameter, and the ball had to be kicked through the hole. It seems that each player took it in turn to kick. There were over seventy kinds of kick, and close dribbling formed part of the game. The opposite side must have been able to interfere in some way, for there were several kinds of foul, but it is not clear how they interfered. The following lines written by the poet Lu Yu (A.D. 50–130) are worth quoting for their delightful moral:

> A round ball and a square wall,
> The ball flying across like the moon,
> While the teams stand opposed.
> Captains are appointed and take their places
> No allowances are made for relationship,
> According to unchanging regulations
> There must be no partiality.
> But there must be determination and coolness
> Without the slightest irritation at failure.
> And if all this is necessary for football
> How much more for the business of life.[1]

Here is something of the true sporting spirit, something very near to athletics. We should like to know more of these Chinese sports.

It was from China according to Professor Giles that the Japanese first learnt the art of jiu-jitzu which in their hands developed into the most scientific system of self-defence and physical training ever devised. It depends on the knowledge of the weakest points in the human body, how to take advantage of these weaknesses, how to grip a limb in such a way as to render it useless. The secrets of this art were until recent years

[1] This account of Chinese sports is taken from two fascinating papers by Professor H. A. Giles in *Adversaria Sinica*, 'Football and Polo in China', 'The Home of Jiu-jitzu', pp. 88, 132. The former was also published in the *Nineteenth Century*, 1906.

jealously guarded by the Samurai, a military cast of small nobles, whose sole business was fighting. They trained themselves for war by all sorts of military and athletic exercises, but these exercises never developed into sports. But sports existed among the common people. Wrestling has always been a popular recreation as in India, and there existed a class of professional

7. Chinese boxers. Compare the bronze of a pankratiast Fig. 195, *Adversaria Sinica*, p. 137.

wrestlers, men trained from childhood so as to attain enormous bulk. But now that jiu-jitzu is no longer kept a secret, it has been proved by actual competition that these giants are no match for the expert in jiu-jitzu, who is usually a small man.

The records which we have considered in this chapter are fragmentary and miscellaneous and often hard to interpret. But one fact emerges clearly. The earliest exercises that can properly be described as athletic are connected with military training and are forms of fighting. These exercises may never develop into athletics, but in them is the germ of athletics. The love of competition is akin to the love of fighting.

III

ATHLETICS IN HOMER

IT is in Homer that we first find the true spirit of sport, the desire to be ever the best and to excel all other men, the joy in the effort. Every Achaean warrior is an athlete and the description of the funeral games in the twenty-third *Iliad* is by far the earliest account of sports that we possess, and for the sheer joy of sport has never been surpassed.

This is no place to discuss the date and authorship of the Homeric poems. It is sufficient to say that while most authorities date the poems not earlier than the ninth century, it is generally agreed that the state of society that they describe existed at least two or three centuries earlier. The fair-haired Achaeans of Homer are not the original inhabitants of Greece; they are immigrants from the North, perhaps akin to other fair-haired giants from central Europe who made their way westward as far as our own islands. As far back as the middle of the second millennium tribes of hardy northerners began to move south along the river valleys and across the mountain passes from the plains of central Europe. Some crossed the Straits to Phrygia and Asia Minor, others made their way by sea to Crete; others, chief among whom were the Achaeans, overran Greece, partly destroying, partly absorbing the Minoan civilization. There they settled, their chieftains occupying Mycenae and other old Minoan strongholds, their clansmen dwelling round them. They were a restless, warlike folk, constantly raiding one another's territories and driving off the cattle in which their wealth chiefly consisted. Their chieftains, 'horse-tamers' and 'shepherds of the people', ruled by hereditary right, but held their power by virtue of their military prowess, their superior armament, and their physical strength. They went to war in chariots, and battles resolved themselves usually into a number of hand-to-hand fights between individual chieftains. In such a society military and physical exercises are the chief part of every boy's training, and the natural recreation of the men. In sport as in war the hero seeks to be ever the best. 'My father', says Glaucus in the *Iliad*,[1] 'bade me ever be far the best and far excel all other men, and not to put to shame my father's lineage.' The spirit which in the Age of Chivalry pro-

[1] *Il.* vi. 208.

duced the Tournament, produced athletics among the Homeric Greeks.

The word athlete (ἀθλητήρ) is first used in a delightful passage in the *Odyssey* describing how Odysseus after being shipwrecked succeeded in reaching the land of the Phaeacians and was hospitably entertained by their King Alcinous.[1] Where Phaeacia was and who were the Phaeacians are questions that do not concern us here. They were probably not Achaeans. But the passage is none the less valuable as showing that Homer regards sports as a natural part of everyday life.

Alcinous has entertained Odysseus at a banquet. After the banquet the minstrel sings of the Trojan War, but Alcinous observes that Odysseus is much affected by the song and proposes quite naturally that they shall adjourn to the agora, where his guest may see the skill of the Phaeacians in sports. There the young men disport themselves with running, jumping, wrestling and boxing, and throwing the diskos. After a while Laodamas, the King's son, invites Odysseus to try his skill in sports. 'Thou art like', he says, 'to have skill in games, for there is no greater glory for a man while he yet lives than that which he achieves by hand or foot.' But Odysseus excuses himself; he is worn out with his sufferings and sick at heart for home. Thereupon one of the young Phaeacians forgets his manners and replies: 'No truly, stranger, nor do I think thee at all like one that is skilled in games whereof there are many among mortals; rather art thou such an one as goes to and fro in a benched ship, a captain of sailors who are merchantmen, one with a memory for his freight, or that hath charge of a cargo homeward bound and of greedily-gotten gains: *thou art no athlete.*'

'No athlete', the words have a strangely modern ring. How often do we hear the expression 'he is no sportsman', and how often is it used by those who like the young Phaeacian are no true sportsmen themselves! Homer, we see, expects every warrior to be an athlete, and the true athlete has nothing to do with ill-gotten gains. Indeed, in these impromptu games there are no prizes, the young men race and wrestle and box for the sheer joy of the contest.

Odysseus is stung by the taunt. He retorts angrily, and picking up a diskos—a stone heavier than those that the Phaeacians were wont to hurl—he lightly slings it far beyond their marks and challenges any of the Phaeacians to beat his throw or to

[1] *Od.* viii. 97 ff.

try a bout with him in boxing or in wrestling. For, he says, he is no weakling in these sports. In archery, indeed, he surpassed all other men, save Philoctetes. Only with the men of old he would not contend, with Heracles or Eurytus 'who contended even with the immortal Gods'. But the Phaeacians have seen enough. Alcinous apologizes for the young man's rudeness and proposes to show his guest a display of dancing. For 'the Phaeacians are no perfect boxers nor wrestlers, but speedy runners and the best of seamen; and dear to us ever is the banquet and the harp and the dance, and changes of raiment, and the warm bath and love and sleep'. No, the Phaeacians are not Achaeans, nor are they athletes in spite of their boasts.

Far fuller is the description of the funeral games held in honour of Patroclus which occupies most of the twenty-third *Iliad*. The custom of celebrating funerals with games is found in many lands; in Etruria, in the Caucasus, in Ireland, even in Siam and in North America. In Greece it was of extreme antiquity and continued all through Greek history. The aged Nestor in the *Iliad* recalls his youthful triumphs at the funeral games of Amarynces. The funeral games of Pelias, the uncle of Jason, were represented on two of the most famous of early works of art—the chest of Cypselus at Olympia and the throne of Apollo at Amyclae. Funeral games are depicted in many early vases, the well-known François vase at Florence and the Amphiaraus vase in Berlin (Fig. 8). Sometimes games were held periodically in honour of some departed hero; and it has been argued that all the great athletic festivals in Greece were originally connected with funerals. Many writers have tried to find a ritual significance in the games themselves. Fighting events have been supposed to be substitutes for human sacrifice, the chariot race a ritual contest for the throne. The celebration of games, it is suggested, was particularly pleasing to the spirit of the departed who had found pleasure in them in his lifetime. There may be some grain of truth in such suggestions, but certainly in Homer we find no hint of any ritual idea underlying the games, nor is there any need of such an explanation. Sports in Homer are part of the daily life and purely secular. Any important occasion would be a natural excuse for holding sports, the gathering of an army for war, the wedding or the funeral of some great chieftain. For where people are gathered together, something must be done to entertain them, and the most natural form of entertainment is some form of competition. In the case of a funeral the practice has the special advantage that it enables the heir to provide mementoes of the dead in the form of prizes, which may be weapons or other objects that belonged to the dead man. In the games of Patroclus, as we shall see, Achilles provides prizes for all the competitors.

The first event in the programme is the chariot-race, and naturally so. For the competitors in these games are the chieftains, who had brought with them from the North their love of horses. Greece is no land for horses but, in the plains of Thessaly, Attica, Argos, and Elis, they bred horses and they prided themselves on their studs. Chariot-races had long become an institution: Nestor recalls the chariot-races of early days. The chariot used was the two-horse war-chariot. In war it was driven by the charioteer while the owner stood beside him and dismounted to fight, but in sport the owner himself drove. There is indeed one allusion in the *Iliad* to a four-horse chariot.[1] Nestor tells Patroclus how he sent a chariot and four horses to compete in Elis for a tripod, and the horses were seized by King Augeas. The passage is probably a late addition to the poem suggested by the chariot-race at the Olympic Games.

For the chariot-race Achilles offers five prizes—'for the winner a woman skilled in fair handiwork and a tripod, for the second a six year old mare in foal, for the third a goodly cauldron untouched by the fire, for the fourth two talents of gold, for the fifth a two-handled urn'. For the five prizes there are five competitors, Eumelus, Diomedes, Menelaus, Meriones, and Antilochus, the son of Nestor, who impresses on his son that a race is won by craft rather than speed, and gives him special advice about the turn. The course is of the simplest, really a cross-country race. The turning point is marked by a withered tree-stump with a white stone on either side and round it is smooth driving. It is out of sight, and Achilles posts here godlike Phoenix to mark the running and tell the truth thereof. To this point the chariots are to make their way over the plain, turn round it to the left and return to the start.

The charioteers draw lots and take their places. All the chariots negotiate the turn safely and on the return journey Eumelus is in front, closely followed by Diomedes. The latter, just as he is about to pass Eumelus, drops his whip; it is Apollo's doing, for Homer attributes all accidents to the gods. But Athene is not behindhand, she restores the whip to her favourite and then in revenge breaks the yoke of Eumelus'

[1] xi. 699.

chariot so that he is thrown to the ground and Diomedes takes first place. Behind him come Menelaus and Antilochus. The track at one point is a narrow ravine, the bed of a winter torrent where there is barely room for two chariots. Menelaus, who is in front, is driving cautiously in the middle of the way, and Antilochus seizes the opportunity to try to pass him by forcing him to the side of the track. Menelaus protests in vain, and drawing aside for fear of an accident allows him to pass. Meanwhile the spectators, who have not seen what was happening owing to the drop in the ground, are quarrelling as to which chariot is leading, and here we have the first and as far as I can find the only example in Greek sports of a bet on a race, Idomeneus offering to wager Aias a tripod or a cauldron.

The prize-giving delightfully illustrates the informal character of these sports. Diomedes of course receives first prize, but when Achilles proposes to give the second prize to Eumelus, who but for his accident might have been first, Antilochus refuses absolutely to abandon his claim. Thereupon Menelaus protests that Antilochus has cheated him of second place by 'boring' his horses. But Antilochus apologizes and excuses himself on the ground of his youthful impetuosity. The quarrel is happily settled, Achilles provides a special prize for Eumelus and gives the fifth prize to the aged Nestor as a 'memorial of Patroclus' burying'.

The next two events, boxing and wrestling, are of peculiar interest. For they are both specialized forms of sport implying the existence of rules or at least customs for their conduct. In Homer they are already arts, practised and handed down by the Achaean warriors, just as jiu-jitzu was by the Samurai of Japan. The descriptions though brief show that the poet thoroughly understood these sports. We may note too how he applies to them the epithet 'grievous' (ἀλεγεινός), the same epithet as he uses of battle. Yet grievous though the contest may be the Homeric warrior 'takes his delight in it' whether in sport or war. These two events as we shall see were at all periods extraordinarily popular among the Greeks.

For boxing Achilles offers two prizes, a 'six-year-old mule for the winner, a two-handled cup for the loser'. At once Epeius advances and in a somewhat braggart speech claims the cup. His challenge is accepted by Euryalus, the son of an old champion who had defeated all comers at the funeral games of Oedipus at Thebes. The two strip and gird themselves with girdles such as

we see represented on a few early Greek vases, then they bind on
their hands not a caestus, such as is depicted in Cretan scenes,
but well-cut thongs of ox-hide, precisely similar to those worn by
Greek boxers in the fifth century. Then they lift up their hands
and fall to. Only the finish is described, and it is an excellent
description of a knock-out blow. 'Noble Epeius came on and as
the other spied for an opening smote him on the cheek', evidently
on 'the mark', 'nor could he much more stand, for his fair limbs
failed straightway under him, and as when the north wind blows
a fish leapeth on a tangle-covered beach and then the black wave
covereth it, so leapt up Euryalus at the blow. But great-hearted
Epeius took him in his hands and set him upright and his dear
comrades stood around him and led him through the ring with
trailing feet, spitting out clotted blood, drooping his head awry.'
The courtesy of Epeius towards his vanquished opponent is a
charming touch especially after his boast before the fight that he
will 'bruise his adversary's flesh and break his bones'. This
courtesy towards the loser is all too rare among the later Greeks.

In the *Odyssey* [1] we have a still more vivid description of a
fight, this time without gloves, which shows how familiar the
Achaeans were with the art of boxing. Odysseus returning home
disguised as a beggar finds at the door of his palace the beggar
Irus who insults him and threatens to beat him. The suitors
overhearing the quarrel are delighted at the prospect of a fight
between a pair of beggars whom they suppose to know nothing
of boxing, 'never before has such a thing happened, such goodly
game the Gods have brought to our house'. They insist on a
fight and promise a haggis to the winner. So the two gird their rags
about them. But when Odysseus strips, the suitors are amazed
at his thighs, goodly and great, his broad shoulders and breast
and mighty arms. Irus too is amazed; but the suitors will not
let him off. So they lead him to the ring and the two put up their
hands. The fight of course is a foregone conclusion. Odysseus'
only doubt is whether he shall kill Irus outright or merely knock
him out. He decides to knock him out. Irus leads off with a
clumsy left hander at his right shoulder, which Odysseus counters
with a blow 'on the neck beneath the ear' which of course knocks
him out. The poet has seen many a fight and knows exactly what
he is talking about.

For wrestling, again, Achilles offers two prizes, a tripod valued
at twelve oxen and for the loser a woman 'skilled in all manner of

[1] xviii. 15 ff.

work' valued at four oxen. Again there are two competitors,
Aias and Odysseus, the types respectively of strength and cunning.
The match was conducted under the rules of what the Greeks
called 'upright wrestling' in which each tried to throw the other
to the ground. Girding themselves the two advanced into the
ring and clasped each other with stalwart arms 'like gable rafters
of a lofty house' (see Fig. 8). It is exactly the attitude adopted
by Westmorland and Cumberland wrestlers to-day and is often
depicted on Greek vases. They try to throw one another in vain.
'Their backs creaked, and sweat ran down in streams and
frequent weals along their ribs and shoulders sprang up.' At
length as the spectators were getting weary Aias suggested that
each in turn should lift his opponent and try to throw him. The
advantage here is clearly with the heavier man, but Odysseus
was equal to the occasion. Aias tried first and lifted Odysseus,
but the latter 'not unmindful of his craft smote deftly from behind
the hollow of Aias' knee', or, in modern parlance, hammed him.
Aias fell backward with Odysseus on the top of him. As both fell
together the bout was inconclusive. Next Odysseus tried to lift
his bulky opponent, but only able to raise him a little from the
ground he crooked his leg inside the other's, a chip known as
'the hank', or perhaps 'the inside click' (see Figs. 154, 164). Both
fell to the ground together, and once more there was no result.
When they prepared to wrestle again, Achilles declared the
match a draw and awarded to each an equal prize.

Next comes the foot-race. The course is like that for the chariot-
race, round some distant mark and back to the starting-place,
close to the funeral pyre where the ground was wet with the blood
of the slaughtered victims. There were three prizes and three
competitors, Aias the son of Oileus, Odysseus, and the youthful
Antilochus. As they near the finish Aias is leading with Odysseus
close behind. Once more a God interferes. Odysseus prays to
Athene and she makes 'his limbs feel light, both feet and hands',
a delightful description of a spurt. But not content with this
legitimate aid she causes Aias to slip in the blood of the victims.
The Achaeans laugh as they see him 'sputtering away the filth',
but there is no ill-feeling. He merely comments that a 'goddess
marred his running', and Antilochus, who comes in last, adds,
'Friends, ye will bear me witness that even herein also the
immortals favour elder men.'

Here probably the original account of the games ended,
though perhaps we may include the competition in javelin throw-

ing with which the book ends. The competition never comes off. For as Agamemnon is one of the competitors Achilles declares a contest useless and awards the first prize to him. The intervening passage is regarded by even the most conservative of critics as a late interpolation. The description is lifeless, and the style far inferior to that of the rest of the book. Three events are described—the armed fight, throwing the weight, and archery.

The armed combat between Diomedes and Aias seems at first sight a murderous form of sport. For Achilles offers a prize to whichever of the two 'shall first reach the other's fair flesh and touch the inward parts piercing through armour and dark blood'. But he evidently has no expectation of a serious or fatal result, for he promises to both a fair feast after the combat. And in reality, when after much brave display Diomedes, perhaps losing his temper, makes persistent thruots at Aias' throat, the spectators stop the contest for fear of hurt to Aias.

The inclusion of this event is remarkable. Such fights were quite alien to the spirit of Greek sports; they were not practised in the gymnasia nor do we find them in any athletic festivals. For we must not confuse these serious fights with the *hoplomachia* which we find taught in the gymnasia in later times by a special *hoplomachos*, harmless contests in the use of arms like our competitions in fencing or bayonet fighting. Yet there must be some ground in tradition or actual practice for the inclusion of this event in the Homeric poem, and though the armed combat was never recognized as a form of sport, we do find it existing in places as a part of funeral ritual, a substitute for the human sacrifice which was actually offered by Achilles on the pyre of Patroclus, a blood offering in which the departed warrior might naturally delight. Such fights were a feature of Etruscan funeral games, and from them developed the gladiatorial shows of the Romans. For Greek lands we have the evidence of a sixth-century sarcophagus from Clazomenae in the British Museum, on which are painted scenes from the funeral games (Fig. 9).[1] Here amid chariots preparing for the race we see pairs of warriors armed with shields and spears fighting to the accompaniment of a flute player. A fight is also depicted as part of funeral games on an eighth-century Dipylon vase.[2] Further, we learn from Athenaeus that

---

[1] It is possible that the scene represented is not a fight but an armed dance. Professor Beazley calls my attention to an Attic b.-f. hydria of *c*. 525 B.C. where a very similar scene represents a dance and not a fight, *A.J.A.* 1923, p. 266.

[2] See *Gk. Athletics*, Fig. 4.

the practice still survived in the fourth century B. C. He tells us that Cassander on his return from Boeotia buried the King and Queen and Cynna, the mother of Eurydice, and among other ceremonies instituted a contest in single combat.[1] Plutarch suggests that armed contests at one time took place at Olympia, and his statement has been used as an argument for the funeral origin of the Olympic festival, but he seems to have little belief in his own suggestion.[2]

Throwing the diskos is one of the most popular diversions in Homer. We have seen that Odysseus proved his might by hurling a diskos heavier than any that the Phaeacians were wont to hurl. So too the suitors of Penelope amused themselves with throwing 'diskoi and hunting-spears', in a levelled place before the palace of Odysseus.[3] It was the recreation of the common soldiery too. When Achilles was sulking in his tent his men 'sported with diskoi, with casting of spears and archery'.[4] So common a sport was it that Homer uses the term 'a diskos' throw' just as we do a 'stone's throw', as a rough measure of distance. But what does he mean by a diskos? He can hardly mean the artificial diskos of the later gymnasium. We cannot suppose that there was a store of such implements of various sizes in the agora of the Phaeacians, or in the camp at Troy. The word 'diskos' merely means 'a thing for throwing', and can be used of any natural object convenient for throwing, especially a stone. Greece was a land of stones, and stones provided a natural weapon in war, and a natural test of strength and skill in throwing. The Homeric warrior in battle hurled rocks that 'two men such as live now could scarcely lift', and when the common soldiery took part in the fight, stones flew fast. The diskoi in the agora of the Phaeacians on the sea-shore may have been flat stones such as fishermen use for holding down their nets or tackle when laid out to dry, or stones for mooring their boats.

The diskos that Odysseus threw was a stone, but at the games of Patroclus the object thrown is described 'as an unwrought mass of metal' (σόλος[5]). This pig of iron, probably the contents of one of the open-air furnaces common in the Mediterranean world, is not only the weight thrown but the prize. It had been taken by Achilles from Eetion of Thebes who used to throw it, and it will provide the winner, says Achilles, with as much iron as his

---

[1] *Ath.* iv. 155a. Most of Athenaeus' long discourse on the single combat has little bearing on the subject.
[2] *Q.C.* 675 c.   [3] *Od.* iv. 626, xvii. 168.   [4] *Il.* ii. 774.   [5] xxiii. 826, 839.

shepherd or ploughman will use in five years. Yet in spite of its weight, the winner hurls it as 'lightly as a herdsman flings the 'bola' [1] when it flies whirling through the herds of kine'.

Stones and arrows are not aristocratic weapons, they are the weapons of the common soldiers and weapons of chase rather than of war. For this reason the bow has a more honoured place in the *Odyssey* than in the *Iliad*. In the *Iliad* even Odysseus figures as 'a spearman renowned' not as an archer. It is for the most part the Trojans who fight with bow and arrow, especially Paris. The Achaean warriors generally regard the bow with dislike and contempt, not unmingled with fear, for the arrow makes no distinction between the brave man and the coward. The Greek hoplite of the fifth century had the same feeling. Hence, though archery was part of the training of the Epheboi and there were local competitions in it, it did not figure in the programme of the great Games. The description of the contest in the *Iliad* is singularly unreal. The prizes offered, twelve double axes for the first prize and two single axes for the second, are suspiciously reminiscent of the *Odyssey*. And the contest itself is absurd. The first prize is to go to the man who hits a dove suspended by a string to a mast, the second prize to him who performs the far more difficult task of severing the cord.

Whenever games are mentioned in Homer we find the true spirit of sport, the joy in the contest. But the Homeric sports are as yet far removed from the sports of historic Greece. In the first place they are, like Homeric society itself, aristocratic. Only chieftains compete, and the principal events, the chariot-race, boxing, and wrestling, seem to be the monopoly of the nobles, though their followers as we have seen have their own recreations. Secondly, the sports are informal and spontaneous. There is no organized training; there are no organized competitions. The nearest parallel to them is to be found in the sports of the Highland Clans, but it is probable that, if we knew more, other parallels might be found wherever a similar state of society has existed. The heroes of the Sagas delight in contests and feats of physical strength; but we have no record of the sports of the warlike tribes of northern and central Europe. In the next chapter we shall see how from the sports of the Achaeans was developed the athletic ideal of the fifth century.

[1] This as suggested to me by Professor Linton Myres is probably the meaning of καλαῦροψ in the passage, 845; *Gk. Athletics*, p. 314.

IV

ATHLETICS AND RELIGION

THE ATHLETIC FESTIVAL

THE most remarkable characteristic of Greek athletics is their continuity. The sports of the eighth century B.C. are the same as those of Homer—the chariot-race, the foot-race, throwing the diskos and the javelin, wrestling, and boxing. These events with certain variations and additions make up the programme of the athletic festivals of Greece during their whole history; they survive the loss of Greek independence, are taken over by Rome, and in places are still found even after the fall of the Roman Empire. This continuity is due in the first place to the practical character of these sports, in the second place to the athletic festival through which athletics were brought within the sphere of religious conservatism.

Athletics were to the Greek far more than mere recreation. To the Homeric warrior they were the means of training and maintaining the physical vigour and activity which he needed in a warlike age. But they were almost equally essential to the Greek of the fifth century. Greece was never a land of peace; quarrels between neighbouring states were frequent; their petty wars required no long preparation; the citizen might at a moment's notice be called upon to take the field and fight, and in the conditions of ancient warfare his safety depended on his physical fitness.

This explains the important place that athletics held in Greek education; it explains too why games, which with us form so prominent and popular a part of school life, never developed to the same extent in Greece. Games have many advantages over pure athletics. They are superior in interest, and they are superior as a training of character, developing the team feeling and unselfishness. But as physical training they are valuable chiefly for those who excel in them; those who have no aptitude for them derive but little benefit. They cannot train a whole nation.

The defect of athletics proper and of all systems of physical drill is that the interest is quickly exhausted. This defect was remedied in Greece by constant competitions, competitions for all ages and not only local but also national competitions. In the latter a new and nobler element was introduced, for the athlete competed not merely as an individual but as the representative of his state.

ATHLETICS AND THE CITY STATE

It was the city state system that made the national athletic festival possible. In Homer we hear of no athletic festivals, hardly indeed of any religious festivals. The conditions of tribal life were too unsettled, too fluid for the growth of organized religion or sport. Of the period that followed we know little, save that all was chaos in Greece. The land was distracted by continuous migrations and wars which destroyed the last traces of the Aegean civilization. For centuries there was a stream of immigrants from the North, some conquering, others settling down peacefully among the older inhabitants. Chief among them were the Dorians, a hardy, warlike, athletic race of mountaineers who made themselves masters of most of the Peloponnese. But the land was too narrow for them all, and as early as the tenth century or earlier, another stream of migration set eastwards. Aeolians, Ionians, Dorians in turn took to the sea and occupied the islands of the Aegean and the coasts of Asia Minor. There they brought the Greek language and civilization, their love of music and of sport. Contact with the kingdoms of the East forced them to closer unity, and the city state arose. In the rich valleys of Asia Minor these cities grew rich and prosperous; commerce, literature, and art flourished. When on the mainland order was at last restored, the rural villages in turn gradually 'grew together', and united in city states. So in the eighth century, when a new period of expansion began which spread Greek civilization over the whole Mediterranean world, the type of polity that the Greek settlers everywhere established was the city state. Between the city states of the Greek world rivalry was keen and this rivalry was the life of the athletic festival.

The cities of Asia Minor developed far earlier than those of the mainland. There, probably, athletics first became part of education, and the athletic festival arose. Sport was no longer aristocratic, for the state required the services of every one of its citizens. Soon every state must have had its sports-grounds (gymnasia) and its wrestling schools (palaestrae). In the settled life of the city religion too became organized, with regular holy days and festivals, and here the national love of competition found free scope. There were sports, music, and dancing, all in the form of competition. As a rule the competitions would be confined to the citizens, but sometimes visitors were allowed to compete.

THE RISE OF NATIONAL FESTIVALS

Again, from earliest times we find certain places recognized as possessing peculiar sanctity as the special home of some particular god, and there festivals would arise which would draw together his worshippers from neighbouring tribes or groups of cities. Thus the island of Delos had in the course of the migrations become the religious centre of the Ionians settled in the Aegean isles and on the coast of Asia Minor. The poet of the Hymn to Apollo, who wrote not later than the eighth century, tells how at Delos 'the long-robed Ionians gather together with their wives and children and delight the god with boxing and dance and song'.[1] Boxing was at all times a favourite sport in the Aegean. We remember the professional boxers of the Cretan vase; it is worth noting too that the first victor in boxing recorded at Olympia was Onomastus of Smyrna, who won the prize in 688 B. C., and was said to have drawn up the rules for boxing at Olympia. Yet in the poet's description of the Delian festival we feel that his interest is not in the boxing, but in the joyousness and grace of the whole scene, especially of the choirs of Delian maidens, chanting hymns to Apollo and Artemis and Leto, and singing the praises of men and women of past days. Even from the mainland choirs came, and Pausanias quotes some lines from the poem written by Eumelus of Corinth in the eighth century for the Messenian choir sent to compete at Delos.[2]

Musical contests were of course peculiarly appropriate to Apollo. The earliest competition at Delphi was musical. Central Greece was particularly the home of the Muses; poetry flourished in Boeotia in the eighth century or earlier, and musical contests were frequent. It may be that the spirit of the Aegean civilization lingered there longer than elsewhere. Hesiod tells us how he competed at Chalcis, at the funeral games of Amphidamas, and won as a prize a fair-handled tripod which he dedicated to the Muses of Helicon, and later legend asserted that his defeated rival was none other than Homer.[3]

The Delian festival was the festival of the Ionians and never

[1] 147 ff.   [2] Paus. iv. 4. 1; 33. 2.
[3] *Works and Days*, 655.

became truly national. For the Panhellenic festival we must turn to the Peloponnese, the true home of Greek athletics, the home too, as we shall see, of the earliest athletic art. The first and the greatest of these festivals was the Olympic. A brief account of its early history will help us to understand the rise of the Pan-hellenic festival, its chief characteristics, and the growth of Greek athletics.

THE OLYMPIC FESTIVAL

Olympia, like Delos, owed its sanctity to its position. It lies a few miles from the sea on the north bank of the Alpheius in the angle formed by it with its northern tributary the Cladeus. North of Olympia and westwards of it stretched the flat coastal plain, the chief highroad into the Peloponnese from the shores of the Gulf of Corinth. Along this plain as far back as we can trace we find tribe after tribe of Northerners who had crossed the Gulf of Corinth pressing southwards. At Olympia their progress was checked by the broad river Alpheius. Here too they found a fertile plain that appealed to their pastoral tastes, and at an early date they established there, on the hill of Cronus overlooking the plain or in the grove of wild olive trees and plane trees at its foot, the worship of the northern sky god, Zeus. Fresh tribes arrived forcing the earlier comers or being forced themselves further south, or eastwards into the mountains. But they were all worshippers of Zeus, and this place, the Canterbury of the Peloponnese, retained for all of them its sanctity. There they would come to consult the oracle at the altar of Zeus, or would gather at his festival, and there at his altar they would hold chariot-races and games.

Greek tradition was unanimous in tracing the origin of the games to Heroic times. Legend connected Olympia with Pelops, who gave his name to the Peloponnese. He was generally sup-posed to be a Phrygian who passed over to central Greece and thence made his way to the Peloponnese. There he defeated Oenomaus, King of Pisa, in the chariot-race which he ordained as the trial for the hand of his daughter Hippodameia. Oenomaus was thrown from his chariot and killed, and Pelops took his kingdom. Pelops was certainly the chief local hero of Olympia. There he had a shrine and was worshipped as a hero. In late times it was supposed that the festival originated in the funeral games held at his tomb. But the general belief in the fifth century connected the games with Heracles. Pindar tells the story in his

Eleventh Olympian Ode. Heracles founded the games after his victory over Augeas. 'Then the mighty son of Zeus, having gathered together all his host at Pisa and all the booty, measured a sacred grove for his sovereign father. Having fenced round the Altis he marked the bounds thereof in a clear space, and the plain encompassing it he ordained for rest and feasting.' 'He set apart the choicest of the spoil for an offering from the war and sacrificed, and he ordained the fifth year feast with the first Olympiad and prizes of victory.' Pindar even tells us the names of those who 'won to their lot the new-appointed crown by hands or foot or chariot'. To Pindar then the festival belongs in the first place to Zeus, and it was founded as a thanksgiving after war.

ATHLETICS AND RELIGION

It is unnecessary here to discuss the value of these legends or the manifold theories that have been proposed as to the origin of the Games. I have endeavoured elsewhere [1] to show that there is no necessary connexion between the founding of a festival and the institution of games. In the case of some festivals founded in historical times we know that athletic sports were instituted from the first. We know too that in other cases games were added later. Thus athletic competitions were not introduced into the Pythian festival till the sixth century, though the festival itself and the musical contests were many centuries older.

Festivals arose from various origins. Many, and those the oldest, were connected with vegetation rites and the farmer's year, others were connected with the worship of some particular god or hero at some particular place. Many festivals originated in funeral games in honour of some chieftain, or soldier, or of those who fell in battle fighting for their country, a practice which we have seen goes back to Homeric times. Others were founded in commemoration of victory. Of this we have an example in Pindar's legend about Heracles at Olympia. In all these festivals games might be added, but there was no ritual meaning in the games themselves which were purely secular. They were added because festivals were times of peace when men gathered together peaceably under the protection of the gods, and the love of competition that characterized the race found its opportunity in such a gathering.

[1] *Olympia*, pp. 63 ff.; *B.S.A.* xxii, p. 85. Cp. Professor H. J. Rose, in *Aberystwyth Studies*, iii, pp. 1 ff.

At the same time it may well be that sports were felt to be particularly appropriate to certain festivals. They were appropriate at funeral games where they might be supposed to be pleasing to the spirit of the deceased who had in his lifetime found his pleasure therein. They were appropriate in games connected with victory. The remnant of Xenophon's Ten Thousand celebrated their return to safety by a sacrifice to Zeus Soter and by games.[1] Sports were appropriate to the festivals of certain gods or heroes, e.g. to those supposed to be the special patrons of sport, Apollo, Hermes, or Heracles. If, as I have suggested, the Olympic festival was from the first the festival of Olympian Zeus, the god of hosts, and was a cessation from war, such sports were particularly appropriate there.

But though the connexion between sport and religion was due to the athletic genius of the race rather than to any ritual significance in the games, we must not underrate the importance of this connexion. Thereby sports were definitely placed under the patronage of the gods, and the victorious athlete felt that he was well pleasing to the gods and owed his success to them. Further, the athlete felt that any violation of the rules of the games, especially any unfairness or corruption, was an act of sacrilege and displeasing to the gods. This feeling undoubtedly tended to preserve the purity of sport at Olympia even when corruption was rife elsewhere. Religious conservatism too tended to check any innovations and accordingly, though additions were made to the programme, the events remained essentially unchanged for nearly twelve centuries. It was to religion that Greek athletics and Greek athletic festivals owed their vitality.

EARLY HISTORY OF OLYMPIC FESTIVAL

Whatever the beginnings of the festival, there is no doubt that Olympia was at an early date a sacred place. There was a village settlement there in the twelfth century, and thousands of votive offerings have been found there dating from at least the tenth century. But times were unsettled. Olympia belonged originally to the Pisatans, but their control was disputed by the Eleans who were later immigrants from the North. In the course of the struggle the games, it is said, were neglected and forgotten. At last Cleosthenes, King of Pisa, and Iphitus, King of Elis, weary of the war, made a truce and revived the festival. The terms of this sacred truce were engraved on a bronze diskos which still existed in the time of Pausanias. The date of this event was fixed,

[1] *Anabasis*, iv. 8. 26.

we do not know how, as 776 B.C., and this year was reckoned as
the first Olympiad. From this date the Games were held every
four years till A.D. 393.

All festivals are times of truce, but the truce is usually somewhat
local. At Olympia the truce was particularly stringent. No one
was allowed during its continuance to bear arms in the territory
of Elis, and the Eleans advanced the claim that their whole land
was sacrosanct. Moreover, after its proclamation, all competitors
or visitors travelling to or from Olympia were under the direct
protection of the god. To violate any such pilgrim was an act
of sacrilege. Even Philip of Macedon was compelled to apologize
and pay a fine because an Athenian citizen on his way to Olympia
had been robbed by some of his mercenaries.[1] The truce in later
times, when the envoys announcing it had to travel to every part
of the Greek world, must have lasted two or three months. We
can easily understand that such a festival, where citizens of hostile
states could meet together in peaceful rivalry, even in times of
war, was a true influence for peace and goodwill.

We can trace the gradual growth of the festival partly in remains of buildings and inscriptions, partly in the Olympic
Register. This work, begun by Hippias of Elis in the fifth century
B.C., contained a list of victors in the games. Later it became the
basis of Greek chronology, the years being dated by the name of
the victor in the stade race, the first event on the list. The records
of the first two centuries are perhaps unreliable in detail, but the
story that they tell is extraordinarily clear and consistent.

For the first fifty years the Olympic festival was mostly confined to the inhabitants of the Western Peloponnese, but one
significant exception is recorded. The Pisatans, resenting the
interference of the Eleans, called in the help of the tyrant Pheidon
of Argos. Realizing the political value of the festival he invaded
Elis and usurped the presidency of the games. Argive control did
not last long. Within the next fifty years the influence of the
festival spread rapidly, to Sparta first, then eastwards to the
Isthmus, to Athens, to Thebes, and even across the sea to Smyrna.
But the chief feature of the period is the number of victories won
by Spartans. The growth of athletics in Greece was largely due
to the Spartans; they are said to have introduced the habit of
stripping naked for games and also the use of oil.[2] For 150 years
they were supreme at Olympia. Out of 81 victories recorded in
this period they are credited with 46.

[1] Demosthenes, *de fals. leg.* ὑπόθ. 335.   [2] Thuc. i. 6.

But meanwhile a greater development was taking place. The age of Greek colonization began in the eighth century, and in the seventh century bands of Greek adventurers were founding city states in every part of the Mediterranean world from the Black Sea to the coasts of Spain and Africa, above all in Sicily and Italy. Nothing proves more clearly the national character that athletics had already acquired than the list of victories won by these colonists at Olympia. Indeed, in the sixth century they almost eclipsed the athletes of the Motherland. At Olympia no fewer than six of the so-called Treasuries were dedicated by colonies.

The political importance of such a festival attracted tyrants and others who wished to increase their own prestige. Among the victors in the chariot-race we find Myron and Cleisthenes of Sicyon, and Periander of Corinth, while Cylon, the would-be tyrant of Athens, won a victory in the foot-race.

According to Pausanias [1] the Games had been forgotten during the dark ages and were revived one by one as men remembered them. So for thirteen Olympiads the only event was the foot-race. We need not credit this improbable story, but rather believe with Pindar that the programme from the first contained the chariot-race, foot-race, throwing the diskos and javelin, boxing, and wrestling. Other events were added later, the two-stade race in 724 B.C., the long distance race four years later. In 708 B.C. the pentathlon was introduced, perhaps in place of separate competitions with the diskos and javelin. In 648 B.C. the pankration was introduced, and in the same year the horse-race. The recorded introduction of the four-horse chariot-race in 680 B.C. perhaps means that at this date the four-horse chariot took the place of the two-horse war-chariot which had probably been used in the earliest games. The first events for boys, a foot-race and wrestling, were introduced in 632 B.C.; boxing for boys was added in 616 B.C. Thus by the beginning of the sixth century the athletic programme was complete, the only important addition being the race in armour, introduced in 520 B.C. Various equestrian events, a pankration for boys and competitions for trumpeters and heralds, were added in later times.

The only prize at the Olympic Games was a crown of wild olive. Phlegon [2] indeed states that this custom was not introduced till the seventh Olympiad, previous to which tripods and other valuable objects were given as prizes. But in this he is probably mistaken. The branches for the crowns were cut with

[1] v. 8.   [2] *F.H.G.* iii, p. 604.

a golden sickle by a boy both of whose parents were living, from the sacred olive tree that grew at the west end of the Temple of Zeus, where even to-day the wild olive may be seen. This looks like a piece of ancient vegetation ritual and suggests that there was an agrarian element in the festival; possibly the four-yearly festival was superimposed on a yearly festival connected with the olive harvest. But whatever its origin this custom of rewarding the victor with no other prize than a wreath of leaves set an example of athletic purity which had an important influence on Greek athletics. The example was followed at the other Panhellenic festivals, and these festivals of the crown (στεφανῖται) acquired such prestige over other festivals where prizes of value were offered that when in Hellenistic and Roman times it was desired to found new games of special distinction they were always festivals of the crown. Indeed, the Olympic crown is a lesson in sportsmanship for all time, reminding us that the true sportsman contends not for the value of the prize but for the honour of victory and not for his own honour only but for that of his country, his state, his school, his side.

THE PANHELLENIC FESTIVALS

The rise of the Olympic festival from a local to a national gathering gave an impulse not only to athletics but to the feeling of nationality, of Panhellenism, which contact with foreign nations was producing among the scattered states of the Greek world. In this festival combining religion and sport the Greeks beyond the sea found all that was most typical of their native civilization. At Olympia none but a freeborn Greek was allowed to compete; nothing, it was felt, distinguished the Greek from the barbarian more clearly than his love of athletics. So in the sixth century new athletic festivals sprang up everywhere, and three of them attained Panhellenic rank.

Delphi with its oracle had long acquired a national or almost cosmopolitan fame, and there a Pythian festival had been held every eight years with musical competitions. But in 582 B.C. it was reorganized as a four-yearly festival with the addition of an equestrian and athletic programme modelled on that of Olympia. At the same time crowns of bay-leaves cut from the Vale of Tempe were substituted for the valuable prizes hitherto given. In the same year an old festival of Poseidon at the Isthmus was reorganized as a Panhellenic festival. It was held not every fourth but every second year and the prize was a wreath of pine leaves. Corinth was the meeting-place of East and West, and the programme seems to have reflected in its variety the influence of that luxurious state, including horse races, athletics, musical competitions, and even a regatta. The last of the four Panhellenic festivals, the Nemea, was reorganized in 573, and like the Isthmia was held every alternate year. The prize was a crown of parsley.

The national character of these four festivals seems to have been recognized from the first, nor was it ever challenged. They were, *par excellence*, the Panhellenic festivals, the sacred games, the games of the crown. They formed a cycle (περίοδος), and the highest distinction that an athlete could win was to be a victor at all four Panhellenic games.

The founding of three new Panhellenic festivals within a few years and the immediate recognition of their national character are signs of a change that was taking place. Hitherto the story of Olympia and of Greek athletics has been one of natural growth, the sixth century is the age of athletic organization. Statesmen realize the value of athletics and do their best to encourage them. Solon makes regulations for the palaestrae, and also offers a reward of 500 drachmae to any Athenian who wins a victory at Olympia. A story told by Herodotus [1] illustrates the spirit of the age. In the reign of Psammetichus, King of Egypt (594–589 B.C.), the Eleans sent an embassy to inquire if the wisdom of the Egyptians could suggest any improvements in the fairness of the regulations for the Olympic Games. The Egyptian wise men having heard their story inquired if they allowed their own citizens to compete, and on hearing that the Games were open to all Greeks, whether they belonged to Elis or to any other state, they replied that this was manifestly unfair, for it was impossible but that they would favour their own countrymen and deal unfairly with foreigners. If therefore they wished to manage the Games with fairness, they must confine them to strangers. The Egyptians were not sportsmen. It is to the credit of the Eleans that even in the decline of sport no such ordinance was ever necessary for athletics, though in the fourth century, owing to a scandal, it was found necessary to forbid the judges themselves entering for the chariot-races. [2]

LOCAL FESTIVALS

Of the countless local festivals that sprang up everywhere in the sixth and fifth centuries we know little beside their names.

---

[1] ii. 160.　　　　[2] Paus. vi. i. 5.

PRIZES

Various objects are represented as prizes on the vases and other monuments; tripods, Figs. 8, 184; amphorae, Fig. 154; armour, Fig. 77; bowls, on the Clazomenae sarcophagus.

10. PRIZE BRONZE BOWL FOUND AT CYME IN ITALY. 6th century. British Museum, 163:

Inscription
'Ἐπὶ τοῖς 'Ονομάστου τοῦ Φειδίλεω ἀθλοῖς ἐθέθην. 'I was offered as a prize at the games of Onomastus, the son of Pheidileus.'
B.M. Guide to Greek and Roman Life, p. 63, Fig. 53.

11. VICTORY BEARING PRIZE HYDRIA. 470 B.C. Lekythos. New York, 07.286.67. Drawing by Professor Beazley. *Attic r.-f vases* in *American Museums*, pp. 75, 76.

12. B.-f. PANATHENAIC AMPHORA IN BRITISH MUSEUM. Early 4th century. Throwing the javelin on horseback. Two epheboi gallop and throw their javelins at a target. The target is a shield with a crown forming a sort of bull's-eye in the centre, supported by a post. The foremost ephebos has thrown his javelin, which is sticking in the bull's-eye. For this competition see P. Wolters, *Zu griechischen Agonen*, Wurzburg Program, 1901.
For Panathenaic Vases in general see G. von Brauchitsch, *Die Panathenäischen Preisamphoren*; Gardiner, *J.H.S.* xxxii, p. 179; E. Schmidt, *Archaistische Kunst*; Beazley, *Vases in Poland*, pp. 7, 8, and *B.S.R.* xi, p. 11; *Arch. Anz.* 1919, p. 76.

From the lists of victories enumerated by Pindar it is clear that every state had at least one athletic festival and states like Athens and Sparta had many. Moreover, at these festivals some of the competitions were open to athletes from all parts. The prizes were tripods or other objects of value; sometimes they were objects of local manufacture, a cloak at Pellene, a shield at Argos, vases of olive oil at Athens; sometimes the victor received a portion of the victim sacrificed, or perhaps the victim itself. The British Museum possesses a bronze cauldron (Fig. 10), dating from the sixth century B.C. which was found at Cyme in Italy, and which was given as a prize at some local games associated with a certain Onomastus. It bears the inscription, 'I was a prize at the games of Onomastus.' Another bronze vase in the British Museum is inscribed in Argive script of the fifth century, 'I am one of the prizes of Argive Hera.' [1]

The most famous of these local festivals was the Panathaea at Athens, though this never attained Panhellenic rank. Its founding in 566 B.C. is usually ascribed to Peisistratus, though, as he had not yet made himself tyrant, Solon may have had a share in it. It was really the remodelling of an old yearly festival, the Athenaea, which continued to be celebrated every year as the lesser Panathaea. But every fourth year from 566 B.C. there was a celebration of special magnificence. The great event of the festival, the procession that bore the *peplos* to the temple of Athene on the Acropolis, is familiar to all from the frieze of the Parthenon. It gave an opportunity for the display of all the forces of Athens. The programme was more varied even than that of the Isthmian Games. Besides athletics and horse-races it included musical contests, recitations, torch-races, Pyrrhic dances, a regatta, and even a competition for good looks. There were open events for all comers and local events confined to Athenian citizens, there were contests for men, youths, and boys. For most of the events the prizes consisted of jars of olive oil. Olive oil was the most valuable product of Attica, and its export was a state monopoly. As many as 1,300 amphorae of oil were distributed as prizes, the winner of the chariot-race receiving 100 amphorae.[2] As an amphora was worth at least 12 drachmae it is clear that these prizes were of considerable value. The Panathenaic vases which contained the oil were painted on one side with the figure of Athene, on the other with a picture of the contest for which the prize was given. Large numbers

---

[1] *J.H.S.* xlvi, p. 257.   [2] *I.G.* ii. 965.

◀ **13. MARBLE STATUE OF GIRL RUNNER.** Vatican. Copy of fifth-century bronze statue about 460 B.C. The trunk and foot-rest are copyist's additions. Photograph from a cast in the Ashmolean Museum from which the modern arms have been removed. The arms as restored in the Vatican statue give to the figure a mincing appearance. When they are removed we realize how vigorous is the movement of the figure. Notice especially the forward swing of the right shoulder as the arm swings forward with the left leg. It has been suggested that the position is that of the start or of the turn in the race. But no such motive is required. Without attempting to reproduce any moment in the actual race the sculptor has set himself the task of representing grace and lightness of movements, and in this he has succeeded.

◀ **14. BRONZE STATUE OF BOY VICTOR, GENER-ALLY KNOWN AS THE IDOLINO.** Mus. Arch. Florence. Possibly an original bronze about 440–430 B.C. The motive has been much disputed, see W. Hyde, *Victor Statues*, p. 141 *sq.* It probably represents a boy victor holding in his hand a libation bowl, and is certainly typical of those statues of boy athletes which were so popular in the latter half of the fifth century B.C.

of these vases have been found in Italian tombs and elsewhere, and they throw considerable light on ancient athletics. There is a particularly fine collection of them in the British Museum (Fig. 12).

The inclusion in the programmes of these festivals of special events for boys is clear proof that in the sixth century athletic exercises were everywhere an essential part of education. At Olympia events for boys were introduced in the seventh century. It is difficult to be sure what was the age limit for boys; most of the evidence is late. An inscription containing regulations for the Augustalia at Naples,[1] a festival closely modelled on that of Olympia, lays down that boys must be over seventeen and less than twenty years of age; and this was possibly the rule at Olympia. But in an age when birth certificates were unknown there must have been considerable elasticity and much must have been left to the discretion of the judges who doubtless took account of each competitor's physical development. Thus we hear of a young Athenian who was disqualified from competing as a boy because he was bigger than his fellows, though owing to the influence of Agesilaus he was finally allowed to compete.[2] Another youth of eighteen, Nicasylus of Rhodes [3] being disqualified as a boy entered for the open competition and won. At the Nemean, Isthmian, and Panathenaic Games there was an intermediate class between boys and men, 'the beardless' (ἀγένειοι), and there is some reason for thinking that the age limits for boys were twelve to sixteen, for the beardless, sixteen to twenty. Elsewhere in purely local competitions there were far more elaborate classifications. At the Athenian Thesea there were three classes of boys. Some competitions were probably confined to schools. Hence the young Greek athlete was from his boyhood continually testing his powers, first in close local competitions, then in open events in his own city or in neighbouring cities, till at last if sufficiently successful he would enter for one of the Panhellenic contests where the picked athletes of the Greek world met.

Athletics were not wholly confined to men and boys. Legend told of the foot-race in which Atalanta tested the prowess of her suitors, and a sixth-century vase represents her wrestling with Peleus (Fig. 158). Athenian women, it is true, were brought up in seclusion and forced inactivity, but it was not so among the

---

[1] *Olympia Inschriften*, no. 56.   [2] Plutarch, *Agesilaus*, 13.
[3] Paus. vi. 14. 1.

Dorians. Spartan girls took part in all the exercises of boys, and they attributed their beautiful complexions and figures to their athletic training. The maidens of Cyrene had foot-races, while Chian maidens wrestled and ran races with boys.[1] At Olympia married women were not allowed even to be present at the festival, but women had their own festival, the Heraea, where there were races for maidens of various ages.[2] The course was 500 feet, or one-sixth less than the men's stade. The victors received crowns of olive and a share of the heifer sacrificed to Hera. They had, too, the right of setting up their statues in the Heraion, and there exists in the Vatican a beautiful copy of a fifth-century statue representing one of these girl victors as described by Pausanias (Fig. 13). They ran, he says, with their hair down, wearing a chiton which came a little above the knee, with their right shoulder bare. The festival of Hera is obviously modelled on the Olympic festival, but we do not know when it was introduced.

NATIONAL IMPORTANCE OF ATHLETIC FESTIVALS IN THE FIFTH CENTURY

The multiplication of athletic competitions gave to athletics a national importance unparalleled in any other age or among any other people. The Panhellenic games were in reality inter-state competitions. Every state encouraged athletics, and in the public gymnasia opportunities for practice and training were provided for all at little cost. Moreover, the valuable prizes to be won at local sports and the rewards heaped on the winners in the national games made it possible for even the poorest to compete. Athletics were in sympathy with the growing spirit of democracy. The poor fisherman commemorated in an epigram of Simonides [3] 'who once carried fish from Argos to Tegea' had the right to compete at Olympia merely by reason of his birth, while Alexander the son of Amyntas had to prove his Greek descent before he was allowed to enter for the foot-race.[4] At the close of the sixth century the Greeks were literally a nation of athletes.

The popularity of athletics reached its height at the time of the Persian wars. The victory of Greeks over Persians was the victory of free city states over oriental despotism; it was the victory of a handful of trained athletes over hordes of effeminate barbarians. So the national triumph found its fullest expression

[1] Athenaeas, xiii. 566.   [2] Paus. v. 16.
[3] Bergk. 163.   [4] Hdt. v. 22.

in the great national games, where in honour of the national gods the picked representatives of the city states competed in friendly contests. The victory of Plataea was commemorated by national memorials at Olympia and Delphi and by the founding of a new athletic festival the 'Eleutheria', 'the Festival of Freedom'. At Olympia the reorganization of the management of the Games dated from this period together with a scheme of building—including that of the Great Temple of Zeus—destined to make the Sanctuary worthy of its national character. Yet almost more significant are the records of the Olympic games of 476 B.C., the first Games held after the war. Themistocles himself was present, the cynosure of all eyes. The list of victors includes names from every part of the Greek world, from Mitylene and the islands of the Aegean, from Sparta and Argos, from Italy and Sicily. Conspicuous among them were Iccus of Tarentum, winner of the pentathlon, quoted by Plato as an example of austerity in training, Euthymus of Italian Locri the boxer, and Theagenes of Thasos the pankratiast, athletes whose names remained household words and in whose honour statues were made by Pythagoras of Samos and Glaucias of Aegina. In the horse-race Hiero of Syracuse was the winner, in the chariot race Theron of Acragas. No fewer than five of Pindar's Olympian odes were written in praise of the victors in this Olympiad.

These Panhellenic festivals were much more than athletic meetings, Olympia above all was the meeting-place of the whole Greek world. At an early date various states, many of them from beyond the seas, sought to secure themselves a permanent standing at the sanctuary by dedicating little temples or treasuries. To the festival itself the cities sent official deputations (θεωρίαι) to represent them at the games and in the great procession on the day of the Full Moon when the official sacrifice was offered on the altar of Zeus. We have noticed too the obvious political value of such a meeting, and it was but natural that records of agreements and treaties between states should be set up at such a sanctuary. But apart from this the gathering of men of all classes and from all parts was a unique opportunity for artists, writers, philosophers, for all who had anything to exhibit or to sell. Such opportunities were rare in the Greek world. The poet or philosopher who wished to make himself known outside his native city had to make a round of other cities. But at Olympia he found a representative audience from all parts. There Herodotus read aloud his Histories from the opisthodome of the

Temple to the assembled crowds, among whom it was said was the youthful Thucydides. His example was followed by Hippias, Prodicus, and other Sophists. In the next century there arose the practice of erecting honorary statues, and those thus honoured included not only statesmen and generals but philosophers such as Aristotle and Anaximenes. These gatherings were natural opportunities too for trade, and the Olympic festival is described by Roman writers as the Olympic fair (*Mercatus Olympicus*).

These manifold interests tended gradually to rival the purely athletic interest. Indeed, from the middle of the fifth century the athletic interest begins to decline in Greece. A change was taking place in the character of athletics. Over-competition and the multiplication of prizes had made the conditions for success too strenuous and too exacting for the private citizen. So there arose a class of professional athletes, and though athletics formed part of the training of the Epheboi the people generally lost the athletic habit and grew content with the role of spectators. The decline of athletics was hastened by the incessant wars between themselves which for more than a century distracted the city states of Greece. Yet the crowds that flocked to the festivals showed little diminution, and, though there was a falling off in the athletic competitions, as spectacles the festivals were perhaps more attractive than ever. Horse-breeding was the fashionable amusement of the wealthy, and from this time the number of chariot-races and horse-races increased. Ambitious politicians like Alcibiades and Dionysius of Syracuse sought to further their own ends and win popularity by the magnificence of their displays at Olympia. Others more patriotic sought to revive the spirit of national unity. It was at Olympia that Gorgias appealed to the assembled crowds to forget their differences and to unite in a crusade against Persia, and his example was followed a few years later by Lysias and Isocrates. Indeed, the value of Olympia was never more clearly demonstrated than in this troublous time; there, in spite of athletic decline and corruption, was kept alive the feeling of Hellenic brotherhood.

THE MACEDONIAN AGE

The rise of Macedon threatened the independence of the city states, and it might have been expected that the athletic festivals would sink into insignificance. But the result was far otherwise. Philip and Alexander, like all who had sought to impose unity on the Greek world, realized the value of the national festivals, and sought to encourage them and to utilize them for their own ends. At Delphi Philip, who had helped the Delphians in the Sacred War, made himself president of the Pythian Games. At Olympia he had himself won a victory in the horse-race which he commemorated on his coins. In Macedonia he founded splendid Olympic Games at Aegae and at Dion. Alexander, in spite of his personal contempt for athletics, regarded Olympia as the capital of the Greek world. There he published the records of his eastern victories and thither in 324 B.C. he sent Nicanor to read before the crowds assembled at the festival the royal rescript ordering the cities of Greece to recall their exiles and acknowledge his divinity. New buildings and monuments testified to the generosity and wealth of the kings of Macedon. We can still see the marble steps of the Philippeion, a beautiful little marble temple begun by Philip and finished by Alexander and containing ivory and gold statues of themselves and other members of their family. Their successors followed their example. From the remains of the palaestra and gymnasium and other buildings we see that all through the third century Olympia maintained its prosperity, and as evidence of the spectacular character of the games we may note that all the buildings of this period were intended to promote the comfort of officials, athletes, and spectators.

Besides the patronage of kings, another cause helped to keep alive the national festivals. Alexander's conquest meant the Hellenization of the East, and Hellenization meant the city state. Everywhere, in Asia, in Syria, and in Egypt, Greek city states sprang up. Their independence indeed was illusory, but they cherished all the more keenly the semblance of autonomy and sought everywhere to reproduce the ideal of the free city state, and of this ideal athletics and athletic festivals were an inseparable part. So the athletic enthusiasm that had died out in the mother country revived in the cities of the East. Everywhere new festivals arose, modelled on and bearing the names of the old Panhellenic games; everywhere elaborate stadia and gymnasia were laid out. The new cities, following the example of better days, sent their champions to compete at Olympia and Delphi.

The records of the Olympic Games during this period are of remarkable interest.[1] We look in vain for victors from the great cities of the fifth century from Athens, Sparta, or Thebes. Their place is taken by Elis, Achaea, Arcadia. The remarkable number

[1] For these records see H. Förster, *Olympische Sieger*.

of local victories is clear proof of the decay of athletics in the rest
of Greece. Still more remarkable is the complete absence of
names from Italy and Sicily, from the Greek colonies that had
played so prominent a part in the sports of the sixth and fifth
centuries. The rise of Rome and Carthage had been fatal to those
states. But from Macedon and from the East there is no lack of
competitors. In the foot-race, the only event of which we have
a complete record, we find no fewer than six victories recorded
from Macedon and Thrace between the years 324 and 268 B.C.
Then they cease, and a similar series of victors from Alexandria
begins. Meanwhile there is an ever-increasing stream of competitors from the cities of Asia Minor and the islands. The new
cities emulate the old. Early in the second-century Alexandria
Troas and Seleucia figure in the lists, while other victors describe
themselves as Carians or Lydians.

ATHLETICS UNDER THE ROMANS

The last chapter in the story of the athletic festivals is perhaps
the most remarkable proof of the hold that they had taken on the
imagination of the ancient world. With the loss of Greek independence in 146 B.C. it seemed as if the very *raison d'être* of these
festivals had disappeared and as if their doom was inevitable, and
indeed the next century was the blackest in their history. The
wars that Rome had waged on Greek soil had impoverished Greece
morally, economically, and socially. The national sanctuaries
were bankrupt and could no longer afford to keep up their buildings or their festivals. At Olympia the competition fell off, and
for a century no athletic statues were erected, for a time even the
chariot-race was discontinued. But the Romans, though they
looked on athletics with contempt, realized the value of these
festivals. It was at the Isthmian Games that Flamininus proclaimed the liberties of Greece, and even Mummius, who destroyed those liberties, celebrated his victory by dedicating at
Olympia a bronze statue of Zeus and twenty-one gold shields
which were attached to the Metopes of the Temple. During the
civil wars matters went from bad to worse, and Sulla actually
attempted to transfer the Olympic Games to Rome. But Rome
had fallen under the spell of Greece, and when Augustus restored
peace to the troubled world a new era of prosperity began. The
old festivals were restored to their former splendour, new festivals
multiplied on every hand, and a wave of athleticism began,
culminating in the second century under Hadrian.

The revival under the Empire was due partly to the policy of Augustus and his successors, partly to the spread of athletics in Hellenistic times in the Hellenized cities of the East. The emperors realized that if they were to secure the loyalty of the various nations of their Eastern Empire it must be by encouraging the one thing that united them, the Hellenic civilization of the city states. They flattered these with a show of local independence and lavish grants of Roman citizenship. Clinging jealously to the tradition of the past, the Hellenic portion of the population who formed the aristocracy of these states still cherished athletics as their distinctive characteristic. They even described themselves as 'those from the gymnasium', or as we might say 'old gymnasium boys', to distinguish themselves from the barbarians.[1] Every city had its gymnasium and stadium, its festivals and competitions. In the days of freedom these competitions had culminated in the Panhellenic festivals which had served to unite the free city states of Greece. The Emperors saw therefore that the city states of their Eastern Empire could be best continued in their unity and loyalty by a revival of the Panhellenic festivals. There was the additional advantage that Greece and particularly Olympia was geographically the natural meeting-place of East and West.

Augustus seems to have had a genuine liking for athletics, unusual in a Roman. He was especially fond of watching boxing, and even street-fights. He had shown his interest in Olympia even before his principate, and under his influence the temple of Zeus and other buildings were restored and the festival recovered its popularity. The chariot-race was revived and even members of the Imperial family deigned to compete in it. Once more victories in the Games were commemorated by votive statues; new buildings and monuments testified to the patronage of the Emperors and the renewed prosperity of the sanctuary. The buildings at Delphi tell the same tale. Once more crowds flocked to consult the oracle or to view the Pythian Games. The Isthmian Games had since the destruction of Corinth languished under the presidency of Sicyon. Corinth, refounded as a Roman colony and once more wealthy and prosperous, resumed control of the Games, and they were celebrated with all their former splendour and magnificence: allusions to them in the writings of St. Paul show how deep was the impression they made on the apostle's mind. The Nemean Games shared in the general prosperity. On coins of the second century the names and emblems

[1] G. Méautis, *Hermoupolis-la-Grande*, p. 94.

of the four Panhellenic festivals are frequently represented. Crowds flocked to them from every part of the Roman world.

While the old Panhellenic festivals were thus regaining their prestige, new festivals were springing up on every side not only in Greece and in the East but even in Italy. Augustus celebrated his victory at Actium by holding Actian Games at Rome, and at the newly founded Nicopolis he instituted a new quinquennial Actian festival intended to rival Olympia. The festival which was closely modelled on the Panhellenic festivals included athletic, equestrian, and musical competitions and also a regatta. The victors received as a prize a wreath, and the Actiads were intended to form the basis of a new chronology which was to supplement that of the Olympiads, an intention which was never realized. In this we see the same spirit of conscious rivalry that made the Romans greet the *Aeneid* as a work greater than the *Iliad*. Romans and Greeks were not yet completely fused as they were in the second century.

This same feeling appears again in the title of *Isolympia*, applied to the Augustalia at Naples. Founded in 1 B.C. they were re-founded in A.D. 2 as a quinquennial festival with the magnificent title of *Italica Romaia Sebasta Isolympia*, and they too were to mark a new era reckoned by Italids. The festival consisted of two parts; the first part, like the Olympic Games, contained only athletic and equestrian events and the prize was a wreath: the second part, modelled on the Nemean and Pythian festivals, contained also musical and dramatic competitions, and some of these were confined to citizens of Naples. The victors in these received sums of money. We have seen that in Hellenistic times many festivals had been founded at various places bearing the name of Olympia, Pythia, Nemea. The right of granting these titles, which had probably been vested in the authorities of these sanctuaries, seems later to have been usurped by the Emperors. In A.D. 86 Domitian gave to the Capitolia which he founded at Rome the title of *Olympia*.

Of the number of festivals old and new we can form some idea from inscriptions recording the victories of famous athletes. One single example must suffice. It is the inscription in honour of Titus Flavius Artemidorus of Adana in Cilicia who won the pankration in the first Capitoline Games in A.D. 86.[1] He was a *periodoneikes* or victor in all the four Panhellenic Games, and his inscription records other victories at the Actia, at Naples,

[1] *I.G.* xiv. 746.

Smyrna, Pergamum, Ephesus, Alexandria, Antioch, Tralles, Sardis, Laodicea, Argos, and other places. Some festivals bear the name of wealthy benefactors who sought thereby to win popularity and immortality themselves. The Balbillea at Ephesus were founded by the astronomer Balbillus in the reign of Vespasian, the Eurycleia at Sparta by a patriotic Spartan, Eurycles, a friend of Herod the Great. Herod himself, in violation of all the traditions of the Jews, erected a theatre and amphitheatre at Jerusalem, and instituted a festival in honour of the Emperor with athletic, equestrian, and musical contests, to which he tried to attract competitors from all parts of the world by the lavishness of his prizes. Not content with this he exasperated the Jews by exhibiting gladiatorial games where criminals were forced to fight with wild beasts. Yet even this did not excite their resentment so much as the trophies in the theatre which they mistook for idols.[1]

The athletic movement initiated by Augustus was, at least as far as Italy was concerned, purely artificial. The athletic festival was to the Romans nothing more than a show. In the first century of our era they still regarded the Greeks with a certain contempt, and despised Greek athletics. To strip naked and to contend in public was degrading in the eyes of a Roman citizen. The populace in the cities of Italy had long been brutalized by gladiatorial shows and craved an excitement which pure athletics could not give. The only athletic events which interested them at all were the fighting events, wrestling, boxing, and the pankration. In the mosaics with which their baths were decorated these are the chief events represented. To make boxing more exciting the competitors were armed with the murderous caestus. Often too these contests were supplemented by gladiatorial shows and fights of wild animals. No effort was spared to enhance the splendour of the Games, to add interest and variety to the programmes, and to ensure the comfort of spectators. An advertisement of games to be held in the Amphitheatre of Pompeii announces that awnings will be provided and sprays of perfumed water (*vela et sparsiones*).[2]

In Greece and in the East the festivals had the same spectacular character. There too we find elaborate stadia provided for the comfort of spectators, there too we find gladiatorial games. At cosmopolitan cities like Antioch and Corinth gladiatorial games were naturally at home, but we even hear of them being held in the theatre of Dionysus at Athens. Still, for the most part, the Greek

[1] Josephus, xv. 8.   [2] *C.I.L.* iv. 1177, 3883.

festivals maintained their traditional athletic programmes. But the rivalry between the city states was gone, nor were the crowds that flocked to the festivals a sign of an athletic nation. The competitors at the national games of Hellas were mostly professionals from Alexandria and the East, men who went about from festival to festival amassing prizes and rewards. How they managed to establish their claim to Hellenic descent, which was still required at Olympia, is a problem. They had no more claim to represent any Hellenic state than hired football professionals from Scotland have to represent an English town. Yet the success of a Cup-tie team hardly evokes greater local patriotism than did the success of those cosmopolitan athletes at Olympia in the city which they elected to represent.

The cosmopolitan character of the competition is shown in inscriptions where competitors are described as drawn from the inhabited world (οἰκουμένη). They are no longer Hellenic but oecumenical. As a rule the competitions are confined to free citizens, but at some local festivals even slaves were allowed to compete. An inscription carved on the rock at Fassiller, a small village in Pisidia, which contains regulations for some local festival, says that if a slave is victorious he must hand over a quarter of the prize money to his fellow competitors.[1]

In spite of its artificiality the athletic movement steadily gained ground. Two causes especially contributed to this result, the revived prestige of Olympia and the pride of Hellenism in the East.

Olympia had from the first inspired the Romans with a respect that they did not usually feel for things Greek. In the dignity of Olympian Zeus they recognized their own Jupiter Optimus Maximus. Livy tells us how Aemilius Paulus as he gazed on the statue of Zeus was deeply affected as if in the presence of the god himself. Under the Empire the ideal of the godhead represented by Pheidias fascinated thinkers and philosophers more and more. The venerable tradition of the Games and the dignity of the ritual also appealed strongly to the Romans. It had been the policy of Augustus at Olympia, as elsewhere, to revive the ideals and to restore the worship of the past, and in this he was ably seconded by the authorities of Olympia. By insisting on exact obedience to the regulations of the Games, by sternly repressing all corruption, they made Olympia an example of athletic honour and of the purity of sport. 'It is strange', says Pausanias, speaking

[1] *American School of Classical Studies*, iii, no. 275; *C.R.* xliii, p. 210.

of one of the rare cases of bribery at Olympia, 'that any one should be found to despise the god at Olympia and to receive or give bribes in connexion with the games.'[1] Such an example was badly needed. Its effect is seen in the reverence that Olympia inspires even in writers who are most emphatic in denouncing the corruption of athletics. In the second century A.D. the festival attracted crowds as great as, or even greater than, in the days of freedom; Olympia was once more the meeting-place of East and West, the centre of Hellenism and of Hellenic religion.

We have noted that most of the competitors at the Olympic Games came from Egypt and Asia. Of the character of professional athletics at this time we shall deal more fully in another chapter. But the evils and corruption that too often degraded athletics must not blind us to the fact that since the loss of Greek independence it was in the cities of the East that Hellenism had found a refuge, and that what survived of the old athletic tradition was to be found there. In the schools and gymnasia athletics were still an essential and valuable part of education, and the athletic ambition was kept alive by competitions for boys of all ages from the local schools at their athletic festivals. If some of these festivals were degraded by the introduction of gladiatorial games and contests of wild beasts, there were others where the old athletic ideal was jealously maintained. We have a striking example in the games held at Daphne, near Syrian Antioch. Founded originally by Antiochus Epiphanes they received from the Eleans the title of Olympia in A.D. 44. The model of Olympia was followed in every particular not only in the programme and administration, but also in the relation existing between Daphne and Antioch which corresponded to that between Olympia and Elis. In the fourth century a fierce dispute arose about a proposal to transfer the festival from Daphne to Antioch. The conservative party headed by Libanius opposed it hotly on grounds of religious sentiment. The innovation, they urged, was an act of sacrilege, a violation of the true Olympia. We have many references to these games in the writings of St. Chrysostom who was presbyter at Antioch, and the festival continued to be celebrated as late as the reign of Justinus in the sixth century.

Nor must we condemn indiscriminately the whole class of professional athletes. We certainly find some at all times who tried to realize the old ideal, who were true sportsmen. Such were Melancomas of Caria and his son of whom Dio Chrysostom

[1] Paus. v. 21. 1 b.

has left a charming picture.[1] Such was Tiberius Claudius Rufus, a pankratiast of the reign of Hadrian,[2] who at Olympia maintained the contest till nightfall against an opponent who had drawn a bye in the previous round. The Eleans passed a decree in his honour recording how he had resided at Olympia for the necessary course of training, had followed the traditional law of the games, and in the contest had given an exhibition worthy of Olympian Zeus and of his own reputation and training.

Under Hadrian and his successors the mainland of Greece regained its prosperity and pre-eminence. Numerous buildings throughout Greece bear witness to Hadrian's interest in the games and to his generosity. At Athens he built a gymnasium, at Corinth he provided baths, at Nemea he instituted a winter festival, while at Mantinea and Argos he founded games in honour of his beloved Antinous. His favourite Herodes Atticus rebuilt the stadia at Athens and at Delphi, and contributed to the comfort of spectators at Olympia by providing a new water-supply terminating in the so-called Exedra. There seems to have been a genuine athletic revival in Greece, and particularly at Sparta. The Panhellenic festivals regained all their former splendour, and maintained their prosperity till the invasion of the Goths in the third century. From this time we hear little more. Yet in the reign of Julian we find them still continuing. The last Olympic victor whose name we know is the Armenian Prince Varazdates, who won the boxing in the 291st Olympiad (A. D. 385). But the end was at hand. The religion to which the Panhellenic festivals owed their life was dying. Christianity was now the established religion of the Empire. These festivals were the last stronghold of paganism, and their very popularity sealed their doom. The oracle of Delphi had been dismantled by Constantine: the Olympic festival was abolished by the express decree of the Emperor Theodosius in A.D. 393. The other festivals probably came to an end at the same time, though in the East some festivals like the Olympia of Antioch still lingered on till the sixth century.

[1] *Or.* xxix, xxx.   [2] *Ol. Inschr.* 54.

V

ATHLETICS AND ART

THE ATHLETIC IDEAL

WE have seen how the joy of effort and the love of competition that characterized the Greeks produced the athletic festival, and how with the multiplication of competitions and the rivalry of the city states the Greeks became in the sixth century literally a nation of athletes. Though we have no means of comparing their athletic performances with those of our own time, it may be safely asserted that no nation ever attained so high a level of physical fitness as the Greeks did at the close of the sixth and the beginning of the fifth century. But the Greeks were also a nation of artists, and in the beauty of the athlete the Greek artist found an inspiration no less strong than that of religion and indeed closely related to it. Thus there arose an athletic art which in its turn refined athletics and helped to produce the athletic ideal which found its highest expression in the sculpture of the fifth century.

The sixth century was an age of organized competition. But though gymnastics were already an essential part of education there was as yet no science of training. Such training as there was was merely traditional, differing little from that of the Homeric warrior, save that all classes now shared therein. Sport was still largely recreational, and was purely amateur. It was in the stage in which football was half a century ago in our schools and universities and clubs, when the game existed for the benefit of the players, not for the spectators and the press.

THE AGE OF STRENGTH

The characteristic of the sixth century is strength. The typical athlete of the period is the strong man, the boxer or the wrestler. These exercises, always the most popular, were also when practised in the true amateur spirit the most practical training for warfare. The great boxers and wrestlers, men whose names became proverbial, Milo of Croton, Glaucus of Carystus, Theagenes of Thasos, all belong to the close of the sixth century and beginning of the fifth century. We hear indeed of great runners, but they are less famous, the popular idea that the foot-race was honoured beyond all other events being purely fallacious. The object of the old gymnasts, says Philostratus,[1] was to produce strength only, and in consequence of their healthy life the old athletes maintained their strength for eight or even nine Olympiads. There was nothing artificial or unnatural about their training: the careful dieting, the elaborate massage, the rules for exercise and sleep introduced by later trainers were unknown. The trainers of those days were themselves athletes and confined their teaching to actual athletics, especially to the art of boxing and wrestling, and the athletes owed their strength to a healthy, vigorous, out-of-door life.

The stories told about these old athletes illustrate this fact. The father of Glaucus we are told discovered his son's strength one day from seeing him hammer in a ploughshare with his naked fist. So Tom Sayers one of the heroes of the prize-ring owed the severity of his punch to his practice in heaving bricks as a bricklayer. Theagenes displayed his strength at the age of nine by shouldering a bronze statue in the market-place and carrying it off. There are many stories of contests with wild beasts that recall the exploits of Samson, but the most characteristic exercise of the period was weight lifting. Milo practised it on most scientific principles with a young bull-calf which he lifted day by day till it was fully grown. But even he was defeated by the Aetolian shepherd Titormus. Challenged by Milo to show his strength he threw off his mantle, seized a huge boulder that Milo could hardly move, raised it first to his knees, then on to his shoulders and after carrying it sixteen yards threw it away. As a further proof of his strength he seized and held fast by the heels two wild bulls.[2]

These stories have been strangely confirmed by discoveries in Greece. At Olympia a block of red sandstone was found weighing 315 lb. with a sixth-century inscription stating that one Bybon with one hand threw it over his head. He must have raised it to his shoulders like Titormus, balanced it on one hand, and then thrown it. A still larger block weighing nearly half a ton (480 kilos) was found at Santorin, bearing the following inscription, also of the sixth century, 'Eumastas, the son of Critobulus, lifted me from the ground.'[3]

Swimming was also a favourite exercise. Tisander, a celebrated boxer of Naxos, kept himself fit by swimming daily out to sea.

---

[1] *Gym.* 43.   [2] Aelian, *V.H.* xii. 22.
[3] *J.H.S.* xxvii, p. 2; *Olympia*, p. 97.

The old athletes, says Philostratus, hardened themselves by bathing in the rivers and sleeping in the open air on skins or heaps of fodder. Living such a life they had healthy appetites and were not particular about their food, living on porridge and unleavened bread and such meat as they could get. The strong man is naturally a large eater; and all sorts of tales were rife about their voracity. Milo, according to an epigram, after carrying a four-year-old heifer round the Altis at Olympia ate it on the same day. The Homeric heroes had equally heroic appetites, probably because meat was not an ordinary part of their diet. These tales are the invention of a later age when the strong man was trained on vast quantities of meat. But this was not the diet of the sixth century. The athletes of this age were healthy, free from disease, preserved their strength, and lived long. Nor did athletics unfit them for the duties of ordinary life and military service. Many of them won distinction in war, and the effects of athletics on the nation were shown in the Persian Wars.

When we turn to the records of art we still find strength the predominant characteristic of the period. We see this in those early nude statues, widely distributed throughout Greece and the islands, which are generally classed under the name of Apollo, though better described by the vaguer term *kouroi*. Whether they represent a god or a man, there is no doubt of their athletic character. In all of them we see the same attempt to render the muscles of the body, whether in the tall, spare type of the Apollo of Tenea (Fig. 16), or the shorter, heavier type of the Argive statues (Fig. 15). It is in the muscles of the trunk rather than of the limbs that real strength lies, and it is the careful rendering of these muscles that distinguishes early Greek sculpture from all other early art, and that particularly characterizes the sculpture of the Peloponnese. The typical figure of the sixth century is that of the bearded Heracles, not the clumsy giant of later days but the personification of endurance and strength, a man, as Pindar says, 'short of stature but of unbending soul'. So he is represented on the black-figured vases (Figs. 149, 194, &c.), and the type survives in the pediments of Aegina and the metopes of Olympia (Fig. 20)

THE AGE OF ATHLETIC BEAUTY

In the art of the fifth century we note a change which is most marked in vase-paintings. On vases of the sixth century the type of athlete commonly represented is the fully grown man (Fig.

PHYSICAL TYPES IN EARLY SCULPTURE

◄ 15. MARBLE STATUE OF CLEOBIS OR BITON (Hdt. i. 31) by Polymedes of Argos. Delphi Museum. About 600 B.C. The attitude is borrowed from Egypt, but in the close study of the forms of the human body the work is thoroughly Greek. The heavy properties are typical of Argive art, see Figs. 25, 26, 27.

◄ 16. MARBLE STATUE OF YOUTH, found at Tenea near Corinth, generally known as the 'Apollo of Tenea'. About 550 B.C. Munich. *Fünfzig Meisterwerke der Glyptothek*, pl. IV.

◄ 17. MARBLE STATUE OF YOUTH (*kouros*) generally known as the Strangford Apollo. British Museum. About 490 B.C.

◄ 18. THE CHOISEUL-GOUFFIER APOLLO. Roman copy of a bronze original of about 470 B.C. British Museum.

◄ 19. FIGURE FROM THE E. PEDIMENT OF THE TEMPLE OF APHAIA, AEGINA. About 490–480 B.C. Munich. The figure is that of an attendant who rushes forward to help his fallen master. The arms are modern. *Fünfzig Meisterwerke der Glyptothek*, pl. XII.

◄ 20. HERACLES AND ATLAS. Metope from the temple of Zeus at Olympia. About 460 B.C. Olympia Museum. Heracles supports the heavens on his shoulders while Atlas brings to him the apples of the Hesperides. Athene stands behind and lends a helping hand.

155); he is usually bearded and, though of ordinary stature, is of powerful physique. The scene depicted is usually some actual competition, particularly in boxing or wrestling. On red-figured vases of the early fifth century the type is that of athletic youth, strong but beautifully developed and graceful. The scene is taken not from competition in the stadium but from the practice of the gymnasium or palaestra, and every variety of sport is depicted, especially the exercises of the pentathlon, throwing the diskos and the javelin, and jumping. The hero of the red-figured vase-painters is not Heracles but Theseus, usually represented as a youthful wrestler conquering his enemies by the art of the wrestling school (Figs. 161, 166, 167). If strength is the key-note of the sixth century, that of the fifth is the union of strength and beauty which belongs especially to the age of full-grown youth and early manhood.

The change may be attributed partly at least to the growth of city life, to the increasing importance of the gymnasium in the life of the city, and to the organized education of the Epheboi. In most states youths between the ages of sixteen and eighteen were enrolled in corps and underwent two years of strict military and athletic training. They learnt to use their weapons and ride, they hardened their bodies by athletics and hunting, and they gained practical experience by serving as patrols on the borders of their state. Much of this training took place in the public gymnasia, which were not buildings so much as recreation or sports-grounds often situated on the outskirts of the city in a grove beside a river. There under special trainers they could ride, run, wrestle, practise any form of exercise. Men of all ages would come to join in the sports or watch the contests of others. So the gymnasia became the daily resort of the whole city.

To the gymnasium is due the intimate connexion between Greek athletics and art. It has been well said that without athletics Greek sculpture cannot be conceived. The gymnasium was the Greek sculptor's studio. There daily he could watch men and boys of every age engaged in every form of sport, and there he acquired that consummate knowledge of the naked human body that is his chief glory. For the Greek, whether in competition or in practice, as the word gymnasium implies, stripped absolutely naked. Even the loin-cloth is rarely seen on sixth-century vases. To be ashamed to be seen naked was to the Greek the mark of a barbarian.

This custom of nudity, which was the Greek sculptor's opportunity, had no little effect on athletics. It is not merely that exposure to the air and the sun-bath are, as doctors now tell us, the very best of physic, but it served as a valuable incentive to the youth of Greece to keep themselves in good condition. The Greek with his keen eye for physical beauty regarded flabbiness, a pale skin, want of condition, or imperfect development as disgraceful, and the ill-developed youth was the laughing-stock of his companions. Of this we have a delightful illustration on a vase in the British Museum (Fig. 21). In the centre is a stool with clothes on it. To the right two graceful youths practise the diskos and the javelin. On the left two ill-developed youths, one lean and skinny, the other pot-bellied, are wrangling. Can it be that the painter is caricaturing two of his contemporaries?

EARLY ATHLETIC STATUES

There was a still closer connexion between athletics and sculpture. As early as the middle of the sixth century the strange custom had arisen of allowing victors in the Great Games to commemorate their successes by dedicating life-size statues sometimes in their native cities, more often in the national sanctuaries, especially at Olympia. How the practice arose we cannot say for certain; possibly it was from the older practice of offering little votive statuettes for victory. At Olympia, among thousands of votive offerings, are miniature bronze chariots and charioteers, mounted horsemen, and statuettes of naked warriors, which may well have been offerings in payment of vows for victory in the Games. The earliest of these victor statues were those of Praxidamas of Aegina, who won the boxing in 544 B.C., and of Rhexibius of Opous, victor in the pankration eight years later. But Pausanias tells us of earlier victors whose victories were commemorated by statues at Olympia, and at Phigaleia he mentions a statue to the memory of Arrhichion, the famous pankratiast of 564 B.C., who died at the very moment that his opponent gave up, but though dead yet received the victor's crown. To the same period belong the earliest of the prize Panathenaic vases with their pictures of the various events in the Games. From this period there was a continuous demand for athletic statues which produced the athletic school of sculpture at Argos and Sicyon and influenced the whole development of Greek art.

There were hundreds of athletic statues at Olympia alone. Yet of all the number there or elsewhere only a few fragments remain.

They were mostly of bronze and were melted down for the sake of the metal. The only victor statue that has survived whole is the bronze charioteer from Delphi. But many are known to us from marble copies of various dates, though the identification of them with particular athletes is purely conjectural. These statues were not as a rule portrait statues. Pliny tells us that only those who had won three victories were allowed to commemorate their success by portrait statues.[1] But this statement

21. Palaestra scene. Attic r.-f. kylix in British Museum E. 6. About 520 B.C. To l. altercation between a fat and a lean youth. In centre stool heaped with clothing. To r. javelin thrower pushing the amentum tight, cp. Figs. 142, 143. For diskobolos, cp. Figs. 122, 129.

can only apply to later times. For before the fourth century portrait statues were almost unknown.

The earliest athletic statues must have been of the type of those early *kouroi* mentioned above. In the sixth century, while strength is always the predominant motive, there is a remarkable diversity of physical type which might tempt us to suppose that the sculptors were trying to represent different types of athlete. Thus in the Apollo of Tenea (Fig. 16), slim and long-limbed with spare flanks and muscular legs, we seem to see the long-distance runner just as he is depicted on Panathenaic vases (Fig. 92). On the other hand, the heavy, thick-set forms of the two early Argive statues from Delphi (Fig. 15), with their powerful limbs and massive heads, obviously represent the strong man. But between the two extremes are numerous intermediate types, such as that

N.H. xxxiv. 16.

22. JUMPER SWINGING HALTERES. Greek work of
early 5th century. Rome, Villa Giulia. This very vigorous
little figure represents a standing jump, See p. 149. Photograph obtained by Mrs. Strong.

23. ATHLETE PUTTING A STONE. Etruscan bronze,
late 5th century. Museo Civico, Bologna. This is as far as
I know the only representation of putting the stone, though
it doubtless was a familiar exercise. Photograph from the
Director of the Museum.

**24. HOPLITODROME IN THE ATTITUDE OF
STARTING.** Height ·164 m. 490–480 B.C. Tübingen. The
shield on right arm and crest of the helmet are lost. For the
position see Figs. 87, 88, 96. Hauser, *Jahrb.* 1887, p. 95; 1895,
p. 182; de Ridder, *B.C.H.* 1897, p. 211; Gardiner, *J.H.S.*
xxiii, p. 269.

25. STATUETTE OF ATHLETE, found at Ligurio in
Argolis, generally known as the Ligurio Bronze. Early 5th
century. Now in Berlin. The heavy jowl and thick sturdy
figure are typical of the Argive School. The object held in
the left hand is probably an apple. See A. Furtwängler, 50*th
Winckelmann's Program*, 1890.

of the Strangford Apollo from Boeotia (Fig. 17), and it would be safer to conclude that the diversity of type is due to the predominance of different physical types in different parts of Greece. For Greek art was widespread as Greek athletics, and everywhere in this archaic art we find, to quote Professor Beazley's words, the same 'loving study and systematic exploration of the human body'. This explanation is confirmed by the continuance of this diversity of type in the more varied and highly developed art of the early fifth century. At the one extreme we have the Choiseul-Gouffier Apollo (Fig. 18), tall, broad-shouldered, with powerful chest and back, essentially a big man. Somewhat similar are the tall, long-limbed forms of the tyrannicides Harmodius and Aristogeiton, a group set up in Athens in 486 B.C. Here perhaps we may recognize the Attic type. At the other extreme are the slim, wiry warriors of the Aeginetan pediments (Fig. 19). Between the two are the Lapiths from the temple at Olympia (Fig. 35) and the sturdy little bronze figure from Ligurio (Fig. 25), short like the Aeginetan, but heavier and more fleshy, which may be taken to represent the Argive type, afterwards developed by Polyclitus. But Greek art like Greek athletics was working towards an ideal, and in the latter half of the fifth century this diversity of type tends to disappear partly owing to the influence of Polyclitus and Pheidias.

But in all this diversity of physical type it is difficult to say what class of athlete, if any, is represented. The fact is that the real specialization of the athlete was only beginning, and the universal athletic training had produced in the first half of the fifth century so uniform a standard of development that, with the possible exception of runners, it must have been difficult to distinguish between the representatives of other events in all of which strength was essential. Hence the early sculptors, in order to indicate in what event victory had been gained, would put into the hands of the statue a diskos or a pair of jumping-weights for the pentathlete, boxing-thongs for the boxer. Later they represented the athlete in some typical position, a boxer sparring with an imaginary opponent or a pentathlete swinging the diskos or jumping-weights (Figs. 22–5, 125–8). An excellent example of this is the little bronze in Fig. 24, which shows an armed runner practising starts.

ATHLETIC STATUES BY POLYCLITUS
AND LYSIPPUS

26. THE DORYPHOROS OF POLYCLITUS. Roman copy in marble of the Bronze *Doryphoros* of Polyclitus, known as the Kanon. About 440 B.C. Found in the old palaestra at Pompeii. Now in Naples Museum. The spear is modern. *Photo. Brogi.*

27. THE DIADOUMENOS OF POLYCLITUS. Athlete binding a fillet round his head, possibly Apollo. Marble copy of a bronze original, about 430 B.C. Found in Delos. National Museum, Athens. *Photo. Alinari.*

28. STATUE OF AGIAS. A late 4th-century marble statue of the pankratiast Agias, found at Delphi, a copy of a statue belonging to a bronze group by Lysippus. The ankles are modern. Museum, Delphi. Photograph from a cast.

29. THE APOXYOMENOS. Athlete scraping himself with a strigil. Marble copy of a bronze statue by Lysippus. Late 4th century. In the Vatican. Photograph from a cast.

MODERN ATHLETIC ART ◥

*Three bronzes by Professor R. Tait McKenzie, Philadelphia,
to whose kindness I am indebted for the photographs.*

30. THE COLLEGE ATHLETE. The figure represents
an athlete holding a dynamometer. The original bronze is one-
quarter life-size and the proportions are taken from the average
proportions of fifty picked athletes.

31. THE DISKOS THROWER. This figure illustrates how
far the style of the modern diskos-thrower approximates to
that of Myron's statue. The chief points of difference are the
more crouching position of the body, the position of the head,
and the turn of the diskos in the right hand.

32. THE STARTER. This represents the modern crouching start. It is stated in various books that the Greeks started
off their hands in this way. There is not the slightest evidence
for such a statement.

K

MYRON AND POLYCLITUS

This naturally brings us to the most famous of athletic statues, the Diskobolos of Myron (Fig. 117). He and his great contemporary Polyclitus both belong to the middle of the fifth century. Their most important athletic statues are known to us from numerous marble copies, and are of peculiar interest because they are not statues made to commemorate victories but are studies in athletic genre, a clear proof that the artists of this age were consciously working out ideals.

Myron, whose work fell between 480 and 440 B.C., devoted himself especially to the study of the athlete in motion. In the Diskobolos he has chosen the only moment that could rightly be fixed in bronze, the only moment that combines stability and motion. At the top of the backward swing there appears to be a momentary pause which suggests stability, while the contorted position of the body and the rope-like pull of the right arm imply the movement that has preceded it and the yet stronger movement that is to follow. Another famous statue by Myron represented the runner Ladas apparently at the very finish of the race straining forward in expectation of victory. We would give much to know how he succeeded in solving this far more difficult problem of fixing in bronze a runner at full speed. For here there is no moment of pause or balance. But, alas, not even a copy of the statue is left to us, possibly because it was quite impossible to transfer it to marble.

Polyclitus, who was a few years junior to Myron, was the most famous of the great Argive school of sculpture. His best-known works, the Doryphoros and the Diadoumenos (Figs. 26, 27), are like the Diskobolos works of athletic genre, but they are studies not of action but of proportion. They are standing figures, but by introducing a new stance, placing all the weight on one leg, and drawing the other back so that it only lightly touched the ground, Polyclitus contrived to give to the standing figure a life and rhythm unknown before. Indeed the Doryphoros is just on the point of moving forward. In this statue Polyclitus embodied his theory of bodily proportion; he called it his *kanon* or rule, and wrote a treatise explaining its proportions. The Doryphoros is of medium height, square set, and solidly built, with body and limbs finely developed, yet without any exaggeration or overdevelopment. The head is somewhat long with a powerful jaw that harmonizes well with the figure. The impression that the statue produces is of power and determination. It is a type equally fitted for athletics or for warfare. He is not a specialist, certainly not a champion runner, though he can probably hold his own with most men in the race, but a good all-round athlete, and we feel that in any competition he will be hard to beat. A severe type possibly; but to Polyclitus as to Pindar athletics were not play, 'victory comes not without toil'. The Diadoumenos represents a somewhat older youth winding round his head the victor's fillet. The attitude is more graceful, with a slight suggestion of weariness after the struggle, the forms are somewhat rounder and softer; yet the proportions of the two statues are similar.

It is interesting to compare with the *kanon* of Polyclitus the fourth-century Apoxyomenos (Fig. 29). The existing statue is probably a faithful copy of the work of Lysippus, who is said to have worked out a new scheme of proportions, and it may certainly be taken as representing this new scheme. The contrast between the two works is obvious. The Apoxyomenos is beautifully developed and in superb condition, but the small head, the greater slimness of body, the greater length of limb, suggest the runner or the jumper rather than the all-round athlete. Still more do we miss the stern resolution of the Doryphoros: there is a restlessness in the attitude, a want of steadfastness, and in spite of his superb physique we doubt whether his heart is in the contest, whether he will finish well if hard pressed.

Lastly, let me set beside these two statues a work by a modern sculptor, Dr. Tait McKenzie (Fig. 30). Himself an athlete, a medical man, and Professor of Physical Culture at Philadelphia, Dr. McKenzie has had the same opportunity that the Greek sculptor had of studying the daily practice of athletes of all descriptions, and the delightful bronzes in which he has embodied the results of his observation are the nearest parallel that the modern world has produced to the athletic art of the Greeks. The College Athlete is a study in proportion. It is based on the average measurements of a number of picked American athletes, and it is remarkable how closely in its general type it agrees with the *kanon* of Polyclitus. On the same plate I have given two other bronzes by Tait McKenzie (Figs. 31, 32), one representing the crouching start, the other a diskobolos in the modern style which it is interesting to compare with Myron's statue.

THE ATHLETIC IDEAL IN ART

The effect of this striving after an ideal is seen in an increasing uniformity of type during the second half of the fifth century. This is but natural. The ideal cannot be found in any extreme of type, in strength or beauty by itself, but only in a combination of the two. His athletic training had taught the sculptor the value of physical strength, systematically trained and developed; his artistic sense taught him that no subject was worthy of his art which did not present beauty of line and proportion. Hence that union of strength and beauty which characterizes the art of this period.

The union of strength and beauty belongs especially to the time of full-grown youth and opening manhood. And it is the ideal of youthful strength and beauty that dominated the art of the Periclean age. Indeed the art of this age has been truly described as the glorification of the Ephebos. The beautiful bronze statue of a youthful athlete at Florence known as the Idolino (Fig. 14) is possibly an original work of this period; other statues are known to us in copies. But the ephebos is best known to us from grave-reliefs, numbers of which still survive, and from the frieze of the Parthenon.

If we would realize how completely athletic experience permeates Greek sculpture in the fifth century we have only to look at those great temple sculptures to which I have already referred. Two examples will illustrate the skill which the Greeks had acquired in representing the human body alike in violent action and repose—the young Lapith on the pediment of Olympia straining every nerve in the struggle, and the so-called Theseus of the Parthenon, a perfect example of strength in repose (Figs. 33, 34).

The influence of athletics is equally marked in the lesser arts, in coins, gems, and above all on vase-paintings. Pl. 35 shows a selection of coin types taken from the Games. It is noticeable that the diskos types and the wrestling types belong to the fifth century. Of vase-paintings I need say no more. To them we are indebted for most of our knowledge of the details of Greek athletics, and from them are drawn the majority of the illustrations in this book.

This intimate connexion between athletics and art had a strong influence on athletics. To it we may ascribe perhaps the most distinctive feature of Greek athletics, the importance attached to

a. Winged figure of Agon holding crowns. Tetradrachm of Peparethus. Early 5th century. *J.H.S.* xxvii. pl. IV. 1.

b. Prize table bearing crowns, five apples, vase and crow. Imperial bronze coin of Delphi. *B.M. Coins*, Delphi, 38.

c. Victory seated, holding in r. hand palm. Olive branch in exergue. Tetradrachm of Elis. 5th century. *B.M. Coins*, Elis, 51.

d. Diskos-thrower (see p. 160) on tetradrachm of Cos. Beginning of 5th century. *J.H.S.* xxvii, p. 30; P. Gardner, *Types of Greek Coins*, p. 116.

e. Crown of bay-leaves of Pythian games. Imperial bronze coin of Delphi. *B.M. Coins*, Delphi, 39.

f. Diskos-thrower. Didrachm of Abdera. Late 5th century. P. Gardner, *Types of Greek Coins*, p. 110. In *B.M. Coins*, Abdera 30, the diskos is described as a patera.

g, h. Wrestlers on staters of Aspendos. 431–371 B.C. P. Gardner, *Types*, p. 144; *B.M. Coins*, Pamphylia, p. 95 *sq.* In g the left-hand wrestler has seized his opponent's left arm with both hands: notice the realistic treatment of the wrist hanging limply down. In h the wrestler to r. seems to be seizing his opponent's thigh.

i. Torch-race on horseback. Silver stater of Tarentum. 3rd century B.C.

j. Mule chariot race. Silver tetradrachm of Rhegium. Early 5th century, commemorating the victory of Anaxilas at Olympia. Head, *Historia Numorum*, p. 108.

k. Naked horseman dismounting from galloping horse (*apobates*). Didrachm of Himera. 5th century.

l. Victorious jockey. Silver tetradrachm of Philip II of Macedon.

m. Wrestlers, Heracles and Antaeus. Alexandria. Bronze coin of Antoninus Pius. This group shows an extraordinary resemblance to the bronze group, Fig. 171.

n. Victorious chariot. Nike crowning the charioteer. In the exergue a shield, helmet, cuirass, and greaves. Silver decadrachm of Syracuse. One of a series of coins connected with the defeat of the Athenians at the river Assinarus, commemorated by the festival of the Assinaria first held in 412 B. C. The arms are doubtless the spoils taken from the Athenians, offered as prizes.

style and rhythm of movement. Of this we shall find abundant evidence in the following pages.

In all these figures the prevailing impression is one of perfect harmony, an absence of all exaggeration. Beauty is not exaggerated into softness, nor strength into coarseness. There is, too, a graceful ease of movement and of action which tells of an education in which music goes hand in hand with gymnastic. The influence of music is especially suggested in the rhythmic poise and movement of the Diadoumenos. Hence these harmonious forms produce an effect deeper than that of mere beauty; they seem to be the expression of the spirit within. The heads, too, are in perfect harmony with the bodies, the heads of healthy, vigorous youths, to whom all activity of body or mind is a joy. Their expression is calm and dignified, but modest withal and without a trace of arrogance or pride (see Frontispiece). We may note the modesty in the downcast eyes of the Diadoumenos as he binds the fillet of victory round his head. This combination of dignity and modesty is what the Greeks called *Aidōs*, the key-note of Pindar's athletic ideal.

THE ATHLETIC IDEAL OF PINDAR

For the spirit of this athletic art we need not depend on mere impression, it is interpreted for us by Pindar. This brings us to another strange custom which illustrates the extraordinary importance attached to athletics and athletic success in the sixth and fifth centuries. Not only were the greatest sculptors employed to commemorate victories in the Games, but the greatest lyric poets also celebrated the victor's praises in Epinikia or hymns of victory to be sung by choirs of boys in the triumphal procession that welcomed the victor to his native city, or else at Olympia on the evening of the victory when in joyous revel victors and their friends went round the altars to pay their vows to the gods or heroes to whom they owed their victory. The earliest writer of Epinikia, Simonides of Ceos, wrote at the end of the sixth century. Of his poems only a few fragments survive. Nor was much more known of his nephew Bacchylides till a few years ago when portions of some thirteen of his poems were found on an Egyptian papyrus. He came of an athletic stock, and he dwells with delight on details of the games, but of their spirit he tells us nothing. For that we must turn to his contemporary, Pindar, the greatest lyric poet of the fifth century, and almost the last writer of

Epinikia. For while the custom of dedicating athletic statues survived even in Roman times, we hear of no hymns of victory after the fifth century.

Pindar's earliest poems were written at the beginning of the century, his last in 444 B.C., but the majority were composed after the Persian War in that great outburst of enthusiasm for athletics which followed the triumph of Greece. He was himself a Theban and an aristocrat, but his muse, he tells us, was a hireling, and he wrote for those who could afford to pay him, for those princes and well-born youths who competed in the chariot-races and in athletics for no mercenary or selfish motive but for sheer joy in the competition and love of fame. 'The shepherd and the ploughman and the fowler and he whom the sea feedeth strive to keep fierce famine from their bellies; but whoso in the games or in war hath won delightful fame, receiveth the highest of rewards in fair words of citizens and of strangers.' [1]

The qualities of the true athlete are summed up in Pindar's eleventh *Olympian Ode* in honour of the youthful boxer Agesidemus: 'If one be born with excellent gifts then may another who sharpeneth his natural edge, speed him, God helping, to an exceeding weight of glory. Without toil there have triumphed a very few.'

First and above all the athlete must be born with excellent gifts. Strength and beauty are the gifts of Zeus, of the Graces, of Fate, and they are bestowed especially on members of ancient and honourable families. But physical beauty must be matched by beautiful deeds; the athlete must not shame his beauty. Natural gifts imply the duty of developing them, and excellence can only be attained, God helping, by 'cost and toil'.[2] Here, as Professor Gildersleeve has well said, Pindar gives a moral dignity to athletics: for the cost and toil are undertaken not by compulsion but for fame. Even the desire for fame is not wholly selfish. Victory is a delight and honour to the victor's city, to his family, even to his dead ancestors. Moreover, the true sportsman 'delights in the toil and the cost'.

The expense of competing in the chariot- and horse-races was naturally far heavier than that of competing in athletic events; yet even these involved considerable sacrifice of time and money for those who competed at the national games. It is true that athletics were hereditary in certain families like that of Lampon

---

[1] *I.* i. 47 ff. The translations are those of Ernest Myers.
[2] *I.* i. 42; iv. 57; v. 10.

of Aegina,[1] whom Pindar describes as a 'whetstone among athletes', bestowing practice on all that he does, and exhorting his
sons to follow the precept of Hesiod, 'Practice perfects the deed'.
But as a rule the services of a professional trainer were called in
and he was doubtless highly paid. The most popular events
among Pindar's patrons were boxing, wrestling, and the pankration, sports which involved not only toil but risk to limbs, if not
to life. But the risk only adds zest to the sport. 'Deeds of no
risk', the poet tells us, 'are honourless whether done among men
or among hollow ships.'[2] It follows, then, that the most necessary qualities for an athlete are courage and endurance. Heracles,
his ideal athlete, is a man of unbending spirit.

But the most characteristic quality of the athlete to Pindar is
what is expressed by that untranslatable word Aidōs, the quality
that wins him the favour of the gods and averts their jealousy.
That jealousy is excited by all excess, by pride, by insolence.
Aidōs is the exact opposite of insolence (ὕβρις): it is the feeling
of respect for what is due to the gods, to one's fellow men, to
oneself; the feeling of reverence, modesty, honour. It distinguishes the athlete from the bully. Strength may tempt a man
to abuse it; success may beget 'braggart insolence'.[3] But aidōs
puts into the heart 'valour and the joy of battle'.[4] No sports
demand so high a standard of honour as boxing and wrestling,
and none are so liable to corruption. But aidōs makes a man
'a straight fighter', the epithet by which Pindar describes Dia-
goras of Rhodes 'who walks in the straight path that abhors
insolence'.[5] It is a feeling incompatible with the commercial
spirit, for 'aidōs is stolen away by secret gain'. It is akin to that
typical Greek virtue of self-control, Sōphrosyne, but is something more subtle and more indefinite, and its comprehension
may help us to understand how even sports that seem to us brutal
are under the special patronage of those fair-haired Graces who
give and grace the victory 'from whom come unto man all pleasant
things and sweet and the wisdom of man and his beauty and the
splendour of his fame'.[6]

Aidōs has much in common with the feeling of honour which
is the essence of that much-abused term, a sportsman. But
though aidōs is a much deeper feeling, we miss in it, or at least
in its practice, that chivalrous generosity towards the loser that is

---

[1] *I.* iv. v; *N.* v.
[3] *O.* i. 56, xiii. 10; *N.* i. 65; *I.* iii. 2.
[5] *O.* vii. 15, 90; *N.* ix. 33.

[2] *O.* vi. 9.
[4] *O.* vii. 44.
[6] *O.* xiv. 5.

perhaps the finest thing in our English tradition of sport. No
Greeks ever shook hands after a fight, no Greek ever was the
first to congratulate his conqueror; defeat was felt as a disgrace,
and for this reason perhaps the Spartans forbade their citizens to
take part in boxing competitions or the pankration, because it
was disgraceful for a Spartan to acknowledge defeat. They could
not feel that it was better to have fought and lost than never to
have fought at all. So the losers got little sympathy from their
fellows. 'By back ways they slink away sore smitten by mis-
fortune. No sweet smile greets their return.' [1]

The Greek ideal is unique, nor are the circumstances that produced it ever likely to occur again. How far was it ever realized
and for how long? Perhaps for a few years under the wave of
patriotic enthusiasm that followed the Persian Wars. But about
the middle of the fifth century a change began, owing to the rise
of professionalism, and athletics fell out of fashion. Yet the ideal
continued to exist as a refining influence, and we find it restated
in the second century after Christ in Lucian's *Anacharsis*. One
illustration must suffice. It is from the *Memorabilia* of Xenophon
written at a time when the word athlete had come to mean a professional.[2] Socrates meets an ill-developed youth and rebukes
him for his very amateurish condition of body. 'Of course,'
replies the youth, 'I am not a professional.' Whereupon the
philosopher reads him a lecture on the duty of developing the
body to the utmost. 'No citizen', he points out, 'has any right to
be an amateur in the matter of physical training: it is part of his
profession as a citizen to keep himself in good condition, ready
to serve his state at a moment's notice. The instinct of self-
preservation demands it likewise: for how helpless is the state of
the ill-trained youth in war or in danger! Finally, what a disgrace
it is for a man to grow old without ever seeing the beauty and
the strength of which his body is capable!' To develop his beauty
and his strength to the utmost is the duty of a citizen. This is
the Greek ideal.

[1] *P*. viii. 86.   [2] *Mem*. iii. 12.

VI

ATHLETICS AND EDUCATION

MUSIC and gymnastic together made up Greek education. Music trained the mind, gymnastic the body. From the day that the Greek boy went to school about the age of seven he spent a considerable portion of each day in the palaestra and gymnasium exercising himself under trained supervision, and he continued to do so till he reached manhood and often indeed much longer.

PALAESTRA AND GYMNASIUM

Before we proceed we must pause and consider what is the difference between the palaestra and the gymnasium. The words are often used loosely even by Greek writers, and they are difficult to define, for they denote as great a variety of institutions as do our words 'School' and 'College'. But there are certain general distinctions. The palaestra is properly the wrestling-school and is essentially a building, of much the same type as an ordinary Greek house with an open courtyard in the centre and some provision for undressing and for washing. The word gymnasium means 'an exercise for which you strip', and so it comes to be used first in the plural, then in the singular as the place where you take exercise. The essential part of it is the running-track, and it is not a building but an athletic ground, but like the palaestra it requires undressing-rooms and bathrooms, and therefore it usually contains a palaestra.

The palaestrae in the gymnasia were public institutions, so were the palaestrae at Olympia and Elis where the athletes trained. But the majority of palaestrae were owned by private individuals, often by schoolmasters. Schoolmasters with only a few pupils would take them in their own houses and hire a palaestra for their physical training, but those with the larger schools had palaestrae of their own where they gave all their instruction. When not required for school purposes the palaestra might be used by older pupils and even by men. Several of Plato's dialogues take place in a palaestra. But for the most part the palaestra was the place where boys received physical training. It was usually within the city, and its privacy made it more suitable for this purpose. The gymnasium being a sports-ground was usually outside the city; it was a public institution and open to all citizens. Young boys might be taken there for running, or throwing the spear, exercises for which there was no room in the palaestra, but its special use was as a training-ground for the Epheboi.[1] There the athletes could train themselves for the public games, while men of all ages could take such exercise as suited them.

First let us look at the palaestra. Its general arrangement is clearly shown in the plan of the palaestra of Olympia (Fig. 36) which, though intended only for the use of athletes at the festival, agrees for the most part with the description given by Vitruvius and may be regarded as typical of most Greek palaestrae. A good idea of its appearance may be formed from the Gladiatorial Barracks at Pompeii (Fig. 37), which are in reality an old Greek palaestra very similar in plan to that of Olympia, the rooms round the colonnade having been replaced by cells for gladiators. The central courtyard at Olympia is 41 metres square and is surrounded by a covered colonnade which probably served as a running-track. There are two principal entrances at either end of the south wall. A pillared vestibule leads into an ante-room opening on the central court. Between the two ante-rooms is a long shallow hall faced by a row of Ionic pillars. It is the *Apodyterion* or undressing-room, which was usually close to the entrance and served as a meeting-place for athletes and their friends. Opposite, on the other side of the court, is another large hall which was probably the *Ephebeion*, a sort of club-room. The rooms on the north are deeper so as to afford more shelter from the sun. In the north-east corner is the bathroom. It contains a large tank 4 metres square and 1·38 metres deep. In the more luxurious palaestra described by Vitruvius there are elaborate hot baths heated by furnaces. But in conservative Olympia such luxuries were unknown, and so they were usually in the fifth century. It is impossible to say for what the other rooms were used. Some of them opened into the courtyard by doorways, but only one, that in the south-east corner, had a door. Possibly it was the porter's lodge. Other rooms served for the storage of oil and athletic apparatus. Most of the rooms were open in front, and several of them were provided with benches. They probably served as lounges where visitors could sit and watch the athletes practising. There are remains of various altars and bases of

[1] The military organization of the Epheboi dates only from the fourth century, but there can be little doubt that there was some sort of organized gymnastic training for youths of this age at a much earlier date.

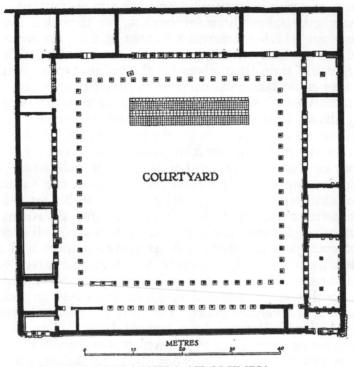

36. PLAN OF PALAESTRA AT OLYMPIA.

37. THE GLADIATORIAL BARRACKS AT POMPEII, formerly a Greek palaestra. The surrounding rooms were converted into cells for the gladiators. *Photo. Alinari.*

38. COURT OF THE STABIAN BATHS, POMPEII, showing stone ball which was used for some game like bowls or skittles. Photograph from Mr. Stanley Casson.

statues. In many palaestrae there were statues of Heracles and Hermes, and also of famous athletes.

The courtyard was covered with fine sand for the convenience of wrestlers, but along the north side is a very curious strip of pavement 24·20 metres long and 5·44 metres broad, formed of alternate bands of ribbed and smooth tiles. The ribbed tiles are arranged in two bands 1·60 metres wide and are separated by a band of smooth tiles 1·12 metres wide. These smooth tiles have a raised edge along the sides and are so arranged that the edges form continuous ridges stretching the whole length of the pavement. The object of this curious pavement is uncertain. We may reject the delightfully humorous suggestions that it was covered with sand and used as a wrestling-ring, or that it was a jumping-track. The most reasonable explanation is that it was a sort of bowling alley. A somewhat similar pavement was found in the large Thermae at Pompeii, and on it some heavy stone balls (Fig. 38).

It is not so easy to find a typical gymnasium. Most of those that have been excavated belong to Hellenistic and Roman times when the gymnasium had developed into a sort of school or college with libraries, class-rooms, and lecture halls. But the true Greek gymnasium was a sports-ground. Shade and water being essential for the comfort of those using it, the site usually selected was a grove beside some stream outside the city. The Platanistas at Sparta was on an island formed by the windings of the river and took its name from the plane trees surrounding it. Athens had already in the sixth century three gymnasia, the Lyceum, the Academea, and the Cynosarges. All three were sacred groves, the Lyceum on the west side, on the banks of the Cephisus, the other two on the east beside the Eridanus and the Ilissus. The two former at least were large enough for riding lessons and cavalry parades. From literature and vase-paintings we can picture the life of these gymnasia, but of the gymnasia themselves we know nothing. The gymnasia at Olympia and Delphi were not, like those at Athens, the daily resort of the citizens, but were intended chiefly for the use of competitors at the festivals. There was therefore no need for spacious parade grounds or shady walks. But from their remains we can form some idea of the necessary buildings. The best preserved is that of Delphi built early in the fourth century. Most of the parts of it are mentioned in an inscription containing the official accounts for work in the stadium and gymnasium for the year 258 B.C.[1]

[1] *B.C.H.* 1899, pp. 564, 612.

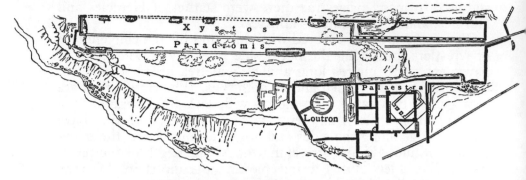

39. PLAN OF THE GYMNASIUM AT DELPHI. *B.C.H.* 1892, pl. XIII.

40. BATH IN THE GYMNASIUM AT DELPHI. In the back wall were placed pipes ending in lions' heads from which water poured into troughs similar to those in Fig. 41, but placed higher. Photograph from the Archaeological Institute, Athens.

41. WASHING TROUGH AND LIONS' HEAD SPOUTS in the gymnasium at Priene. *Priene*, Fig. 278.

The gymnasium at Delphi is a good example of the skill with which the Greeks adapted their buildings to the nature of the ground (Fig. 39). It is constructed in two terraces on the steep slope overlooking the gorge of the Pleistus. The upper terrace is 180 metres long and 25 to 30 metres deep, and contains a covered running-track or *Xystos* 7 metres broad, and parallel to it an uncovered track or *Paradromis*. From the inscription we learn that they were dug up, rolled, and covered with fine white sand. Six picks were provided for the work, and a similar inscription at Delos mentions the purchase of rollers for the gymnasium.[1] The length of the track is approximately that of the Delphic stadium, which was 177 metres.

The lower terrace contains an irregular enclosure consisting of the baths and palaestra. The latter is a small court 14 metres square surrounded by a colonnade on to which various rooms open. One of these is the *apodyterion* or undressing-room, two are *sphairisteria*, rooms or perhaps open courts for ball play. The inscription states that in one of these the ground is to be dug up, raked over and rolled, and finally covered with black earth. There is mention, too, of a wall. Among the various games of ball we find some which consisted in bouncing a ball against a wall or on the ground and striking it back with the hand as it rebounded.

The bathroom is especially interesting (Fig. 40). One side of it is formed by the retaining-wall of the upper terrace. In this wall are constructed a row of fountains. The water was supplied from a conduit in the upper terrace and issued through eleven bronze spouts in the shape of animals' heads placed at such a height as to fall conveniently over the head and shoulders of the bathers in the same manner as depicted in Fig. 58. It was caught below in eleven basins which were used for washing (cp. Fig. 41). In the centre of the enclosure was a circular plunge bath, 10 metres in diameter and 1·80 metres deep, the sides formed of a series of steps. There were no warm baths in the old gymnasium, though some seem to have been added in Roman times.

Vitruvius, who wrote just before the beginning of our era, gives a full description of the gymnasium. His plan differs from that we have described chiefly in the addition of elaborate hot baths. Indeed these tend to encroach so much that it is sometimes difficult to distinguish the palaestra from the bathing establishment which always has an open court for ball play and other exercise. On these we need not dwell, but two of the rooms

[1]   *B.C.H.* 1890, p. 397, ll. 98, 99.

which he mentions are of interest, the *Elaiothesion* or oil store, and the *Konisterion* or dusting-room.

Oil played a very important part in Greek training. Not only did the Greek oil himself before and after the bath, but athletes, especially wrestlers, carefully rubbed themselves with oil before exercise. The very names *Paidotribes* or 'boy rubber' and *Aleiptes* or 'oiler' indicate the importance of oil and massage. Athletes are sometimes described as 'those who oil themselves'. In the fifth century every one brought his own oil flask and strigil. But at times of festival oil was provided free for all competitors, and in later times a free supply was provided for the use of the Epheboi in training, and indeed for all who used the gymnasia. Enormous quantities were required. A Spartan inscription referring to some athletic contest directs that the gymnasiarch shall provide daily four *kyathoi*, about a third of a pint, for each man, three for each youth, two for each boy.[1] The gymnasiarch, one of those honorary officials of whom we shall speak later, often showed his generosity by providing oil at his own expense, or even by leaving a sum of money to serve as an endowment for the purpose. The oil was kept in amphorae or in tanks. A picture of such a tank is shown on the funeral stele of one Diodorus of Prusa, a gymnasiarch who had probably celebrated his term of office by providing oil (Fig. 42). It is a large circular vessel supported on three elaborately wrought legs, and on its side hang three ladles holding a kyathos each that were used for measuring out the oil. Under the empire the provision of oil was a heavy burden for the gymnasiarch or even for the state.

The *Konisterion* was the room where athletes powdered themselves before exercise. The powder (κόνις) must not be confused with the lye (κονία) which was used in washing to form a lather. Its effects on the body were regarded as hardly less beneficial than those of oil.[2] It closed the pores of the skin, checked excessive perspiration, and kept the body cool. There were special kinds of powder credited with special virtues. One of a clayey nature was supposed to be particularly cleansing, another resembling brick-dust produced perspiration on bodies that were overdry, a third of a bituminous nature warmed the skin. Two sorts, a black and a yellow earth, were prized for making the body supple and sleek. The powder was kept in baskets, and ought, we are told, to be applied with a supple wrist and open fingers so as to fall like fine dust, but these are refinements for the few. The

[1] *I.G.* v. i. 20.   [2] Philostrat. *Gym.* 56.

ordinary youths contented themselves with common earth or
sand. In later times the earth was mixed with water to form a
sort of mud-bath in which the athlete rolled. This was popularly
known as *ceroma.*

Some idea of the magnificence of later gymnasia can be
gathered from the plan of the great gymnasium at Pergamum
(Fig. 43). In the reign of Tiberius there were five gymnasia at
Pergamum, and a sixth was added later. The one illustrated was
built originally in the second century B.C., but the existing

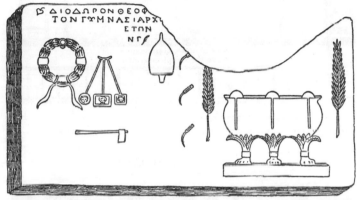

42. Stele of Diodorus, gymnasiarch of Prusa, showing crown, votive
tablets, wrestler's cap, strigils, palms. Hanging on the side of the
oil tank are ladles (kyathoi) for measuring the oil. Imperial Period.
Berichte der Sächsischen Gesellschaft d. Wissenschaft, 1873, pl. I.

remains belong mostly to the second century after Christ. It
consists of three, or originally four, terraces cut out of the steep
face of the hill. The lowest terrace, about 80 metres long, was
the gymnasium of the boys. On the northern wall, which is the
retaining-wall of the middle terrace, was found a list of boys who
had passed out into the ranks of the Epheboi. To the latter
belonged the middle gymnasium, and its walls were covered with
lists of their names. The great upper gymnasium is that of the
young men, and to the east of it, not shown on the plan, are
the Thermae or hot baths. Along the south side is a covered
running-track 200 metres long. The great court, 36 by 74 metres,
was surrounded by a Corinthian colonnade and adorned with
numerous statues. The rooms opening on to the colonnade
include a theatre, and a great pillared hall, dedicated to 'the
Emperors and the Fatherland'. Of life in the public gymnasia
and the palaestrae of Athens in the fifth century we can form

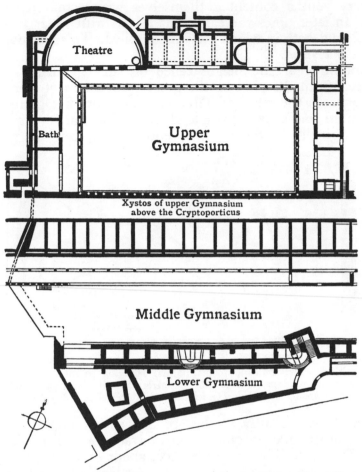

43. PLAN OF GYMNASIUM AT PERGAMUM. *Gk. Athletics*, Fig. 189, simplified from *Ath. Mitt.* xxix, pl. VII; xxxiii, pl. XVIII.

◀ **44. SCENE FROM THE UNDRESSING ROOM.** Attic r.-f. calix-krater. Late 6th century. Berlin 2180. To l. boy removing thorn from a youth's foot. Another youth pours oil from an aryballos into his hand, a third has just taken off his himation and is about to hand it to a slave boy. F.R. 157.

◀ **45. SCENES FROM THE UNDRESSING ROOM.** Attic r.-f. kylix. About 480 B. C. Copenhagen, Thorwaldsen Museum. On either side pillars with very broad capitals suggesting a building; javelins lean against the wall. Hanging on the wall are strigils, oil flasks, a diskos in its sling, a hare. Groups of epheboi and trainers, some standing, some sitting. Photograph from Professor Johansen.

MASSAGE

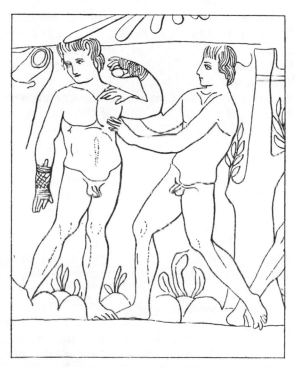

some idea from the dialogues of Plato and the scenes on the red-figured vases. With their aid let us try to picture the scene in the Lyceum or the Academea.

LIFE IN THE GYMNASIUM

The gymnasium, as we have said, lies by the riverside and is laid out with shady avenues and walks. There is a palaestra with baths similar to those at Delphi or Olympia but probably more spacious. Outside are running-tracks, jumping-pits, ranges for throwing the diskos and the javelin, open spaces for riding lessons and parades. We enter and find ourselves in an anteroom where perhaps is a statue of one of the gods of the palaestra, Hermes or Apollo. Passing through it we enter the *apodyterion* or undressing-room, a long narrow hall looking out on the colonnade and the court. Round the walls are benches, and on them hang all sorts of athletic apparatus, diskoi in their slings and jumping-weights, wrestling caps and boxing thongs, oil flasks, sponges, and strigils. Leaning against a pillar are some of the long blunt javelins used for practice. Some of the young men have hung up their belongings on the walls; here is a basket and here a strange object, a hare. Perhaps one of them has caught it and brought it as a present to the trainer or has himself received it as a present or a prize (Figs. 44, 45).

The room is full of people, mostly, it would seem, youths from fifteen to twenty years of age, but there are older men, too, who have come for exercise or to talk with those they meet there. For, like a cricket pavilion, the *apodyterion* is a general meeting-place. Here we may see a mathematician drawing figures in the sand as he demonstrates to a group of youths some new problem. Here talking with some friends is an ugly, snub-nosed man whom we recognize at once. Two middle-aged men enter, greet him, and pass out into the colonnade, take two or three turns round it by way of exercise, and rejoin the group. They are sophists, and with mock humility the snub-nosed man consults them on the nature of true wisdom.

But most of the younger men are less seriously engaged. Those who have not yet taken their exercise or who have finished it are standing or sitting about talking. Two boys in a corner are playing knuckle-bones. Some of the fashionable young men have brought with them their fighting quails or their pet animals. Two of them are setting a cat and a dog to fight for a wager (Fig. 54).

Others are dressing or undressing. Here is a group of youths undressing. One of them has a thorn in his foot and is standing with his mantle thrown over his shoulders leaning on his stick while a small attendant picks it out (Fig. 44). Another is carefully folding his mantle and is about to hand it to an attendant to look

49. Punching the korykos. Scene from the Ficoroni cista, Italian work made at Rome by Novios Plautios. 3rd century B.C. Rome, Villa Giulia. Pfuhl, *Malerei*, iii. 254.

after. It is a wise precaution. 'Clothes-snatchers' are as common in the baths and the palaestrae as pick-pockets at a modern race-meeting. Solon even imposed the penalty of death on any one who stole from the gymnasium a cloak, or oil flask, or any other object worth more than ten drachmae. Still, many of the youths leave their clothes on stools or benches. Here is one who has laid his mantle down and is oiling himself before going out to wrestle. He holds the oil flask high up in his right hand and lets the oil drip into his left hand. A youth with his hands bound with boxing thongs is being massaged by a friend. Sometimes a trainer is employed for oiling and massage, but in the fifth century these are still simple processes, there is no elaborate system (Figs. 46, 47, 48). Other youths are picking up the sand and throwing it at one another, a simple means of powdering. Those who have finished their exercise are scraping off the oil and dirt with strigils (Fig. 60).

If we look into one of the other rooms we may see some of the older men exercising themselves with ball play. They are bouncing the ball against the floor or the wall and striking it back with the flat of the hand, trying to do so as many times as possible. One wonders that two of them did not try doing this alternately and thus evolve some game like fives. Perhaps they did. We know strangely little about Greek ball play.

In another room we see some very familiar objects. It is the *Korykeion*, and from the beams of the ceiling hang various sorts of punch-ball (κώρυκος). The Greek boxer used the punch-ball for practice much as the modern boxer does. It is a bag or skin filled with fig-seeds, meal, or sand, and is hung on a level with the head. There is another larger punch-ball like a wine-skin, hung about two feet from the floor, which is used by pankratiasts. It is not unlike the sacks sometimes used to teach boys to tackle in football. There may also be dummies which a boxer may use if he can find no one to spar with (Figs. 49, 50).

The courtyard is full of athletes boxing, wrestling, or practising the pankration. There are picks lying about, and one youth is loosening the ground with the pick so as to make it soft for the wrestlers. The use of the pick is much recommended as an exercise (Figs. 52, 56). The ground for the pankration has been watered into a soft mud. Trainers are watching the practice, clothed in long mantles and holding in their hands their badge of office, long forked rods with which they enforce discipline and punish any clumsiness or unfairness. Outside in the open park other youths are running races 'mid a fragrance of smilax and leisure and white poplar in the springtime when the plane tree whispers to the elm'.[1] Others are practising for the pentathlon, throwing the diskos or the javelin, or jumping. A flute-player stands by giving them the rhythm for their movements. Some boys are trundling hoops (Fig. 55) or engaged in one of the many ball games. In an open space we may see a ground marked out much like a football ground where teams of boys are playing a sort of ball game. In another part a company of Epheboi

[1] Aristoph. *Nub.* 1008.

are learning to ride. One of them is practising mounting by means of a sort of vaulting-pole while the trainer looks on (Fig 58). He is naked—but other Epheboi are dressed in their gay cloaks and broad-brimmed hats, and are going through some cavalry manœuvres. Some on horseback are practising javelin-throwing at a target.

After exercise comes the bath. Under the trees is a pleasant gabled building with fountains much like those at Delphi. A

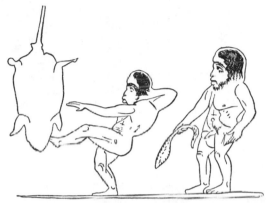

50. Dwarf as pankratiast punching and kicking large *korykos*. B.-f. pelike. About 420 B.C. Petrograd, Hermitage, 1611. *Annali*, 1870, Pl. R.

number of youths are washing. One of them is oiling himself, another is pouring into his hand some powder to rub on the body and form a lather. Various sorts of powder are used: a sort of lye formed from wood ashes, an alkali called *litron,* and fuller's earth. Other youths stand under the fountains and let the water pour over their head and shoulders (Fig. 57). The strigil of course is in constant use. In a room of the palaestra we see another method of washing. A group of youths stand round a large basin. One of them is splashing himself, another has got a friend to sluice him with a bucketful of water (Fig. 60). In some gymnasia there is a plunge bath, as at Delphi (Fig. 40), but the river itself is more convenient for those who want a dip.

OFFICIALS AND TRAINERS

The gymnasia, being public institutions, were usually under the control of public officials, gymnasiarchs.[1] At Athens the con-

[1] For a reference to the numerous inscriptions relating to the Gymnasiarchia see Dar-Sag. *s.v. Gymnasiarchia, Gymnasium*; *Gk. Athletics*, p. 500.

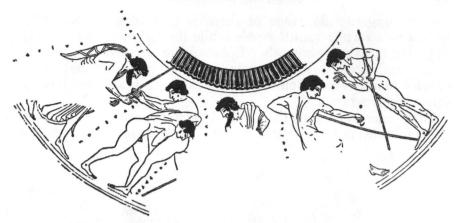

51. A WRESTLING LESSON. Attic r.-f. psykter. Late 6th century. Boston 01.8019. *Antike Denkmäler*, ii. 20. To l. trainer giving lesson in wrestling. One of the wrestlers has allowed the other to obtain his hold and with outstretched hands awaits the word of command. To r. javelin throwers; see Fig. 143 from the same vase.

52. PALAESTRA SCENES. Attic r.-f. kylix. About 480 B.C. Ashmolean Museum, Oxford. *Corpus Vasorum, Oxford*, ii. 5; vi. 1, 2. *a.* Wrestlers, cp. Fig. 164: trainer with forked rod: youth with pick; boxer measuring his boxing thong. *b.* Three boxers, trainer, youth exercising with halteres. In centre youth holding javelin, and in his right hand the amentum; he seems to be stepping out the ground. Youthful trainer with walking-stick and forked rod watches him. Notice how the rod is curved to fit the space: the same thing sometimes takes place with the human figure, e. g. Fig. 114.

53, 54. TWO SIDES OF A STONE BASE FOUND AT ATHENS in 1922. Late 6th century. See also Figs. 212, 213. *J.H.S.* xlii, p. 104, pls. VI, VII; xlv, p. 164. Photographs from casts.

53. ATHLETES PRACTISING. To l. runner in the attitude of the start (see p. 135). Two wrestlers; one of them has seized the other's left arm with both hands, intending to turn round and swing him over his shoulder. The other frustrates this move by placing his right hand against his shoulder. To r. javelin thrower adjusting the thong, cp. Fig. 143.

54. CAT AND DOG FIGHT. Two epheboi seated set a cat and a dog to fight, two others standing watch with interest.

55. BOY WITH HOOP. Interior of Attic r.-f. kylix. About 500 B. C. Ashmolean Museum, Oxford. *Corpus Vasorum, Oxford*, i. 8.

56. BOY WITH PICK FILLING A BASKET WITH SAND, perhaps for the use of the wrestlers. Interior of Attic r.-f. kylix. About 490 B. C. Brussels. *Corpus Vasorum, Brussels*, III. i. c, pl. IV. 1. Photograph by Mrs. Beazley.

57. WASHING AT A FOUNTAIN. B.-f. hydria. Late 6th century. Leyden 14 e. 28. The scene is at a fountain under a portico in a grove. The athletes have hung their clothes on the boughs of a tree. The water issues from two lions' heads (cp. Figs. 40, 41) under which stand two men. On the left two youths are preparing for the bath: one of them holds an oil-flask high in his r. hand (cp. Fig. 44). To the r., not shown in the photograph, two youths, one of whom holds an oil-flask in his left hand. Photograph by Professor Beazley. Beazley, *J.H.S.* xlvii, pl. XI, pp. 63, 64.

58. A RIDING LESSON. R.-f. kylix. About 480 B.C. Munich 2639. A youth preparing to vault on a led horse by means of a pole. To l. trainer giving instruction or order. Part of the boy on horseback is restored. New photograph obtained for me by Dr. Sieveking.

59. BRONZE STRIGILS AND OIL FLASK in the British Museum, 337. *Guide to Greek and Roman Life*, p. 115, Fig. 126.

60. YOUTHS WASHING AND SCRAPING THEM-SELVES WITH STRIGILS. Attic r.-f. kylix in British Museum, E. 83. About 430 B.C. New photograph. For interior see Fig. 47.

trol of education and therefore of the gymnasia was vested in a board of ten Sophronistai, and in the fourth century a magistrate called Kosmetes was appointed for that purpose. The duties of the gymnasiarch were confined there to the training of teams for the torch race. But elsewhere the gymnasiarch appears as a sort of minister of education. Sometimes he is a duly appointed magistrate, often he is one of those honorary magistrates chosen from the ranks of the richer citizens to perform expensive public services. In either case he was expected to spend his own money freely, in organizing displays and competitions, in improving the gymnasia, especially in providing oil and, in later times, fuel for the furnaces to heat the hot baths.

The actual training was given by the Paidotribes and the Gymnastes.[1] The former, as the name denotes, was properly the trainer of boys, and is usually coupled with the schoolmaster. He was a private teacher often with a palaestra of his own. His fee for a course in the fourth century was a mina, about £4. Parents took considerable pains in choosing a paidotribes for their sons. Paidotribai were also employed in the gymnasia to train the Epheboi. In Hellenistic times they had a number of assistants for special exercises, the *sphairistes* who taught ball play, the *akontistes* and *toxotes* who gave instruction in the use of the javelin and the bow, and the *hoplomachos* who gave lessons in the use of arms. The paidotribes may sometimes have trained athletes, but this was properly the work of the gymnastes. The earliest gymnastai of whom we hear were boxers and wrestlers who gave practical instruction in these exercises, but in the fifth century they developed a science of training or gymnastic which aimed, by means of rules for diet, massage, and exercise, at producing the physical condition required for athletic success.

The science of gymnastic was closely connected with that of medicine. The trainer, like the doctor, required a knowledge of diet and of the effects on the body of certain kinds of food: he required some knowledge of anatomy and of the effects of different kinds of exercises; he required, too, to be a judge of the human animal and to be able to recommend to any individual the sort of athletics that he should take up and the training suitable for him. Unfortunately the trainer was not as a rule a scientific man, and his training was vitiated from the first by a false ideal. It aimed at producing not general physical excellence but the

[1] For the distinction between the Gymnastes and Paidotribes see Jüthner, *Philostratus*, p. 1; *Gk. Athletics*, p. 503.

artificial condition required for some particular event. At the same time, under the paidotribai and gymnastai there arose in the fifth century a science of medical gymnastics. It was the invention, according to Plato,[1] of one Herodicus of Selymbria, a paidotribes, who suffering from a mortal disease, discovered a means of treating it by strict rules of diet and exercise. 'By a combination of training and medicine he found out a way of torturing first himself and then the rest of the world by the invention of a lingering death.' Another invention with which these trainers are credited is that of medical massage (ἰατραλειπτική). But these developments need not be discussed here.

PHYSICAL TRAINING IN THE FIFTH CENTURY

Physical training was, as we have seen, an essential part of Greek education. In most Greek states education was voluntary, but the Greeks were enthusiasts for education, and few who could afford it failed to avail themselves of the services of the schoolmaster and the paidotribes for their sons, at least till the age of fourteen, when the elementary course of education usually ended for the poorer classes. The well-to-do, however, continued their education, attending the lectures of mathematicians, rhetoricians, grammarians, and practising in the palaestra or gymnasium till the age of seventeen or eighteen. Then they were enrolled in the ranks of the Epheboi. The two years' training of the Epheboi was the only part of education that was compulsory, and they were two strenuous years. 'Rods and toils unmeasured' were then their lot, says the author of the Platonic treatise *Axiochos*. Thus the Greek boy's physical education extended over twelve years or more.

Of the system of this physical education we know very little, especially in its early stages. It is sometimes stated that the Greek boy was carefully taught at home the correct method of standing and walking, and a most ingenious theory of physical training has been built up on this conjecture. Unfortunately there is no evidence for it either in literature or art. It is true that, as Aristophanes tells us, the Greek boy was taught the correct way of sitting and of getting up, and not to sit with crossed legs.[2] But those were questions of good manners, not of physical training. The Greek had no more need to learn how to stand and how to walk than an animal has. The modern child acquires bad habits

[1] *Rep.* 406 B; *Protag.* 316 D; Aristotle, *Rhet.* i. 5.   [2] *Nub.* 966.

of standing and walking owing to his sedentary life and the cramping effects of clothing and boots, and he therefore requires appropriate exercises to correct these bad habits. The Greek, living a freer, more natural life, needed no such correction. The object of his physical training was to develop his strength and activity. It was no artificial or scientific system, it grew up naturally from those athletic exercises that were the tradition and the delight of his race.

We do not know in what order the exercises were taught and we know little about the method of teaching. We may be sure, however, that the system was progressive. Plato recommends that races for boys shall be only half the distance of those for men, and races for 'the beardless' only two-thirds. Further, the difference in the weights of existing diskoi and jumping-weights indicates that light weights were used by boys. The fact that the pankration for boys was not introduced at Olympia till the second century B.C. suggests that the Olympic authorities at least did not regard it as a suitable competition for boys, and though elsewhere, even in the fifth century, there were competitions in this event for boys, we may infer that it was taught later than wrestling or boxing.

The only exercise as to which we have definite information is wrestling. Teaching in wrestling was, as the name palaestra indicates, the most important part of physical education. It was taught progressively as a sort of drill. First boys were taught to perform the separate movements or figures (σχήματα), then to combine them. Such instruction could be given to a pair of boys, or to a whole class arranged in pairs. We have preserved in a papyrus from Oxyrrhynchus a fragment from a manual of instruction in wrestling.[1] It is in the form of a drill for various holds and throws. The instructor gives one or more orders to each of the pupils or pairs of pupils in turn, ending each group of orders with the order 'engage' (πλέξον) or 'throw' (ῥεῖψον). Unfortunately the papyrus is much mutilated and the interpretation of many of the terms is very obscure. One simple example of these orders must suffice. Addressing one of the pair, whom we will call A, the instructor says, 'Put your right arm round his back'. Then to B, 'Take an underhold'. Then to A again, 'Step across and engage'. In Fig. 51 we see an excellent illustration of such a wrestling lesson. One youth has taken his hold, the other waits for the instructor's next order.

[1] *Ox. Pap.* iii. 466, cp. Jüthner, *Philostratus*, p. 26.

This method of instruction, which is quite familiar to us in the present day, was equally applicable to the 'hits' and 'guards' of boxing, or to the more complicated movements of the pankration. When the pupil had thoroughly learnt the movements and their combinations he would be allowed to proceed to 'loose play' as it is called in fencing. Similarly the preliminary movements of throwing the diskos and the javelin, or swinging the weights before the jump, could all be taught as drill. Indeed they were probably taught as a musical drill, for, as we have seen, the time in these exercises was commonly given by a flute-player. The jumping weights were in later times used much in the same way as dumbbells, and it seems not unlikely they were already so used even in the fifth century: for athletes are often seen swinging them in attitudes which can hardly have any connexion with jumping.

The training of the Epheboi must have had an important influence on the national physique. Besides gymnastic exercises it included riding and the use of all weapons, and during the second year the Epheboi gained hardihood and experience by acting as patrols on the frontiers.

The interest in this training was kept alive by innumerable competitions, arranged for boys of different ages. Further variety was added by ball play and other games which probably occupied a more important place in the life of the palaestra than we realize. Nor must we forget the influence of the dance in giving grace of carriage and movement. Greek dancing was closely connected with religion and formed part of all religious festivals and processions. From an educational point of view the choral competitions between the tribes at Athens were particularly valuable. Each tribe was represented by a choir of fifty boys who were trained free of charge by some rich citizen appointed as *choregos* for the purpose. This free training was especially useful to the poorer citizens. If all the tribes were represented, five hundred boys must have received this free training every year. The dance was dramatic and imitative and exercised every part of the body. Some dances were definitely athletic or military in character. In the gymnopaidia at Sparta the dancers imitated all the movements of wrestling. The Pyrrhic dance was an imitation of war. The dancers, armed with shields and javelins, went through the various actions of attack or defence (Fig. 69), some pretending to hurl spears or javelins or strike their opponents, others bending to one side, crouching down, leaping up in the air to avoid the missiles. The torch-races again (Fig. 65), though they can hardly be described as athletics, gave a certain amount of free training to a number of youths. Here again teams were trained free of charge by wealthy citizens.

The conditions of life in fifth-century Greece favoured a healthy physical development to a degree that we can hardly realize. It was a life of natural activity in the open air. If a Greek attended the Assembly, or a religious ceremony, or a theatrical performance, he was all the time in the open air, and more often standing than sitting. He did not spend hours in the vitiated atmosphere of halls, or churches, or theatres, nor did he sit for hours cramped at a desk or in crowded workshops and factories. His clothing was loose and let the air reach every part of his body, even when he was not partially stripped. He was abstemious in his food and drink; there was little luxury in Greece proper. Hence the heavy artificial diet of the professional athlete was the more injurious in its effects. The military training that he received as an ephebos, the conditions of ancient warfare all tended to promote activity. The Greek learnt to ride bare-back, to throw missiles and ward them off, to use his weapons and defend himself in close combat. All this was an excellent physical training. Hunting, too, was general. At Athens, indeed, owing to the increase in population and cultivation, game became scarce towards the close of the fifth century, but in most parts of Greece there were ample opportunities for hunting, especially in the Peloponnese.

SWIMMING AND ROWING

Most of the Greeks lived near the sea or near some river, and in the maritime states at all events most boys, and girls too, learnt to swim and to dive and were quite at home in the water (Figs. 61–5). Not to know how to swim was as much the mark of an uneducated man as ignorance of letters. The Greek loss at Salamis, says Herodotus, was small because the Greeks could swim, and when a ship was sunk the crew swam across to the island. At Sphacteria divers succeeded in bringing provisions to the Spartans in the island by swimming under water, towing baskets behind them. At Syracuse the Athenians sent down divers to destroy the stakes which the Syracusans placed under water.[1] It was perhaps because swimming and diving were so universal, so natural to the Greeks, that we never hear of any instruction in these exercises. Children learnt to swim from one another, or

[1] Hdt. viii. 89; Th. iv. 26; vii. 25.

61. SWIMMING. Detail from the François vase, Florence. Attic b.-f. column-krater. About 560 B.C. F.R. 13. The ship is the ship of Theseus who has come to Crete to free the Athenian hostages from the Minotaur, below it is a man swimming ashore—using the crawl stroke.

62. DIVING FROM A ROCK. Scene from Etruscan wall painting in the 'Tomba della Caccia e Pesca'. 6th century B.C. Weege, *Etruskische Malerei*, p. 64; *Mon.* XI, XII, xiv.

63. YOUTH PREPARING TO DIVE FROM A BOAT. Attic b.-f. oenochoe. Late 6th century. British Museum B. 508. New photograph.

64. BRONZE STATUETTE OF DIVER. Early 5th century. Munich. Photograph from Dr. Sieveking. Hekler in *Jahrb*. xxxi. 101 wrongly describes this as the figure of a jumper.

The somewhat scanty evidence, literary and monumental, about swimming and diving has been recently collected by Dr. Erwin Mehl in *Antike Schwimmkunst*, and a summary of his conclusions is given in his article on 'Schwimmen' in Pauly-Wissowa. From an athletic point of view the results are meagre, for though there is abundant evidence that swimming was an almost universal accomplishment of the Greeks and Romans, competitions in swimming and diving seem to have been unknown.

65. RUNNERS IN THE TORCH RACE. The runner in the centre is just about to take the torch from the runner behind him. Attic r.-f. oenochoe. About 400 B.C. Louvre. Photograph from Professor Beazley.

from their elders, much in the same way as they learnt to walk. It was perhaps for the same reason that competitions in swimming were so rare: indeed the only competition that we hear of was at Hermione. As to the style of the Greek swimmers, it appears from representations of swimming that the Greeks preferred the hand-over-hand stroke, possibly the modern crawl, though the action of the legs as represented is not very clear. They employed also the side stroke and the breast stroke, but less frequently. They knew how to float, swim on the back, and tread water: they had games of some sort in the water.

In the maritime states every boy must have learnt to row. At the Isthmian festival, at Athens, and many other places there were boat-races, or rather ship-races. Legend said that the first race at the Isthmian Games was won by the ship *Argo*. At Athens there were boat-races at various festivals. Some of these races must have been between triremes, for a speaker in Lysias claims to have won a race off Sunium with a trireme, and to have spent 15 minae on equipping it. This suggests that there were races between the ships equipped by different trierarchs. At the Panathenaic festival there was an inter-tribal race.[1] The winning tribe received 200 drachmae to pay for a feast or bump-supper, besides three oxen valued at 300 drachmae for the sacrifice. There was a second prize of 200 drachmae. Here the boats used were probably the light boats with a single bank of oars which always accompanied the triremes as tenders. These are probably the boats which we find represented in Ephebic inscriptions of Imperial times. The number of the crew varies. In one very short boat only three rowers are represented, one of whom holds a crown. On another longer boat we have five rowers. A far more suitable boat for racing is represented on a somewhat earlier stele. Here by a curious accident there is a crew of eight; they are naked and sitting at ease, and bow, who is the smallest of the crew, holds a palm branch. There is no cox, though the steering-paddle is represented. The number of rowers is clearly determined by artistic considerations of space and no reliance can be placed on such evidence (Figs. 66–8).

GALEN ON PHYSICAL TRAINING

The life of all this athletic activity lay in the spirit of emulation and love of competition. There was little system or science of physical culture in the fifth century. The training of the palaestra

[1] *I.G.* ii. 965.

BOAT RACES

66-9. THREE RELIEFS FROM ATTIC EPHEBIC IN-SCRIPTIONS OF IMPERIAL TIMES, see P. Gardner, *J.H.S.* ii, pp. 90, 315; xi, p. 196.

66. Athens, National Museum. Svoronos, cx. 1470. At bottom of the stele relief of boat containing three men, one of whom holds a crown. At top relief referring to torch race.

67. Athens, National Museum. Svoronos, cxi. 1468. At the top of the stele, not shown in our illustration, are three figures standing, a draped figure in centre probably the gymnasiarch who trained the crew, on his right a man in a chlamys crowning him, on his left a youth bearing a palm.

68. Athens, National Museum, not shown in Svoronos. The inscription, *I.G.* III. i. 1129, gives the names of the Archons for the year A.D. 164-5. Boat-races are not actually mentioned in the inscription. New photograph obtained for me by Mr. A. M. Woodward.

PYRRHIC DANCE

69. RELIEF from the Acropolis Museum, Athens. 4th century B.C. *Photo. Alinari.*

had grown naturally like the games and sports of our public schools in the last century from which the modern athletic movement has developed. Its value lay in its spontaneity, in its freedom. There was no conscious balancing of light exercises and heavy, of quick exercises and slow. Such theorizing belongs to a later age when life has become more artificial and luxurious. The earliest science of gymnastic arose in connexion with the training of athletes for athletic competitions when athletics were already becoming a profession; from it developed the science of medical gymnastic, and at a later period that of educational gymnastic. Of the history of the latter we know nothing, but we can gather some idea of its character from Galen.

In Galen's treatise on the Preservation of Health he discourses at length on the exercises suited to youths between the ages of fourteen and twenty. He distinguishes exercises for the legs, the arms, and the trunk. He further classifies exercises into those which exercise the muscles and give them tone without violent movement, quick exercises which promote activity, and violent exercises. As examples of the first class he mentions digging, driving, carrying heavy weights, rope-climbing, and exercises of resistance such as holding the arms extended while another person tries to pull them down. Among quick exercises he enumerates running, sparring, the use of the punch-ball, ball play, rolling on the ground 'either alone or with others', and a variety of leg and arm movements, many of which are well known in modern systems of physical drill. The exercise called ἐκπλεθρίζειν is the familiar running figure in which the runner runs in an ever-decreasing circle till he reaches the centre. Another exercise (πιτυλίζειν) consists in marching on the toes and at the same time swinging the arms. The leg exercises include jumping up and down and raising the legs alternately backwards and forwards. The arm exercises are the usual dumb-bell movements, performed rapidly without dumb-bells, with the hands open or clenched. Finally any of the exercises of the first class may become violent if practised rapidly and without interruption, and quick exercises become so if performed with weights or in heavy armour. Galen further lays down elaborate rules for the time of exercise and for massage both before and after exercise.

Here we have a regular treatise on physical culture very similar to those that abound in our own day. There is indeed little in our modern systems which we do not find anticipated in Greek medical writings. We do not know how far Galen's principles were ever put into practice. But we may be sure that such physical training could not do for Galen's contemporaries what athletics had done for their ancestors. Physical training is a valuable part of education and necessary in artificial conditions of life. But physical training is not sport, nor can it ever take the place of sport. There is no joy in it. It may develop the body and impart habits of discipline, but it cannot impart those higher qualities—courage, endurance, self-control, courtesy—qualities which are developed by our own games and by such manly sports as boxing and wrestling when conducted in the true spirit of manly rivalry for the pure joy of the contest; it cannot train boys 'to play the game' in the battle of life.

VII

PROFESSIONALISM

THE very popularity of athletics was their undoing. Excess begets Nemesis: the Nemesis of excess in athletics is professionalism, which is the death of all true sport.

HONOURS PAID TO ATHLETES

Even in the sixth century there is an element of excess in the honours paid to the victor at the Panhellenic games. Of the two most significant of these honours, the Statue and the Hymn of Victory, we have already spoken. It is true that these were paid for usually by the victor himself, sometimes by his friends or the city, and that the statue was really a votive offering. But the mere right to erect such a statue at Olympia placed the victor on a pedestal above other men. Similarly on his return home he was received with triumph as great as if he were a general returning from a campaign. But he received still more substantial rewards. Solon, as we have said, offered a reward of 500 drachmae to any Athenian victor at Olympia, and lesser sums for victors at other festivals. At Athens, too, and elsewhere, the victor had the right of a front seat at all public festivals, and sometimes of free meals in the Prytaneion. In later times he was exempt from taxation. At Sparta, which at this time seems to have stood aloof from the athletic movement, he had the privilege of fighting next to the king. In later times these honours grew more and more extravagant, especially in the rich cities of the West. As an instance of such extravagance it is recorded that Exaenetus of Agrigentum, who won the foot-race at Olympia in 412 B.C., was drawn into the city in a four-horse chariot, attended by three hundred of the chief citizens in pair-horse chariots. In the fifth century, which was characterized by a revival of the worship of the dead, we even find a few cases of athletes worshipped as heroes.[1]

The excessive honour shown to the athlete did not escape criticism, and we are fortunate in possessing the protest made by that remarkable thinker, Xenophanes of Colophon. Born in 576 B.C. he left his native city at the age of twenty-five and for sixty-five years travelled about the cities of Greece and the West.

[1] For a full discussion of these honours see *B.S.A.* xxii, pp. 88 ff.; *Olympia*, p. 67.

He had therefore in his long life seen the whole growth of the athletic movement, and he clearly saw the danger. After enumerating the honours paid to the athlete, the front seats at festivals, free meals, grants of money, he continues:

'Yet is he not so worthy as I, and my wisdom is better than the strength of men and horses. Nay this is a foolish custom nor is it right to honour strength more than excellent wisdom. Not though there were among the people a man good at boxing, or in the pentathlon or in wrestling, nay nor one with swiftness of foot which is most honoured in all contests of human strength, not for his presence would the city be better governed. And small joy would it be to a city should one in contests win a victory by the banks of Pisa. These things do not make fat the dark places of the city.'

Wisdom is better than strength. We find the warning put into the mouth of Diogenes by Dio Chrysostom six hundred years later, we have heard it often in our own day. It is not good for a state, it is not good for a school, when sport takes the first place. Neither is it good to neglect the body. To cultivate mind and body alike, to keep the balance between music and gymnastic, was the ideal of Greek education, but like all ideals it is hard to realize.

OVER-COMPETITION

The real evil in the sixth century was over-competition, and it was a danger not only to the state but to the athlete. The multiplication of competitions and of prizes was making sport a source of profit. The rivalry between cities was partly responsible. It is related that Croton, a city famous for its athletes, or according to another account its luxurious rival Sybaris, tried to found a festival that would eclipse Olympia, and to attract competitors by the magnificence of its prizes. The story told of Astylus, a famous runner from Croton,[1] suggests that inducements were sometimes held out to athletes to compete for some state other than their own, even as a football professional is induced to change his club. Astylus had won the stade race and the diaulos in two successive Olympiads, 488 and 484 B.C. At the next Olympiad he allowed himself to be proclaimed a Syracusan 'to please Hieron', the tyrant of Syracuse.[2] His fellow citizens, indignant at what must have seemed almost an act of sacrilege, destroyed the statue they had erected in his honour and turned his house into a common prison.

[1] Athenaeus, 522, 523.   [2] Paus. vi. 13. 1.

Thus, early in the fifth century there arose 'the pothunter', who spent most of his time travelling from city to city, picking up prizes. Theagenes of Thasos is said to have won some 1,400 prizes. For such a man athletics were no longer a recreation, but an absorbing occupation which left little time for other duties. When the 'Shamateur' makes his appearance, professionalism is not far off. Meanwhile, the very causes which encouraged the pothunter were discouraging the ordinary man who, unwilling to devote all his time and energy to sport, and feeling it useless to compete, gradually lost personal interest in athletics and contented himself with the role of spectator.

RISE OF PROFESSIONALISM

In these circumstances competition rapidly became more strenuous, and the would-be champion had from boyhood to devote himself to training. He soon found that it was necessary to concentrate on some particular event, to specialize, and that different events required different development and different training. So a new art of training arose. The old trainers were mostly boxers or wrestlers who imparted their own skill to their pupils and for the rest encouraged them to live a natural healthy life that produced all-round development; the new trainers aimed at producing a special state of development and for that purpose took control of the whole life of their pupils, especially of their diet.

The diet of the old athletes had been, like that of most Greek country folk, mainly vegetarian, consisting of figs, fresh cheese from the baskets, porridge, and meal cakes with only occasional meat as a relish, and wine. The frequently repeated statement that the athlete's diet was regulated by the law of the Games, and that he was not allowed to drink wine is entirely groundless. But shortly after the Persian Wars a change took place. A meat diet was introduced by some trainer, probably Dromeus of Stymphalus, who twice won the long race at Olympia (460, 456 B.C.).[1]

The object of a meat diet was to produce the bulk and strength supposed to be necessary for the boxer or wrestler. In Greece classification by weight was unknown, and in boxing and wrestling the heavyweight has a natural advantage. Therefore, to produce bulk, the trainer prescribed enormous quantities of meat, which had to be counteracted by excessive exercise. Eating, sleeping,

[1] Paus. vi. 7. 3; Diogen. Laert. viii. 13; Pliny, *Hist. Nat.* xxiii. 7.

and exercise occupied the athlete's whole time and left little leisure for other pursuits.

Thus an artificial distinction arose between the life of an athlete and that of the ordinary citizen. By the time of the Peloponnesian War the word 'athlete' had come to mean a professional, while athletics were out of fashion among the young men generally. Aristophanes sadly contrasts the pale, narrow-chested youths of his day with the men who fought at Marathon.[1] The wrestling-schools and gymnasia were deserted for the marketplace and the baths. The gilded youth of Athens found their sport in quail-fighting and horse-racing. They preferred to be spectators of the deeds of others rather than doers. Meanwhile the competitors at Olympia were drawn more and more from the hardy countrymen of Thessaly and Arcadia, who found that they could make a profitable livelihood out of athletics. For though the character of the competitions was changing, the popularity of the festivals as spectacles and the rewards of athletes only increased. 'There is no source more profitable to Plutus', says Aristophanes, 'than holding contests in music and athletics.'[2] And Plato in the myth of Er represents the soul of Atalanta as choosing to enter into the body of an athlete, on seeing the great rewards bestowed on them.

For the general neglect of athletics there was sufficient excuse in the vicious and unscientific character of the new training. It might produce strength but it was at the sacrifice of activity, health, and beauty. In the case of the young it tended to stunt the growth. Few boy victors, says Aristotle, distinguished themselves as men.[3] The body was no longer evenly developed. 'The runner', says Socrates, 'had over developed his legs, the boxer the upper part of his body.'[4] Athletics were little use as a training for war and were condemned by generals such as Epaminondas, Alexander, and Philopoemen. Plato, a keen advocate of physical training, can find no place for the athletics of his time in his ideal state, and in his *Laws* proposes a new system of athletics based on the requirements of war. The artificial habit of life makes the athlete unfit to withstand the vicissitudes of campaigning. 'His nature', he says, 'is sleepy and the least variation from his routine is liable to cause him serious illness.'[5] His verdict is confirmed by Hippocrates of Cos, 'the father of medicine', who

[1] Aristophanes, *Nub.* 961–1022; *Ran.* 1086.   [2] Aristophanes, *Plutus*, 1161.
[3] *Pol.* 1339 a.   [4] Xenophon, *Symposium*, 2. 17.
[5] *Rep.* iii. 404 A.

declared the high state of training produced by athletics to be a dangerous and unstable condition of body.[1]

The whole case against the professional athlete is summed up by Euripides in a fragment of his lost play *Autolycus*.

'Of all the countless evils throughout Hellas none is worse than the race of athletes. . . . Slaves of their belly and their jaw they know not how to live well. . . . In youth they strut about in splendour, the idols of the city, but when bitter old age comes upon them they are cast aside like worn-out cloaks. I blame the custom of the Hellenes who gather to see such men honouring useless pleasures.'

Then, echoing the words of Xenophanes, he continues:

'Who ever helped his fatherland by winning a crown for wrestling, or for speed of foot, or hurling the diskos or striking a good blow on the jaw? Will they fight against the foe with diskoi in their hands, or driving their feet through the foemen's shields chase them from their land? . . . Crowns should be given to the good and wise, to him who guides his city best, a temperate man and just, or who by his words drives away evil deeds, putting away war and faction.'

RESULTS OF PROFESSIONALISM

'Aidōs is stolen away by secret gains.' When money enters into sport corruption is sure to follow. Early in the fourth century we find more cases of 'transfer' at Olympia.[2] The emissaries of Dionysius, tyrant of Syracuse, bribed the father of the boy boxer, Antipater of Miletus, to induce his son to proclaim himself as a Syracusan. Antipater refused, but in 380 B.C. one Sotades of Crete, who at the previous Games had won the long-distance race, accepted a bribe to proclaim himself an Ephesian, for which offence he was rightly banished by his countrymen. Worse than this, victory was actually bought and sold. In 388 B.C. Eupolus of Thessaly bribed his opponents in boxing to allow him to win the prize. The offence was discovered and the guilty parties were all fined. Out of the fines were made six bronze statues of Zeus, called Zanes, which were placed at the entrance of the stadium with inscriptions warning competitors that not with money but with speed of foot and strength of body must prizes be won at Olympia. The vigorous action of the authorities of Olympia had its effect, and throughout the history of the festival very few cases of corruption are recorded. But when corruption

[1] Galen, Προτρεπτ λόγ. ii.   [2] Paus. vi. 2. 6; vi. 18. 6; v. 21. 5.

was even possible at Olympia, we may be sure that it was pre-valent elsewhere.

Thus within a century the whole character of athletics was completely changed. From this time there is little to record save that all the evils which we have described grew more and more pronounced. The festivals became more purely spectacular, the competitions became more the monopoly of professionals and their training more artificial and unpractical, and the result is visible in the deterioration of their physical type. Yet all through the decline the old ideal was maintained at Olympia and it never wholly lost its influence. At all periods we find men of position competing as genuine amateurs in a manner worthy of the old tradition, men like the founder of the Achaean league, Aratus of Sicyon, or the statesman, Gorgus of Messene, both of whom won victories in the pentathlon, that all round competition which best expressed the ideal of Greek sport, but which appealed least of all to the professional. Such men were the exceptions. Further, as has been already mentioned, there was real value in the athletic movement that accompanied the spread of Hellenism in the East.

A symptom of the spectacular character of athletics, which is familiar to us all to-day in England and still more in America, was the increased expenditure on athletic buildings, which reached its height under the Roman Empire. In the fifth century stadia and gymnasia were of the simplest, but side by side with the decay of athletics in the fourth century we hear everywhere of old stadia being improved and new stadia constructed largely for the convenience of spectators. Here too Olympia has a lesson for us. The only change made in the stadium at Olympia was to raise the embankments round it so as to provide room for more spectators, but even to the last they had to sit or stand on the bare ground. From the same period we may date the construction of elaborate gymnasia. At Athens Lycurgus rebuilt the Lyceum gymnasium where Aristotle walked and taught, and planted it with trees. But these gymnasia were really social clubs. There the Athenian gentleman would betake himself in the afternoon to get an appetite for his evening meal. There were bath-rooms, dressing-rooms, club-rooms, shaded colonnades where he could take his exercise when the sun was too hot or the weather was wet, rooms for ball play, and for the more strenuous, wrestling-rings and running-tracks. The gymnasia had long been the resort of philo-sophers, and gradually the social and educational side prevailed over the athletic. The gymnasium which Ptolemy Philadelphus built at Athens in the third century was provided with a library and lecture-rooms where philosophers and rhetoricians still lectured in the time of Cicero.

The evil effects of professionalism are worst in those fighting events, boxing, wrestling, and the pankration, where the feeling of aidōs or honour is most essential. Here again the history of modern sport tells the same tale. Wrestling which was once a national sport in England has been killed by professionalism. Amateur boxing is of modern date and owes its existence to the encouragement it receives from the Army and Navy, the Universities, and the Public Schools, but it is overshadowed by professional boxing, and the amateur is continually tempted to turn professional by the enormous sums that he can earn as a public entertainer. For though the prize-ring is dead and the term 'prize-fighter' is a term of reproach, the professional champion is the hero of the sensational press and earns in a single night's exhibition sums that the old prize-fighter never dreamt of. When a boxer will not fight unless he is guaranteed a huge purse whether he wins or loses he forfeits all claim to be called a sportsman.

In Greece the evil was increased by the absence of classification by weight, which made these events the monopoly of the heavy-weight athlete. They became in consequence less scientific and more brutal. This deterioration, as we shall see, can be traced in boxing in the gradual change from the soft boxing thongs to the murderous caestus of Roman times, and in the consequent deteri oration of the style of boxing. In wrestling we have an example of sheer brutality in a fourth-century wrestler, Sostratus of Sicyon,[1] who defeated his opponents not by skill in wrestling but by seizing and breaking their fingers.

As brute force became more important and science less, competition fell off, and we find the same competitor amassing prizes in two or three events. Thus Cleitomachus of Thebes at the close of the third century won all three fighting events at the Isthmia in one day. At Olympia he was defeated by Caprus of Elis, who by winning the wrestling match and the pankration was considered to have emulated the fabled performance of Heracles, who was supposed to have won both these events at the first Olympic Games. In consequence he took to himself the proud title of Successor of Heracles.[2] The title was gained by six other strong men till it was abolished early in the Empire. In the foot-races also we find one Leonidas of Rhodes[3] in 164 B.C. winning the

[1] Paus. vi. 4. 2.   [2] Paus. v. 21. 10, and Africanus.   [3] Paus. vi. 13. 4.

stade race, the diaulos, and the long race at Olympia on the same day and so winning the title of Triple Victor (*Triastes*), and not only so, but he repeated the performance in four successive Olympiads. The love of advertisement is seen in the titles bestowed in late inscriptions on distinguished athletes, *Periodoneikes*, 'All-round champion' given to those who had won victories in all Panhellenic festivals, *Paradoxos*, 'Marvellous' or 'Record-breaker', a title that suggests the advertisements of a music-hall.

It is interesting and instructive to trace the degeneration of the physical type in art. Take for example the boxers represented on fifth-century vases (Fig. 173) and compare them with those on a Panathenaic vase dated 336 B.C. (Fig. 175), typical heavy-weights with small heads and heavy clumsy bodies. Pass over two hundred years or more and look at the bronze statue of a seated Boxer in the Terme Museum at Rome (Fig. 72), which we now know to be a work of the first century B.C. by the Greek sculptor Apollonius. Here we have the typical bruiser with his scarred face and brutal features, 'the successor of Heracles'. And if we would see the last stage of degradation, we shall find it in the prize-fighters represented in the Mosaic from the baths of Caracalla (Fig. 74). Or better still compare the true idea of strength represented in the Theseus of the Parthenon (Fig. 33) or the Apollo of Olympia with the false idea of Glycon's Farnese Heracles (Fig. 73). To Glycon strength consists in bulk, and in bulging over-developed muscles, which even at rest are not relaxed. His Heracles in fact is hopelessly muscle-bound.

PROFESSIONALISM UNDER THE EMPIRE

During the last century of the Roman Republic competition and the profits of athletics diminished steadily and there was little inducement to take up athletics as a profession. But the revival under the Empire produced an extraordinary development of professionalism. The competitors at the innumerable festivals in Italy and throughout all the eastern provinces were with few exceptions professionals, i. e. men who had adopted athletics as a means of livelihood. There were few Romans or Italians among them, they were mostly Greeks or at least citizens of the Hellenized cities of the East.

These athletes formed a special class with privileges of their own. Augustus,[1] we are told, confirmed and increased these

[1] Dio Cassius, lii. 30; Suetonius, *Augustus* 45.

privileges. A victor in the Sacred Games had a right to free sustenance or, in lieu of it, to a pension. He was also exempt from
taxation, from civil and military service, especially from the
leitourgiai which were such a burden to wealthy citizens in Greek
states. The conditions qualifying for these privileges seem to
have varied. Maecenas advised Augustus to confine the right of
free sustenance to winners at Olympia or Delphi. A decree of the
Emperor Diocletian, preserved in the Code of Justinian, lays down
that exemption from public service was only granted to men who
had spent all their lives in athletics and who had won at least three
victories in Sacred Games, one of which must have been in Rome
or in Greece, to which is added the significant proviso 'without
bribery or corruption' (*non aemulis corruptis ac redemptis*).[1]

The history of professional athletics under the Empire is full
of interest and instruction for the present day. We find the
athletes even before the Empire organizing themselves in synods,
or trades unions for the maintenance of their privileges. When
Mark Antony[2] visited Ephesus in 41 B.C. he met his friend and
trainer, M. Antonius Artemidorus, who brought with him the
priest of 'the synod of sacred victors and winners of the crown
from the inhabited world'. The latter appealed to Antony to
maintain the rights of the athletes and to grant them the privileges
of exemption from military service, from liturgies, and from the
billeting of troops. He further requested that the Ephesian
Games should be regarded as a time of sacred truce. A letter
written by Antony to the Greek community in Asia granting this
petition is preserved on a papyrus in the British Museum.

ATHLETIC GUILDS

In the first century after Christ nearly every city in the East
had its athletic union, its 'Sacred Synod of the Xystos', so called
from the Xystos or covered colonnade which was a part of the
gymnasium. The most famous of these guilds was the 'Synod
of Heracles', originally perhaps formed at Sardis, where it seems
to have been regarded as the chief guild in the East.[3] But Rome
was the centre of the Empire, and in the reign of Hadrian the
Synod of Heracles seems to have been dissolved and transferred
to Rome, where a similar guild had long existed. One M. Ulpius
of Ephesus, a distinguished pankratiast, who was Xystarch or

---

[1] Justinian, x. 53 (54).   [2] *C.R.* vii. 476; Hermes, xxxii. 509.
[3] *I.G.* xiv. 1102–10.

70. **SCENES IN GYMNASIUM.** Mosaic found at Tusculum. Late Roman work. *Mon. d. I.* vii, pl. 83; *Annali*, xxxv, p. 397. In left-hand corner trumpet with mantle swathed round it and a shell-shaped object of uncertain use; prize table with bust of some benefactor or famous athlete, underneath an amphora. Below table defeated athlete sitting in a dejected attitude. To his r. official crowning the victor who holds a palm while a small, fat-bellied slave boy acclaims his master. Next, a pankratiast standing over his fallen opponent while an official rushes towards him with whip in his r. hand. In r.-hand corner two boxers with typical caestus. In the next row to r. two wrestling groups, one standing, the other on the ground. In each case one wrestler has jumped on the other's back (κλιμακισμός, see p. 220), to the l. a jumper starting to run, in centre another jumper running at full speed with cylindrical *halteres* in his outstretched hands. To the r. a runner. In top line boxers, wrestlers, diskos-throwers.

71. **TERRA-COTTA RELIEF REPRESENTING HALL OF GYMNASIUM,** found in the Garden of Sallust. Berlin, 8739. Rohden and Winter, *Die antiken Terracotten*, iv, p. 144 sq.; v. pl. LXXXII. One of a numerous class of terra-cotta reliefs which served as ornaments in the gymnasia of the Empire. In the centre Heracles, to l. two boxers, to r. athlete using strigil, and athlete holding palm. Other reliefs have as central figure Hermes or an athlete, and in the side niches vases, or herms.

72. **BRONZE STATUE OF BOXER.** Terme Museum, Rome. The name of the sculptor, recently deciphered on the caestus, is Apollonius, the son of Nestor. Date 1st century B.C. The face is scarred, the nose broken, the ears swollen. For the caestus see Fig. 176.

73. **THE FARNESE HERACLES,** by Glycon of Athens. About A.D. 200. Naples. A very free copy in marble of a bronze statue by Lysippus. While we may attribute to Lysippus the pose and conception of the statue, we cannot hold him responsible for the gross exaggeration of the muscular development which, though alien to Greek art of the fourth century, is quite in accordance with the degraded taste of Glycon's time. Found in the baths of Caracalla, for which it was possibly made. *Photo. Anderson.*

president of the Synod, petitioned the Emperor for quarters at Rome, and we possess two letters, one from Hadrian, another from Antoninus, granting this petition. A house was granted them where they could keep their records and their sacred things, near the baths of Trajan and conveniently situated for the great Roman Games, the Capitolia. Here they had a gymnasium and a council chamber where they could discuss all matters concerning the welfare of athletes, the holding of competitions and the erection of honorary statues. Like all associations they had their own religious cults. With the worship of Heracles they combined that of their benefactors, Hadrian and Antoninus, and that of the reigning Emperor who, as *Agonios*, lord of the contests, is the representative of Hermes Agonios, the god of the palaestra. The activity of the Synod was not confined to Rome. As the title περιπολιστική, 'Itinerant' or 'Nomad', indicates it helped in organizing competitions and no doubt exercised some sort of control over the local festivals in all parts of the Empire. Its members were drawn from 'the inhabited world' and its officials were the most distinguished athletes of the time. Thus in practice, if not in theory, the Synod of Rome became the head-quarters for all the athletic unions of the Empire, and as such enjoyed the peculiar favour of the emperors who saw in its organization an invaluable instrument for securing the loyalty of the various cities.

A papyrus in the British Museum [1] throws an interesting light on the activity of the Athletic Synod at Rome and the character of the members. It is a diploma of membership issued to the members of the Synod notifying them that one Herminus of Hermopolis also known as Moros, 'the fool', has paid his entrance fee of 100 denarii and is admitted as member of the mess (σύνδειπνος). Whether the mess was free to members, and if so, where the funds came from, we do not know. The diploma was granted at Naples in the year of the 49th celebration of the Augustalia, A.D. 194. A later addendum states that Herminus paid a further fee of 50 denarii when he officiated as priest at the games of Asia at Sardis. Representatives from the central synod seem to have been sent sometimes to officiate in the provinces.

The diploma records various marks of imperial favour, and at the same time demonstrates the loyalty of the Synod. First comes a letter from the Emperor Claudius written in A.D. 46, to thank the Synod for sending him a gold crown on the occasion

[1] *B.M. Papyri*, iii. 1178.

of his victories in Britain. In a second letter Claudius expresses his gratification at the way in which the Synod had organized the games given in his honour by the Kings of Commagene and Pontus, probably in connexion with the *Ludi Seculares* in A. D. 47. Lastly Vespasian in an undated letter confirms the privileges granted to the Synod by Claudius.

There is also a list of the officials, the most important of whom also sign the diploma. There are three high-priests, who are also Xystarchs for life and overseers of the Imperial Baths, of whom only one officiates for the year. There are also two Archons of the Xystos, a treasurer, a secretary, and an assistant secretary. These officials are all eminent athletes from different parts of the Empire, and are all described as 'marvellous' (παράδοξος). One of the archons is a runner from Mytilene, the other a wrestler from Ephesus, the treasurer is a distinguished trainer from Mytilene. The three Xystarchs are especially interesting because two of them are well known to us from other inscriptions. They are M. Aurelius Damostratus Damas of Sardis, twice periodoneikes as pankratiast, and also an invincible (ἄλειπτος) boxer, M. Aurelius Demetrius of Alexandria, periodoneikes as pankratiast, and also a marvellous wrestler, and lastly M. Aurelius Chrysippus of Smyrna, periodoneikes in wrestling.

RECORDS OF PROFESSIONALS

Let us look at the record of Damostratus. It is given in two inscriptions, one found at Rome, the other at Sardis.[1] The former is a decree in his honour from the Synod of Heracles at Rome, and possibly belonged to the basis of a statue. It describes him in the same terms as the papyrus, but adds that he was a citizen of Alexandria, Antinoe, Athens, Ephesus, Smyrna, Pergamum, Nicomedea, Miletus, and Sparta. Why he was honoured by so many cities we shall see from the inscription on the base of his statue in his native city of Sardis. It contains a list of his victories and honours. He was, it tells us, a record breaker, having won a record number of victories in the Sacred Games in Italy, Greece, Asia, and Alexandria. Again, 'he was the first and only man since time began to win 20 victories as a boy in the Sacred Games and 48 as a man'. How many he won at other games we do not know, for the inscription is broken, but it is clear that he must have made a very handsome fortune as an athlete.

[1] *I. G.* xiv. 1105; Keil and Premerstein, *Reise in Lydien*, no. 27.

Greek festivals, it will be remembered, were divided into those of the crown where the only prize was a wreath of leaves and those in which prizes of value were given. The Sacred Games were still games of the crown, but the crown was often of gold, and it certainly did not exclude more valuable prizes. The number of Sacred Games had multiplied enormously and was still growing steadily. The Sacred Games in which Damostratus won victories included, besides the four Panhellenic festivals, the games at Argos, the Capitolia at Rome, games at Puteoli, Naples, and Actium, no fewer than four festivals at Athens, games at Rhodes, Sardis, Ephesus, Smyrna, Pergamum, Alexandria, and the triumphal games celebrated by Marcus Aurelius and Commodus in A. D. 176. Further we learn that several games where he had won prizes as a young man had since then been raised to the rank of Sacred Games. The distinctive feature of these games, however, is no longer the crown, so much as the triumph implied in the strange adjective *iselasticus* (εἰσελαστικός) 'having a triumphal entry', applied to them. In Pindar's time the victor's fellow citizens had welcomed him in triumph on his return to his native city. This spontaneous welcome has now become a formal triumph which the professional victor can claim as a right. We actually possess a letter in which Pliny [1] solemnly consults the Emperor Trajan as to whether an athlete has a right to the title 'isclasticus' before he has actually had his triumph, to which the Emperor with equal seriousness replies that he cannot claim the title until he has made his triumphal entry. Shall we ever see the day when a victorious Cup Tie Team returning to its city—I can hardly say its native city—will be entitled to a public reception by the Mayor and Corporation and to a pension for life?

To return to Damostratus our inscription further gives us a list of the honours conferred upon him by the Emperors. His athletic career began under Marcus Aurelius. From him and Commodus he received the special honour which only an Emperor could confer, the citizenship of Alexandria. He was also appointed as Xystarch to preside at the Capitolia and several festivals in the East. With these appointments we may probably connect the rights of citizenship accorded to him at various places. He received similar appointments from the Emperors Severus and Caracalla. To these Emperors he applied for the high priesthood of the Synod at Rome and the Xystarchy, which was granted to him and also to his sons after him. It was these sons who between

---

[1] *Epist.* cxviii, cxix.

the years 212 and 217 A.D. erected his statue at Sardis, whither he
may possibly have returned to end his days.　His sons were also
athletes and describe themselves as 'marvellous' and champions.
These inscriptions illustrate the extraordinary interest taken by
the Emperors themselves in the athletic guilds and festivals.
The Emperor himself appoints the Xystarch and Chief Priest of
the Guild at Rome, and he too appoints Xystarchs to preside at
festivals in the provinces.　It is the emperor who grants to the
Guilds their privileges, and questions concerning these privileges
are referred to him personally.

　　The spirit of ostentation and advertisement, and the love of
record-breaking which distinguishes this age are still better
illustrated in the inscription on another athlete, Asclepiades of
Alexandria, also a High Priest of the Synod at Rome, and the son of
that Demetrius who was a colleague of our friend Damostratus.
He erected a statue to his father at Rome, and in a long inscription
he tells us the story of his career.　In the list of his titles he tells
us that he was 'chief of the temple guardians of Great Sarapis,
a citizen of Alexandria, Hermopolis, and Puteoli', and not only that
but 'councillor of Naples, Elis, Athens, and many other cities'.
Then follows the description of his unbeaten record as a 'pankratiast invincible, immovable, unrivalled'.　'I neither challenged
any nor did any one in my time dare to challenge me, nor did I
divide the crown with any nor did I decline a contest, or enter
any protest, nor did I abandon any contest nor take part in any
contest to please royalty, nor did I gain a victory in any new
fangled games but in all the contests for which I ever entered my
name I was crowned in the actual ring and was approved in all
the preliminary trials.'　The list of his victories is very similar in
character to that of Damostratus.　He was a periodoneikes, and
his victory at Olympia was won in A. D. 181.　In enumerating his
victories he constantly records how he brought all his opponents
to a standstill (στήσας) from the start, or after the first, or second
heat, phrases which suggests that they scratched after the first or
second round, or even allowed him a walk-over.

　　The meaning of some of the terms in this inscription is not
very clear, but it undoubtedly indicates that sport was not very
clean, that protests were frequent, that matches were arranged
beforehand, and that the petty princes of the East exercised
a somewhat unwholesome influence.　His emphatic insistence
on the cleanness of his own record is an answer to malicious
attacks and charges brought against him by his rivals.　For he tells

us that at the age of twenty-five he retired from athletics, 'owing
to the dangers and jealousy that beset him'. After an interval
of some years he was induced to reappear and won the pankration
at the sixth Olympiad (A. D. 196) of the Olympic Games of
Alexandria, founded by Marcus Aurelius.

PROFITS OF PROFESSIONALS

Of the pensions of athletes we learn some interesting details
from some papyri of Hermopolis belonging to the reign of
Gallienus (A. D. 253-60).[1] A victor in any of the Sacred Games
had a right secured by the law of the Empire to receive a pension,
obsonia, from his city. He had only to present to the Council
a demand, made out in triplicate, and the Council had no
option but to grant it. The amount of the pension was from 180
to 200 drachmae a month. Most of the athletes mentioned were
local athletes and their victories were won in local games, for
example at Sidon, Gaza, Bostra, which can only have been places
of secondary importance. Moreover, an athlete could enjoy two
or more pensions together. One of them received for two victories in the course of four years, 2 talents and 3,900 drachmae. Of
the value of these pensions we can judge from the fact that
workmen engaged on building a public stoa, presumably therefore skilled men, received only 4 drachmae a day, and the average
wage for a day's labour must have been about 1 drachma. When
an ordinary athlete could earn such a pension, what must have
been the pension of an Asclepiades or Damostratus?

Another valuable privilege was exemption from taxation and
from those public services which rich citizens were forced to
undertake. One of the most burdensome of these was the office
of gymnasiarch, or president of the state gymnasium. Among
other expenses he had to provide the oil required for daily use in
the gymnasium and baths, sometimes too to provide for the
heating of the baths. In the third century A. D. it was not easy to
find citizens willing or even able to undertake such services, and
a number of gymnasiarchs were appointed who took it in turn
to provide oil. From such expenses the athlete and even his sons
had a right to claim exemption. At Hermopolis a young orphan
son of an athlete, Aelius Asclepiades, and descended from a famous
athlete of the same name—it was a common name in Egypt—

---

[1] Méautis, *Hermoupolis-la-Grande*, 152 sqq., 174, 199. *C. P. Hermopoli-
tanorum*, 53, 54, 69, 70, 72, 73, 75, 76, 78, 79, 81.

had been appointed to some liturgy. He appealed to the Imperial Commissioner, Ploution, himself an athlete of Hermopolis who had gone to live in Rome and had been sent back by the Emperor to his native city to settle some dispute connected with the gymnasiarchy. Ploution referred the appeal to the Emperor, who granted it and exempted the boy from all taxes and state service. The prefect communicated the Emperor's decision to the Council so that they might learn in future to respect the rights of athletes.

What, one naturally asks, was the social status of these athletes, and why did they receive such extraordinary honours? It is seldom that we have definite information as in the case of Ploution quoted above who, though holding the office of *ducenarius* and a member of the Museum, was yet in receipt of an athlete's pension. But from the names of the athletes and the honours conferred on them by the Emperors and by the cities, we cannot but conclude that they were drawn mostly from those 'old gymnasium boys' who formed the Greek aristocracy of the Eastern cities. The rewards of athletics must have made the athlete's profession very attractive to young men of good position. For the *pax Romana* had left life in the city state sadly void of interest, and the young man who did not enter the service of the Emperor could find little scope for his ambition at home. When there was an appeal to Rome on even trifling matters, civic liberty was a mere illusion. Hence the amazing popularity of hollow rhetorical displays and equally hollow athletic displays, and all the extravagance lavished on them. They supplied some substitute for those contests which had been the life of the city states of Hellas.

THE ATHLETE IN THE THIRD CENTURY A. D.

The extravagant claims advanced by the professional athletes might tempt one to suppose that they were a race of supermen. But we can test the value of all their bombast and self-advertisement from the works of contemporary authors, not from mere casual references but from treatises dealing with athletics and physical culture.

Our first witness is Galen, who was born at Pergamum in A. D. 180 and was actually for a time medical officer to a school of gladiators at Alexandria. He was an ardent advocate of exercise, the true principles of which he expounds admirably in his delightful essay on 'Exercise with the Small Ball'. But for athletes, the professional athletes of his day, he has not a good word to say.

In his 'Exhortation on the Choice of a Profession' he discusses
the profession of an athlete. Does the athlete's life benefit himself
or the state? To this question he emphatically answers 'no'.
Here are his reasons.

'The mind is higher than the body, for the mind we share with the Gods,
the body with the animals. In the blessings of the mind athletes have no
share. Beneath their mass of flesh and blood their souls are stifled as in
a sea of mud. Nor do they enjoy the best blessings even of the body.
Neglecting the old rule of health which prescribes moderation in all things
they spend their lives in over-exercising, in over-eating, and over-sleeping
like pigs. Hence they seldom live to old age and if they do they are crippled
and liable to all sorts of disease. They have not health nor have they
beauty Even those who are naturally well proportioned become fat and
bloated: their faces are often shapeless and unsightly owing to the wounds
received in boxing and in the pankration. They lose their eyes and their
teeth and their limbs are strained. Even their vaunted strength is useless.
They can dig and plough but they cannot fight. They cannot endure heat
and cold, nor, like Heracles, wear one garment winter and summer, go
unshod and sleep on the open ground: in all this they are weaker than
new-born babes.'

If any one thinks that Galen is exaggerating let him look at the
mosaics from the baths of Caracalla (Fig. 74). These portraits of
the famous professional athletes of the time, these 'heroes of the
Stadium' as they are described with unconscious irony in a well-
known work, might have been made to illustrate the physician's
description. There we see them, row after row, with their
clumsy, over-developed bodies, their small brainless heads, and
brutal expression. They have not health nor have they beauty.

Galen's charges are fully confirmed by Philostratus who wrote
in the first half of the third century, and his evidence is the more
valuable in that his work *De Arte Gymnastica* is really an answer to
Galen's attack on athletics. But while he defends athletics, he
fully admits the degeneracy of the athlete of his day. The fault,
he says, is not in the man nor in athletics but in the vicious
system of training, and for this he blames the doctors. Trainers
had borrowed from them quack rules for diet and developed
hard and fast systems of training which they applied indifferently
to all alike, without any regard to age or individual requirements.
He finds the remedy in a return to the more natural and simpler
system of the olden times.

The worst evil of professionalism is corruption. We have seen
how it entered into Greek athletics from the beginning of pro-

fessionalism, and how the authorities of Olympia strove hard to repress it. How prevalent it was under the Empire we learn from Philostratus. There was no attempt at concealment. Victories were publicly bought and sold: even trainers encouraged the traffic, lending money for the purpose to their pupils at exorbitant rates of interest. He quotes a single example from the Isthmian Games. A competitor who had promised his rival 3,000 drachmae to let him win, refused to pay on the ground that he had won on his merits. Recourse was had to the oath and the defeated athlete swore openly in a loud voice before the altar of Poseidon that he had been promised the money if he allowed himself to be defeated. 'When this could happen at the Isthmian Games, what', asks Philostratus, 'might we not expect in Ionia or Asia?'

ADDENDUM. That parents and guardians in choosing a profession for their boys seriously considered the claims of athletics is clear from the following letter.[1] It was written in 257 B.C. by one Hierocles, the keeper of a palaestra at Alexandria, to Zenon, the agent of a wealthy land-owner, Apollonius, under Ptolemy Philadelphus. Zenon has sent a boy named Pyrrhus to be educated by Hierocles, and has written to him telling him if he is sure that the boy will win a victory, to continue training him; otherwise not to incur useless expense or keep him from his letters. Hierocles replies that only the gods can be certain that the boy will win, but that Ptolemaeus his trainer considers him superior to others who had been a long time in training, and 'I hope', he adds, that in a short time *you* will be crowned. He further asks Zenon to send the boy some clothes and bedding and also some honey, which seems to have been a staple article of diet. The palaestra in question seems to have been founded by Apollonius, probably for the benefit of the numerous Greeks on his estate. To this class the boy Pyrrhus belonged. His father apparently was dead, and his mother, like many other Greeks in Egypt, was in straightened circumstances and in receipt of a pension from Zenon. At all events the latter undertook the expense of the boy's education, but not entirely from philanthropic motives. It is not Pyrrhus, but Zenon who will be crowned, if the boy is victorious. In other words, Zenon will get the prize, while if the boy does not turn out an athlete his education may make him useful on the estate in other ways.

[1] *Cairo Papyri*, 59060, 59098; *P.S.I.* 443.

VIII

ROMAN SPORTS

THE Romans of the Republic despised athletics, but like all vigorous people they were fond of strenuous exercise. They rode, hunted, swam, boxed sometimes, or wrestled, but without any science. But these sports they regarded merely as exercise and recreation and attached no further importance to them. For competitions they had no liking, nor had athletics any place in Roman education. There was indeed no organized education at Rome; it was left to the parents to give their children such education as they thought fit, and this education was strictly practical. Old Cato taught his son not only to throw a dart, fight in armour, and ride, but also to box and to endure both heat and cold and to swim the most rapid rivers.

ROMANS AND GREEKS

If we compare the history of Greece and Rome we can easily understand the difference in their attitude to sport. The athletic spirit took its rise in the heroic age of the Greeks, but the Romans had no heroic age. Nor was Italy a land of city states. Such city states as existed were Etruscan and Greek, and from them the Romans borrowed most of their sports. Most of Italy was inhabited by more or less kindred tribes dwelling in scattered villages in the hill country. A stock of hardy farmers, all their energies were occupied in a grim struggle with the forces of nature and in wars with their neighbours. Fighting, hunting, the work of the farm, provided them with bodily exercise; they had no need of organized training like dwellers in cities. They had, no doubt, their rustic sports, but these sports never developed, and indeed with the decay of country life after the Punic wars they tended to disappear. There was, moreover, no cohesion, no sense of a common nationality, like that which united the scattered city states of Greece. Nationality in Italy was imposed by Rome, and in the Roman idea of nationality athletics had no place. For centuries the Romans had been engaged in continuous wars, and in the struggle they had developed a grim seriousness which made them despise all that was not practical. This was their attitude towards Greek athletics. Exercise was necessary for health, recreation was necessary, but to devote to sport the time necessary to achieve athletic success, to submit for months to the tyranny of a trainer, often a man of low birth, to make an exhibition of oneself before one's fellow citizens, was felt to be quite incompatible with the dignity of a Roman. It was the nudity of Greek athletes that especially revolted the Romans. 'To strip naked among one's fellow citizens', says Ennius, 'is the beginning of vice' (*flagiti principium*). Centuries later in the reign of Nero we find the same feeling in the protests of the old school against the introduction in Rome of an athletic festival on Greek lines: 'The youths were degenerating under the influence of foreign tastes, passing their time in athletics, in idling or low intrigue. What remained for them but to strip themselves naked, put on the caestus and practise such battles instead of the arms of legitimate warfare?'[1]

There was much justification for the Roman point of view. Even at their best there was an element of exaggeration and of danger in Greek athletics. The honours paid to athletic success were out of all proportion to its desert; the time required to secure such success was more than an amateur could or ought to afford. Athletics are not an end in themselves; the production of champions is not the true end of sport; there is a limit to the usefulness of competitions. It is this feeling that makes many people in England so lukewarm towards the revived Olympic Games and the multiplication of championships and international competitions. We feel that they confuse our values, and give to sport an unreal place in our life. Yes, the Romans had much justification. Moreover, all their athletics had not saved the Greeks. When the Romans first came to know them well, the nation was degenerate and their athletics were degenerate. The competitors at the great Games were professionals whose training made them useless as soldiers. The gymnasia, instead of producing useful citizens, had indeed become schools of idleness and immorality.

The Romans, it is true, had public games in abundance; games held in honour of the gods, some of which according to tradition went back to the very beginning of the city. Games, too, were frequently vowed to the gods in time of war, of civil strife or pestilence. At a later date distinguished citizens were sometimes honoured with funeral games. The chief events in these games in the earliest times seem to have been chariot- and horse-races, sometimes fights between boxers, more rarely other athletic

[1] Tac. *Annals*, xiv. 20.

contests. Dramatic performances were introduced in 361 B.C. Gladiatorial shows were first exhibited in 264 B.C. by Marcus and Decimus Brutus at the funeral games of their father, and are frequently mentioned after this date as an addition to funeral games.

These Roman games, however, were very different from the athletic festivals of the Greeks. The difference is implied in the very word '*ludi*'. The Greek meetings are never described as games but as contests (ἀγῶνες). Whether dramatic, musical, equestrian, or athletic they are contests, competitions between free citizens; and they exist primarily for the competitors. The Roman games are *ludi*, amusements, entertainments, and the performers are slaves or hirelings; they exist for the spectators. Tarquin, who is said to have been the first to mark out the Circus Maximus at Rome, imported his chariots and boxers from Etruria. From Etruria, too, came the actors (*ludiones*) when *ludi scenici* were first introduced at Rome. There can be little doubt that the gladiatorial shows originated in Etruria. The gladiators themselves, says Livy,[1] were usually conscripted from slaves and people of servile origin, and he particularly contrasts the games given by Scipio at Carthage in memory of his father, where the gladiators were volunteers, many of them of high birth, from the various tribes of Africa.

ETRUSCAN GAMES

There is no reason to doubt the truth of the tradition connecting the earliest Roman games with Etruria. The Etruscans first made their appearance in Italy in the ninth century B.C., and most modern authorities are now agreed that Herodotus was correct in stating that they came by sea from Asia Minor. There they must have been familiar with the sports of the Asiatic Greeks, and from these they may have borrowed the practice of holding funeral games. In Italy by their superior weapons they quickly subjugated the semi-barbarous native tribes. The Etruscan nobles who formed the governing class formed a close exclusive aristocracy. Under them great cities rose; agriculture, commerce, and art were developed. By the fifth century the Etruscans had extended their power across the Apennines to Bologna, and southwards as far as Campania; a Tuscan dynasty ruled in Rome. Their fleet was mistress of the Western Sea, which was called from then the Tyrrhenian Sea.

The luxurious life of the Etruscan nobles is vividly pictured

---

[1] xxviii. 21.

on the walls of their tombs. It was their pious belief that the
dead would enjoy hereafter the pleasures they had enjoyed in life,
and among these pleasures games occupy a prominent place. Their
favourite sport was chariot-racing. The Etruscans were famed
for their horses and cavalry and were probably the first to introduce chariots into Italy. Boxing and wrestling are constantly
depicted, other sports less frequently. But we may doubt whether
they had any science even in boxing or wrestling or cared for
them otherwise than as spectacles. In one bloodthirsty contest,
where a man armed with a club with his head entangled in a
mantle is attacked by another man with a ferocious bloodhound,
we have perhaps an anticipation of gladiatorial sports. These
paintings, of which the earliest belong to the seventh century B.C.,
show strongly the influence of contemporary Greek vase-painting,
and scenes and exercises from the Greek palaestra are sometimes introduced incongruously; but on the whole they give a
faithful picture of the Etruscan games, and it is not a Greek
picture. There can be no doubt of the spectacular character of
these games. For while in other frescoes we see the Etruscan
nobles and their families going out hunting, banqueting, or
making love, the riders, dancers, athletes are evidently, from their
physical type and features, men of a lower class, slaves or hired
performers. In the Tomba delle Bighe at Corneto we see the actual
stands full of spectators watching the games, a scene hardly
paralleled in Greek art, though, as already noted, similar scenes
are represented in Minoan Crete.

The frescoes of the Tomba delle Bighe (Fig. 75) may be dated
about 500 B.C. and are probably the work of a Greek artist. At
either end of the frieze of the back wall and once on each of the
side walls the stand is represented. It is a platform supported by
wooden posts, and over it we see draped a curtain or awning,
like the *vela* of the Roman Amphitheatre. On the platform are
seated the Etruscan nobles and their families, men and women,
young and old, all appropriately dressed and eagerly watching the
sports. On the ground, under the stand, sprawl the common
people paying but little attention to the games. The most interesting scene of all is on the right wall where we see the preparation for the chariot-race and the parade of chariots before the
grand stand. First come two horses led by their riders or grooms,
then three youths preparing to harness the horses to a *biga*, then
the actual parade, the horses of the first chariot just starting, the
second moving somewhat more quickly, the third as it nears the

stand at a brisk trot. On the back wall between the two stands
are two boxing-matches, a wrestling group, a mounted horseman
leading a second horse with a rider preparing to leap on it by
means of a pole, other athletes apparently waiting their turn. On
the left wall we see a pankration scene and the judge with uplifted
whip preparing to punish some breach of the rules, an armed
dancer, various diskos-throwers, and other draped figures, obvious
imitations of scenes from the Greek palaestra so common on Greek
vases, but here incongruous.

The palaestra scenes in Etruscan tombs were often the work
of Greek artists, but that the sports themselves were utterly
alien to northern Italy is clear from the mistakes made by native
artists in reproducing them. For example, a most extraordinary
boxing scene is depicted with hardly any variation on a group of
situlae or bronze buckets, found at Bologna and Este and exported
thence to the Tyrol and Austria. The earliest of these situlae
dates from the close of the sixth century, the one illustrated in
Fig. 76, which comes from Watsch, is perhaps half a century
later. The scenes on these situlae are taken mostly from Etruscan
life, the boxing group undoubtedly is derived from Greek vase-
paintings, possibly through Etruscan copies. Two boxers con-
front one another holding in their hands what seem to be dumb-
bells. Between them is a helmet supported on a curious stand,
perhaps meant for a tripod. A pair of combatants with the prize
placed between them is a familiar scheme on seventh-century
vase-paintings from the Aegean World. In Fig. 77 we see a pair
of warriors fighting; between them is a suit of armour, helmet,
buckler, and greaves, the prize or perhaps the spoils of victory.
In Fig. 184 two boxers are fighting over a tripod which is of
course the prize. In the Tomba degli Auguri at Tarquinii we
see a similar group of wrestlers, the prizes, three cauldrons, being
placed between them. But what of the dumb-bells? They are
nothing else but jumping-weights. It is true that they are straight
like dumb-bells, not curved like the Greek jumping-weights, but
that they are really jumping-weights is proved by a relief on a
marble chair in the Lateran (Fig. 78), a work probably made in
central Italy not earlier than the fourth century. Here we have
the same boxing group reproduced so closely that it is clear that
it must be derived from the same Etruscan prototype as the
situlae. But here the jumping-weights have their proper shape.
We can only conclude that the Italian artist familiar with them
on Greek vases or in Etruscan paintings but ignorant alike of

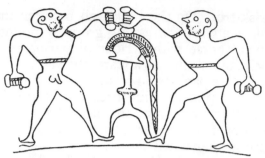

76. BRONZE SITULA FROM WATSCH. Jüthner, *Ant. Turn.* p. 75. Hoernes, *Geschichte der Bildenden Kunst*, pl. XXXV. 1. Other situlae on which the same group occurs are:

1. Benvenuti situla from Este. MacIver, *Iron Age in Italy*, p. 33, dates it 540–500 B.C.
2. The Arnoaldi situla from Bologna, about 450 B.C. Montelius, pl. C: the drawing of the trophy and helmet is very rough, the artist does not understand the helmet.
3. Situla from Matrei. Hoernes, *op. cit.* pl. XXXV, 4, 6.
4. Situla from Kuffarn, N. Austria. Hoernes, pl. XXXIII, p. 661.
5. Situla from Styria. Hoernes, p. 663.

On the Certosa situla (Hoernes, pl. XXXII), a pair of diminutive boxers are placed facing one another at opposite ends of what seems to be a long couch. A more vigorous pair of boxers armed with similar implements are found on a terracotta relief from Este (Hoernes, XXXVI. 8). Boxers are also represented in reliefs on stelai of Felsina (Ducati, *Mon. dei Lincei*, xx. 685), but there is no indication on these stelai of anything resembling the dumb-bells of the situlae. On one stele, no. 169, the boxers seem to be wearing gloves similar to those represented on Greek fourth-century vases.

◄77. TWO WARRIORS FIGHTING OVER TROPHY. Island, so-called Melian Amphora: 7th century. Conze, *Melische Gefässe*. The scheme is identical with that on the situlae and on the Corsini chair. Athens, Nat. Mus. 475.

◄78. CORSINI CHAIR. Lateran. *Mon. d. I.* xi. 9; *Annali*, li (1879), 314; Ducati in *Mon. dei Lincei*, xxiv, 401 sq., from which our illustration is taken: 4th or 3rd century. The chair is like the situlae funerary in character and the games are probably funeral games. Besides the boxers there are two groups of wrestlers.

boxing and of Greek athletics thought these weights were a sort of weapon for fighting and armed his boxers with them. Some Italian archaeologists prefer to see in them an Italian weapon from which the caestus was derived. If it is so, it argues a still more complete ignorance of boxing or athletics; for it is hard to conceive any people inventing a weapon so clumsy and so inappropriate for boxing.

ATHLETIC SHOWS AT ROME

Athletic contests, by which we may probably understand wrestling matches in the Greek style, were, says Livy, first exhibited at Rome in 186 B.C.[1] at the games provided by M. Fulvius after the Aetolian war, and here, too, we note the same spectacular character that marks the Etruscan games. For the actors and athletes were brought from Greece. Moreover, to provide more exciting sport, lions and panthers were imported from Africa, and the games, says Livy, were celebrated with a variety and magnificence hardly inferior to those of his own day. In the last century of the Republic the number and splendour of the games grew apace. The increasing crowd of unemployed in the city needed amusement, and politicians vied with one another in the variety and extravagance of the shows by which they sought to win the favour of the mob. We can judge what those shows were like in Livy's time from the account in Suetonius of the games provided by Julius Caesar.[2]

Besides a variety of musical and dramatic performances there was a gladiatorial show in the Forum, games in the Circus, and a sea fight. In the gladiatorial show, in defiance of public opinion, two prominent citizens fought, Furius Leptinus, a member of a praetorian family, and Quintus Calpenus, an ex-senator. The Pyrrhic dance was performed by noble youths from Asia and Bithynia, and one Decimus Laberius, a Roman knight, actually performed in a farce of his own composition. At the games in the Circus youths of noble birth gave a display of chariot-driving and riding, including the Game of Troy, of which we shall have more to say. Five days were occupied in *Venationes* or combats with wild beasts, and there was a sham fight between two forces, each consisting of 500 foot-soldiers, 30 cavalry, and 20 elephants. A temporary stand was erected in the Campus Martius where athletic competitions took place lasting five days.

[1] Livy, xxxix. 22.   [2] *Julius Caesar*, 39.

Lastly a huge artificial lake was constructed in which biremes, triremes, and quadriremes from Tyre and Egypt joined in mimic battle.

How purely spectacular these athletic contests were, we can learn from the words of Augustus himself. In the record of his reign that he wrote himself, preserved in the temple of Ancyra, he enumerates the numerous shows he gave: eight gladiatorial shows in which about 10,000 gladiators fought; six and twenty venationes of wild beasts from Africa, 3,500 of which were killed; a sea fight between 30 triremes and numerous small boats, the crews numbering 5,000, for which a huge lake was constructed across the Tiber. 'Twice I provided for the people in my own name an exhibition of athletes collected from all quarters, and a third time in the name of my grandson'—*athletarum undique accitorum spectacula.* So runs the Latin text: its evidence is conclusive.[1]

Every town in Italy had its own shows of the same sort. Take, for example, the funeral inscription on A. Clodius, three times elected Duumvir at Pompeii.[2] In it his wife enumerates the various shows that he gave in honour of his election. On his second election, at the games of Apollo, he gave two days' shows, on the first day in the forum, 'a procession, bulls, bullfighters, common pugilists; on the second day in the Amphitheatre, 30 pairs of athletes, 5 pairs of gladiators, 35 pairs of gladiators, venationes, bulls, bull-fighters, bears, boars, and other animals'. By 'common pugilists', *pugiles catervarii*, we may probably understand pugilists who fought in troops like gladiators, but unarmed, as opposed to boxers of the Greek type who are described as *pyktae*. The term is also used in describing fights of street roughs. The 'pairs of athletes' suggests that they were wrestlers, that being the usual meaning of the word in Latin.

THE IUVENES

We saw in another chapter how Augustus and his successor revived the splendour of the athletic festivals of Greece, how they organized similar festivals in Italy and in Rome, and how they encouraged the guilds of athletes. But these festivals had no effect upon the Romans, nor did they promote athletics in Italy. The athletes were professionals from all parts of the Empire, and

[1] *Monumentum Ancyranum*, xxii.
[2] *C.I.L.* x. 1074 d; della Corte, *Juventus*, p. 46; to the latter work I am indebted for much of the information contained in the following pages.

the festivals were to the Romans only additional spectacles, and as such less entertaining than the sports of the Amphitheatre. But there is one movement encouraged, if not initiated, by Augustus that must have exercised a great and wholesome influence on the youth of the Empire. In most of the cities of Italy and in many of the provinces we find in the early Empire associations or clubs of boys and youths known as *Iuventus*. The members, *Iuvenes*, were drawn from the chief families of their townships, and the object of the associations was to train them for the Army or the Civil Service. The training given was chiefly military and athletic, and was probably copied from that of the Greek epheboi. Indeed it seems that in some of the Greek cities in Italy, or in cities like Pompeii where Greek influence had been strong, similar associations had long existed. But there can be little doubt that the revival, if not the origin, of the movement was due to Augustus. In his own record of his reign he especially relates how his destined heirs Gaius and Lucius Caesar were in the years 5 and 2 B.C. saluted by the whole body of Roman knights as *Principes Iuventutis*, and he celebrated the occasion with games in their honour. The institution indeed bears no little resemblance to that of our Boy Scouts, except that it was exclusively aristocratic. It is interesting, too, as the only organized attempt in Italy at making physical training a part of education.

Though united in the service of the Empire, all these clubs were absolutely independent. Like all such associations they had their own cults, usually the cult of the chief local deity. Thus the members of the Pompeian Club called themselves *Iuvenes Venerii Pompeiani*, 'the Young Men's Venus association of Pompeii', Venus being the patron goddess of the place. They were also known by the aristocratic title of the Nine Hundred (*Nongenti*). Other clubs were allowed to take the name of the reigning Emperor, as *Traianenses*, *Antoniniani*. Each club had its own officials: its President (*magister*), usually some influential citizen who had belonged to the club; its Captain (*praefectus*), who was responsible for their training; its Treasurer (*procurator*), who looked after the funds and property of the club. These funds were kept up by monthly subscriptions, donations, and legacies. But the expenses were heavy; the upkeep of the club buildings, arrangement of assaults-at-arms, displays, processions, provision of prizes all cost money. So the clubs, just as our own clubs do, would try to secure some wealthy man as their patron (*patronus*) in the hope that he would repay the honour shown him by his generosity;

and in this they were seldom disappointed. There was a wonderful public spirit among the rich citizens at this period.

We know nothing of the athletic training of the Iuvenes. It was probably similar to that in Greek gymnasia. At Pompeii they had as their head-quarters a gymnasium and palaestra of the regular Greek type near the theatre in the oldest part of the city; while close to the Amphitheatre they had an up-to-date gymnasium provided with elaborate baths and a club-house. Their chief training was military: they learnt the use of weapons of all

79. Game of Troy. Drawing on 6th-century Etruscan vase found at Tragliatella. *Annali*, liii (1881); See Benndorf, *Über das Alter des Trojaspiels*, 'Sitzungsberichte der kais. Akademie der Wissenschaften', cxxiii. K. iii; Dar.-Sag. s.v. *Ludus Troiae*; M. della Corte, *Juventus*. For a full publication and discussion of this oenochoe which is in a private collection in Rome, see article by Quirino Giglioli in *Studi Etruschi*, iii, p. 111.

sorts, and ex-gladiators were sometimes employed to train them. At Pompeii their *salle d'armes* has been excavated in the Via dell' Abondanza. All around it are cupboards where their equipment could be kept, and painted on the walls at the entrance are two gladiatorial trophies. The champions of the Iuvenes, not satisfied with their own bloodless contests, used sometimes to risk their lives against the professional gladiators of the Amphitheatre.

But the most characteristic part of their training was in horsemanship. The Italians have always been great riders, and the horse is prominent in early Roman ritual and legend. One of the oldest festivals of Rome was the *Equiria* when horses raced in the Campus Martius. At the *Ludi Magni* the procession was headed by companies of youths on horseback, and at the games given by Julius Caesar the noblest youths gave displays of chariot-racing and horsemanship, leaping from horse to horse, or leaping down and remounting at full gallop. A double company of boys, younger and older, performed the Game of Troy, a sort of military ride similar to those which are such an attractive feature of our own Military Tournaments. It is this that Virgil describes in one of the most charming passages of the fifth *Aeneid*. His description of the other games is rhetorical and artificial. He has no real knowledge of athletics, but in the Game of Troy he is describing what he knows and loves. When the other sports are finished Aeneas bids Ascanius marshal his youthful companies. The course is cleared and the youths advance in three companies of sixteen each and pass in parade before the admiring gaze of their elders. Then at a signal the three companies break away, then gallop back, then part again, retreating and charging, weaving circles within circles in mimic warfare, in maze-like figures or like dolphins sporting in the sea. Such, says Virgil, is the game Ascanius taught the Latins, and even now it is called Troy.

Virgil is right. Troy is one of the oldest games of Rome; but it has nothing to do with Troy. On a sixth-century Etruscan vase we see it represented (Fig. 79). There are two horsemen shown, and behind them is the Maze or Labyrinth itself, represented as we see it scratched on the walls of Pompeii six hundred years later, and between the lines of the maze we read the real name, the Etruscan word TRUIA, which the Romans mistook for Troy. From Pompeii, too, we have the record of a very similar military ride, 'the serpent game'. It is in an inscription consisting of four verses in praise of one of the *Iuvenes* of Pompeii called Septimius, and the inscription, written in the form of a serpent, may be freely rendered: 'If you have seen the skill with which Septimius performs the serpent ride, whether you are a lover of the shows or of horses, you can hold the scales level', i.e. you will be equally satisfied.[1] There is nothing competitive in such rides, merely skill in horsemanship. But the Italians loved shows, and loved horses as they do to-day.

---

[1] *C.I.L.* iv, pl. XXXVIII. 1.

THE STADIUM AND THE FOOT-RACE

IN Homer the competitors in the foot-race ran to some mark in the distance, turned round it, and ran back to the starting-point. In historic times the Greeks always raced up and down a straight track, not round a curved track. Here we have the essential difference between the Greek racecourse or *Stadium* [1] and the modern running-track. The stadium was so called because the track for the straight race or sprint was exactly a stade long, other races being all multiples of a stade. In practice, however, the distance varied, because the standard of measurement was not the same in all places. The track of Olympia, said to have been stepped out by Heracles, was 192·27 metres long, that at Epidaurus 181·30 metres, that at Delphi 177·5, while at Pergamum we have the exceptional length of 210 metres. Time records would clearly have been useless even if the Greeks had had stop-watches.

The Greek stadium was therefore a long parallelogram, some 200 yards long by 30 yards wide. The start was in its simplest form marked by posts (νύσσαι) or a line (γραμμή) drawn in the sand, and the finish or turning-point (καμπτῆρες) was similarly marked. It was usually enclosed by an embankment, natural or artificial. At Olympia the stadium lay along the foot of the hill of Cronus, and the other side and the ends were artificial. At Epidaurus advantage was taken of a shallow trough between two low ridges, the eastern end being raised by an embankment. The space enclosed was of course actually longer than a stade, there being a space of some 15 metres left at either end. The end might be square as at Epidaurus, or curved into a theatre (σφενδόνη) as at Delphi and Athens. Some late stadia have a sphendone at both ends, thus approximating to the Roman circus. But the shape of the ends only affected spectators. The track itself was rectangular.

The most interesting of the earlier stadia is that of Epidaurus [2] (Figs. 81, 83). It was laid out probably in the fifth century and continued to be used in Roman times. Finish and start are

---

[1] For the Stadium see Krause, *Gym.* pp. 131 ff.; *J.H.S.* xxiii, pp. 261 ff.; *Greek Athletics*, pp. 251 ff.

[2] Πρακτικά, 1902, pp. 78–92.

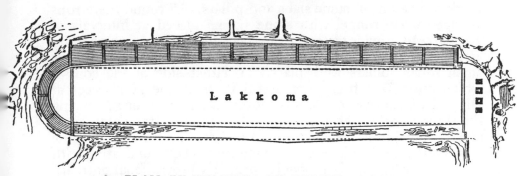

80. PLAN OF STADIUM OF DELPHI. *B.C.H.* xxiii
(1899), pl. XIII.

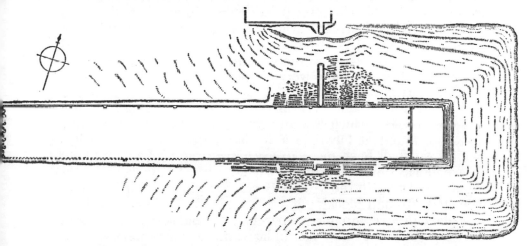

81. PLAN OF STADIUM OF EPIDAURUS. *Πρακτικά*,
1902, pl. I.

82. VIEW OF STADIUM OF DELPHI, showing the
curved sphendone.

83. VIEW OF STADIUM AT EPIDAURUS, showing the
starting lines. Photograph from the Archaeological Institute,
Athens.

marked by a line of stone slabs and pillars. All round there runs
an open stone runnel with stone basins placed at intervals of
30 metres to provide water for the spectators. There was a similar
arrangement at Olympia. At intervals of a plethron or 100 feet
small square pillars were placed on either side of the course,
which must have been very useful if, as in the girls' races at
Olympia, a shorter course was required, and also for measuring
the throws of the diskos or spear. The rows of stone seats were
mostly added in Macedonian times or later. In the centre of the
seats on the north side was an arched tunnel communicating with
a square enclosure. It probably formed a processional entrance
for officials and competitors. Opposite to it on the south side
there seems to have been a platform, and here we may conjecture
stood the table on which the prizes were laid and here the victors
received their prizes. In earlier days there were probably a few
stone seats, and these were reserved for officials. Most of the
spectators sat or stood on the ground. At Olympia, even to the
close of its history, there were no seats for spectators.

The starting arrangements at Epidaurus are particularly interesting. Finish and start alike are marked by a pair of stone
pillars, between which lies a line of grooved stone slabs similar
to those found at Olympia and elsewhere. This stone sill, of
which we shall have more to say later, was probably added in
Macedonian times. Originally the start must have been marked
by a line drawn in the sand between the pillars. But in front of
the stone sill and blocking it are five pillars, having on each side
a shallow groove, intended apparently to hold some sort of bar or
starting-gate. We know that in late times runners were stationed
behind a rope (called ὕσπληξ) or a bar, the dropping of which
was the signal for the start.[1] A sort of starting-gate was used in
the Roman Circus, but there is no evidence of any such practice
in the fifth or fourth centuries.

Far more elaborate is the stadium at Delphi (Figs. 80, 82, 85),
the best preserved of all Greek stadia and the most romantic in
its situation.[2] It lies on a rocky terrace above the sanctuary, with
the cliffs of Parnassus rising sheer above it to a height of 800 feet,
while deep below lie the valley of the Pleistus and the Crisaean
plain. It was constructed originally in the second half of the fifth
century when the terrace was cut out of the mountain-face. The
lower side was supported by a massive retaining-wall on which

[1] For a discussion of the ὕσπληξ see *J.H.S.* xxiii, p. 263.
[2] *B.C.H.* 1899, pp. 601–15.

THE STADIUM

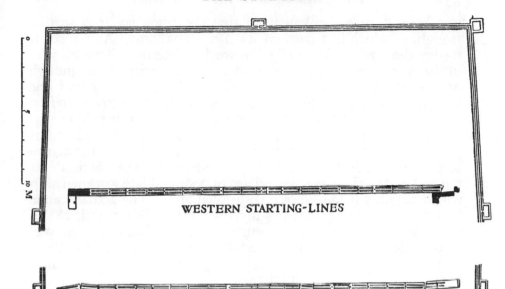

WESTERN STARTING-LINES

EASTERN STARTING-LINES

84. STARTING-LINES AT OLYMPIA. *Olympia*, p. 284.

85. VIEW OF STARTING-LINES AT DELPHI. The pillars behind the stone sill probably belong to some sort of triumphal arch and are a late addition.

86. THE PANATHENAIC STADIUM AT ATHENS as restored for the modern Olympic Games. The two pillars mark the line of the original starting line, the track round is an attempt to adapt the stadium to modern conditions.

was heaped an embankment so that the track lay in a sort of trough, to which fact it owed its name Lakkoma. As we see it to-day the stadium is chiefly the work of Herodes Atticus, who in the second century after Christ reseated it with stone, though not, as Pausanias says, with marble. The two sides and the shallow curved sphendone at the western end are surrounded by tiers of stone seats raised on a stone basement 5 feet high and providing room for 7,000 spectators. Flights of steps placed at intervals of half a plethron gave access to the seats. In the centre of the north side were the seats of honour for the officials. At the east end are four massive pillars of poor and late workmanship which possibly belonged to a triumphal arch. The actual course is 177·5 metres long and 25½ metres wide at either end, 28½ in the centre. The object of this curve which we find elsewhere was to provide a good view of the whole course to spectators. Start and finish were marked by a line of grooved stone slabs similar to those at Epidaurus and Olympia.

In earlier times the stadium at Delphi must have been much simpler. In the intervals between the festivals the track must have been overgrown with weeds and perhaps was used for pasture. When the time for the festival approached the track had to be put in order and the work was put out to contract. We possess various records of these contracts. The most interesting of those is in the accounts of the Archonship of Dion[1] (258 B.C.), in which are enumerated the various items of work to be done in the stadium and hippodrome and gymnasium.

First the course itself and the embankment were cleared of weeds and rubbish. This cost 15 staters. Then the track and jumping-places were dug up and rolled at a further cost of 110 staters. Finally it was covered with 600 medimnoi of white sand, which at 1⅔ obols per medimnos amounted to 83 staters 4 obols. Next a barrier was erected round the course at a cost of 5 staters, and a scaffolding of seats for 29 staters. This erection was clearly a temporary structure intended for a few privileged spectators and officials. Thirty-six staters were expended on the starting-line and turning-posts, and 8 staters on arrangements for the pentathlon, presumably for throwing the diskos and the spear. The comparatively large sum of 77½ staters spent on the boxing-ring suggests that some sort of platform was erected to enable the spectators to have a good view of this popular event. It is not easy to guess the value of these figures. The stater was equal

[1] *B.C.H.* 1899, pp. 564, 613.

to two drachmae, and in the time of Pericles a drachma was a day's wage for an artisan: a labourer would not have received much more than half a drachma, or a quarter of a stater per day.

The Panathenaic stadium at Athens (Fig. 86) was recently restored for the revived Olympic Games,[1] and we can realize something of its splendour, though an ancient stadium owing to its narrowness can never be satisfactorily converted into a modern track. Constructed originally by Lycurgus in the fourth century B.C. it was rebuilt like that of Delphi by Herodes Atticus, but with far greater magnificence. There were forty-six rows of marble seats raised on a marble basement nearly 6 feet high, and capable of holding 50,000 spectators. The start was marked by two stone pillars between which were remains of a stone sill. Between the pillars, too, stood four double-headed Herms. These were square shafts about 6 feet high crowned by two heads, said to represent the youthful Apollo and the bearded Dionysus. The square shafts were divided to the height of 3 feet by a narrow slit through which, as at Epidaurus, may have passed the rope or bar used in later times for the start. More probably some barrier may have been fastened in them for use when the stadium was employed, as we know it was in Hadrian's time, for dangerous shows such as fights with wild beasts.

To return to the stone sills which, we found, marked the start and the finish at Olympia, Delphi, and Epidaurus, and were probably universal in the fourth century B.C., if not earlier (Figs. 84, 85). These sills at Olympia[2] are about 18 inches wide and extend the whole breadth of the course. They are divided at intervals of 4 feet by square sockets, evidently intended to hold posts. At Epidaurus there were traces of lead in these sockets. Between each pair of sockets two parallel grooves are cut in the stone 7 inches apart at Olympia, 4 inches at Epidaurus, 3½ at Delphi. Their object was clearly to mark the place where each runner stood. There were twenty of these sections in the western sill at Olympia, twenty-one in the eastern, one of which is incomplete. Each section evidently afforded room for a single runner. The reason why these lines are alike at both ends is obvious. In the stade-race the runners finished at the opposite end to that from which they started, in other races they finished at the starting-place. As it was clearly desirable that the finish should be always at the same place, the stade runners must have started

[1] Frazer, *Pausanias*, ii. 205.
[2] For the Olympic Stadium see *Olympia*, p. 284.

THE FOOT-RACE

87. START OF THE RACE IN ARMOUR. Attic r.-f. amphora. About 470 B.C. Louvre, G.214. *J.H.S.*xxiii, p.270; *Bull. Nap.*, new series, vi. 7. The two figures are placed, as often, on either side of the vase. The drawing between them is the vase itself. Cp. Figs. 24, 96.

88. RUNNER PRACTISING A START. Attic. r.-f. kylix. About 460 B.C. Now in Boston. This vase, formerly in Naples, had till recently disappeared, and was known only from Krause's drawing, which I reproduced in Fig. 48 of *Gk. Athletics*. The lines of the face are worn away. Photograph from Mr. C. T. Seltman.

89. THE STADE RACE. B.-f. Panathenaic amphora, about 525 B.C. Metropolitan Museum, New York, 14.130.12. Compare the photograph in Fig. 94.

90. DIAULOS RACE. Fragment of b.-f. Panathenaic amphora. About 550 B.C. National Museum, Athens, 761. The inscription is *ΔΙΑΥΛΟΔΡΟΜΟ ΕΙΜΙ*, I am a prize for a diaulos-runner. New photograph obtained for me by Mr. A. M. Woodward.

at the far end or turning-place. Hence it was necessary to have similar starting-lines at both ends.

Two questions naturally present themselves. What was the object of the posts? What was the object of the parallel lines?

It is tempting to suppose that the course was roped as it is to-day for short races, but we have no evidence either for or against this suggestion. But apart from this it is obvious that in a straight two hundred yards' race the runner must have some point to fix his eye on if he is to run straight, and a post with a distinguishing mark would have been of great value as a guide. In the two-stade race, as we shall see, the runner turned round the post.

The object of the parallel lines is harder to understand. Here again the suggestion has been made that the runners started off their hands and placed their fingers in the grooves. But though we have several representations of runners in the attitude of starting, we never see them or hear of them starting off their hands. And even then, why two grooves? The only explanation that I can offer is that for some reason or other the runners had all to start with the same distance between the feet, whether because the Greeks thought it fairer that all the runners should start in exactly the same position or because it would prevent poaching at the start. At all events this explanation accords with the actual practice of Greek runners, who seem always to have started with one foot only a few inches in front of the other, a position recommended by many modern runners.

The best representation of a starter is that in Fig. 88. A youthful runner stands ready to start beside a pillar which marks the starting-line, and opposite to him stands a young trainer with his forked rod ready to correct him if he starts too soon. More upright is the position of the armed runner, represented in Fig. 24. The shield which he carried on his left arm is broken away. The same attitude is reproduced on an amphora in the Louvre (Fig. 87). Here, too, we see an armed runner, while opposite to him stands the trainer with his right arm extended and hand turned somewhat upwards. It is a singularly appropriate gesture. We can almost hear him say, 'Steady on the mark'. The attitude of the armed runner hampered by his shield is somewhat stiffer and more cramped than that of the unarmed runner. But in these and in all other representations of the start (e.g. Figs. 53, 96) the runners stand with both knees slightly bent and feet close together. The position is accurately described in an old song where the herald summons the competitors 'to take their stand foot to foot at the balbis'.[1] The signal to start was given by the herald calling 'Go' (ἄπιτε),[2] or perhaps by a blast of the trumpet as in the chariot-race. Runners would try to poach a yard or two at the start. But the position of starting made this difficult, and Greek methods were more drastic than ours. 'Those who start too soon are beaten', says Adeimantus to Themistocles in the historic council before Salamis.[3] The long forked rods used by officials to keep order at the Games and in the gymnasia are familiar objects on vases. In Fig. 188 we see the rod in use to chastise an offender.

The length of the various foot-races was determined by the length of the stadium. The stade race was a single length of the course, about 200 yards. The *diaulos*, once up and down the course, was two stades or about 400 yards. The long-distance race or *dolichos* is variously given as 7, 12, 20, 24 stades, probably because the distance varied at different competitions. At Olympia the evidence is slightly in favour of 24 stades or about three miles. Occasionally we hear of a *hippios* or horse *diaulos* of 4 stades, so called because the length of the hippodrome was twice that of the stadium. There were different races for different ages, and possibly the races for boys were sometimes shorter than those for men. We know that in the girls' races at Olympia the course was one-sixth shorter than the usual course.

There were, as we have seen, places for twenty starters at Olympia. In the stade race where the field was probably large there were preliminary heats, apparently of four runners, only the winners running in the final.[4] Heats were undoubtedly run in other races where necessary.

In the stade race, a single length of the track, the runners naturally ran straight for their own posts. But how did they run in the *diaulos*, or in the long race? Did they run in parallel tracks turning each to the left round his own post, or did they all turn round one post in the centre? At Olympia the central socket in the stone sill is larger than the rest, and from representations of the long-distance race it seems probable that the turns were made round the central post at either end as they undoubtedly were in chariot-races. But in the shorter *diaulos* the runners on

---

[1] Pomtow, *Poetae Lyrici Graeci Minores*, ii. 154; Julian, 318.
[2] Aristophanes, *Eq.* 1161.
[3] Hdt. viii. 59.
[4] Pausanias vi. 13. 2. The text unfortunately is corrupt.

the outside would be at a serious disadvantage if all had to turn round a central post. In the crowding at the turn a runner might easily lose three or four yards, a matter of vital importance for this distance, but of less importance in a three-mile race where the runners spread out rapidly. Moreover, the Delphic inscription already quoted speaks not of the 'turning-post' but of the 'turning-*posts*'. We may probably conclude, then, that in the *diaulos* each runner raced to and turned round his own post. The turn was always to the left. The name *diaulos* meaning the double-pipe, fitly describes the course.

The styles of the sprinter and the long-distance runner are clearly distinguished on the prize vases given for these events at the Panathenaic Games, which date from the sixth to the fourth century B.C. The style of the long-distance runner is excellent (Figs. 92, 93): his arms close to the sides yet swinging freely without any stiffness; his body slightly inclined forward, with chest advanced and head erect. He moves with a long, sweeping stride, running on the ball of the foot without raising the heel unduly. At the finish he too, like the sprinter, swung his arms vigorously in making his spurt, 'using them as wings', says Philostratus.[1] This violent action of the sprinters (Fig. 89) makes these early drawings of them seem at first sight grotesque, and the Greek sprinter has been described as 'advancing by leaps and bounds with arms and hands spread-eagled'. But it must be remembered how extremely difficult it is to draw a sprinter, and, moreover, that the movements of the sprinter as revealed by the camera are hardly less grotesque. Indeed the Greek artists have succeeded in reproducing the essential points of the sprint. The runners run well on the ball of the foot, the heel somewhat higher than in the long race, their knees are well raised, and their bodies erect. The action of the arms is hardly more violent than that of the modern sprinter. 'The arms', says a well-known American trainer, 'are of great service in sprinting, and the importance of this fact is generally underestimated. They are used in bent form and moved almost straight forward and back, not sideways across the body.' This is just what we see on Greek vases. Indeed a comparison of the vase-paintings with the photographs of modern races (Figs. 94, 95) shows how amazingly accurate the Greek drawings are and how excellent is the style. The real reason why these pictures seem grotesque is that in the sprint the early vase-painters, perhaps for purposes of symmetry,

[1] *Gym.* 52.

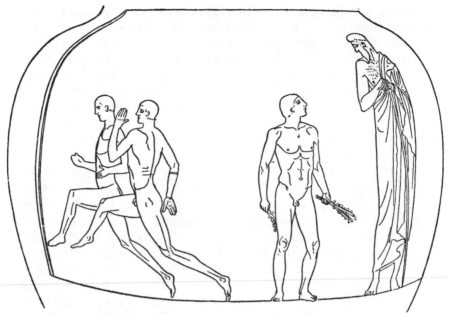

91. BOYS' RACE. B.-f. Panathenaic amphora. About 400 B. C. Bologna. Drawing from a photograph. *J.H.S.* xxxii, p. 179. The drawing of the two runners is vigorous: the leader seems to be running well within himself, the other is spurting in order to pass him. Notice that the drawing of the arms and legs is here correct, the right leg and left arm moving together. The youth holding in his hands sprays of some plant is perhaps a victor in another race.

92. LONG DISTANCE RACE. B.-f. Panathenaic amphora. About 470 B. C. Collection of the Marquis of Northampton, Castle Ashby. Photograph by Mrs. Beazley. The runners are just reaching the turning-post and are about to turn round it to the left.

93. LONG DISTANCE RACE. B.-f. Panathenaic vase. Archonship of Niceratus, 333 B. C. British Museum B. 609. New photograph.

94, 95. These two illustrations are selected from the large collection of athletic photographs in the possession of the Sport and General Agency.

94. PHOTOGRAPH OF THE 100 YARDS RACE BETWEEN OXFORD AND CAMBRIDGE AT QUEEN'S CLUB. The photograph is taken about half-way in the race. The arm action of the winner, J. W. J. Rinkel, Cambridge (3rd from the left), is identical with that of the leader in Fig. 88 and the second runner in Fig. 91. The second runner from the left has his hands open, which is unusual in modern racing. If these four figures were brought close together and silhouetted, we should have an effect very similar to that on the Greek vase. The only real difference is that the Greek for some reason or other makes right arm and right leg move together.

95. PHOTOGRAPH OF THE 5,000 METRES RACE BETWEEN ENGLAND AND FRANCE AT THE STADE PERSHING, PARIS. A comparison of this with Figs. 92, 93 shows how similar the Greek style was to the modern style, and illustrates the accurate observation of the Greek draughtsman.

make the right leg and right arm move together, whereas in reality the right arm swings forward with the left leg, and vice versa.

The only certain representation of a *diaulos* runner or quarter-miler seems to show that his style, as we should expect, is similar to that of the sprinter but with less violent action of the arms (Fig. 90). In Fig. 91 we have a picture of a boys' race; from the style it must represent a stade race, or perhaps the finish of the long-distance race. The vase from which this illustration is taken is comparatively late in date, and we may note that the movement of the legs is here correct, the right leg and left arm moving together.

We have no means of estimating the performances of Greek runners or comparing them with those of our own times. The Greeks kept no records. We hear of a runner who could outpace and catch hares, of another who raced a horse from Coronea to Thebes and beat it. Various feats of endurance are recorded. Herodotus tells us how Pheidippides ran from Athens to Sparta in two days, a distance of a hundred and fifty miles. It was the same Pheidippides who is said to have brought to Athens the news of the victory of Marathon, a story commemorated in the modern Marathon race which is of course a purely modern event unknown to the ancients. But all this is too vague to be of any value for comparison. Such scanty evidence suggests that the Greeks generally attained a high standard of running, especially in long distances.

Towards the close of the sixth century a race in armour was introduced. It was, strictly speaking, a military exercise, and its introduction was perhaps an attempt to restore to athletics the practical character which under the stress of competition was in danger of being lost. It was an event that appealed to the whole body of citizen soldiers rather than to the specialist. It may be compared to such events as the obstacle race and the race in uniform which are a useful and popular feature of our own military sports. Its picturesqueness made it a favourite subject with Greek vase-painters.

There are many varieties of the armed race, differing from one another in distance, in equipment, and in rules. At Olympia and Athens the race was a *diaulos* of two stades, at Nemea it was a four-stade race. The longest course was at Plataea; it was fifteen stades long, nearly two miles, and the runners were clothed in complete armour. The victor deservedly was proclaimed 'Best

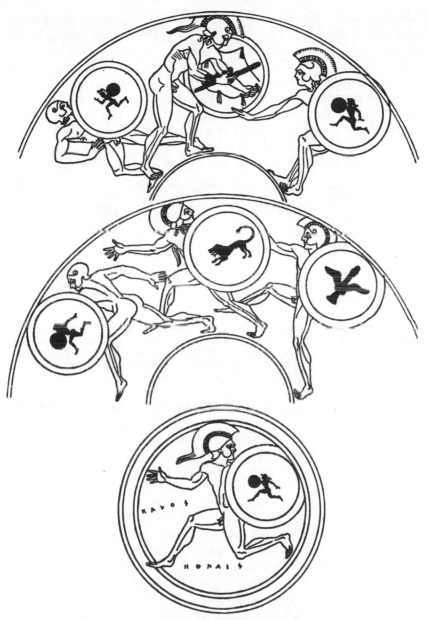

96. The race in armour. Attic r.-f. kylix. About 480 B.C. Berlin, 2307.
Gerh. *A.V.* 261.

of the Greeks.'[1] More usually the runner wore helmets and greaves and carried shields. The wearing of greaves was discontinued after 450 B.C. On a cup in Berlin (Fig. 96) we have a complete picture of the race. To the right is a runner starting, in the position already illustrated. To the left is a runner who has just reached the post and is in the act of turning. The third runner has completed the turn and is just starting on the return. Below we see three runners in full career, one of whom is committing an unpardonable offence, he is looking round. Perhaps the runner in the centre is the winner: if so, his position is excusable.

97. Armed runner. Attic r.-f. kotyle. About 470 B.C., formerly in Bourguignon Collection, Naples. *Jahrb*. x, p. 191, Fig. 16; *J.H.S.* xxiii, p. 285. Dr. Hauser considers that this represents the start off the hands; de Ridder regards it as a gymnastic exercise. I would suggest that it may have been a fancy variety of start for the race in armour.

Some of the variations depicted of this popular competition can hardly be regarded as serious. We have seen, for example, the position of the armed runner at the start. In Fig. 97 we see him stretched forward and supporting himself on his right hand. Has he overbalanced, or is he really a starter, and was it sometimes ordained that the competitors in this race should start in this awkward position just as competitors in an obstacle race or a sack race are sometimes placed lying on the ground at the start? Anyhow, this picture is slender evidence for the theory that the Greek runners started off the hands. Again, in Fig. 98 we see some of the runners carrying their shields before them, others without shields. This suggests a race where the runners put down their shields at the end of the first lap and ran the second lap without them. But of course this is mere conjecture.

With the torch races (Fig. 65) we are not really concerned.

---

[1] *Revue des études anciennes*, xxxi, p. 13. The title occurs on several inscriptions from Sparta and elsewhere, and L. Robert shows conclusively that it refers to the winner of the race at Plataea.

They were really ritual performances, the object being to bring the new pure fire as quickly as possible to the altar. There were torch races in many Greek States. At Athens there were torch races on horseback and on foot, individual races, and team races. In the individual races the runners started from the Academy outside the city, and the runner who came in first with his torch alight received the prize. The efforts of the runners to keep their torches alight were the cause of vast amusement to the spectators who sped them on their way with resounding slaps. The team race, well known to all readers of the *Agamemnon*, was a relay race. The teams represented the different tribes, and the members of each team were posted at intervals along the course. Though not serious athletics, the training for the torch races provided a large number of youths with excellent exercise.

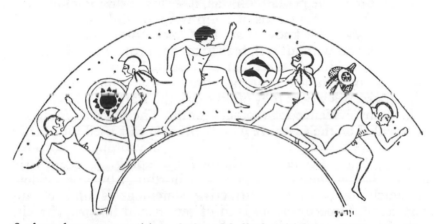

98. Armed runners practising. Attic r.-f. kylix, late 6th century. Munich, 2613. *J.H.S.* xxiii, p. 284, Fig. 11. The objects hanging on the wall suggest that the scene is in a gymnasium. Here we have another fancy performance.

X

JUMPING

JUMPING[1] was not a military exercise, and in Homer it is only mentioned as one of the recreations of the Phaeacians. In later times it was one of the events of the pentathlon, but there were as far as we know no separate competitions in it, at all events at the great festivals. Yet it must always have been a popular recreation. It was regarded as a very strenuous exercise and as the most typical event of the pentathlon. In the gymnasium it occupied a very important place, owing perhaps to the value which the jumping-weights acquired for physical training.

The jump in the pentathlon was, it seems, a running long jump with weights. Other forms of jump were, doubtless, practised in the gymnasia. We know that the Greeks practised a standing jump with and without weights (Figs. 99, 110). For a high jump there is no evidence: the pillar represented in Fig. 99 is not an object to be jumped over but one of the pillars familiar in palaestra scenes where they often mark the start, or take-off. Nor is there any evidence for the pole jump. The poles so frequently represented on the vases are merely blunt spears used for practice. A pole or spear was used, as we have seen, in vaulting on horseback (Fig. 58), but not as far as we know for jumping. A recent writer has stated that the Greeks practised hurdling, but the evidence on which he bases this attractive statement is unfortunately worthless.[2] Greece was no land of fences and hedges: the chief obstacles were streams and ditches. Hence comes the pre-eminence of the long jump.

For the long jump a firm hard take-off was provided called the Threshold (βατήρ).[3] We do not know whether it was of wood or stone. In vase paintings the take-off is marked by spears stuck in the ground or by pillars similar to those used to mark the start of a race. Possibly the stone sills of the stadium were used for this purpose.

The ground in front of the take-off was dug up and levelled to a certain distance. This was called the Skamma (σκάμμα, or τὰ

---

[1] See *Gk. Athletics*, pp. 295 ff.; *J.H.S.* xxiv, pp. 70, 179.

[2] Schröder, *Sport im Altertum*, p. 107. The relief of which he gives a drawing is lost. But apart from this, the object which he regards as a hurdle is obviously nothing else but a prize table.   [3] *J.H.S.* xxiv, pp. 71 ff.

ἐσκαμμένα). 'To jump beyond the skamma or the dug-up' was a proverbial expression for an extraordinary feat. Phayllus, the hero of the fabulous jump of 55 feet, is said to have jumped five feet beyond the skamma, and we are not surprised to learn from one commentator that he broke his leg in the performance.

The ground of the skamma was soft so as to take the impress of the feet. The jump was measured by rods (κανόνες), and the

99. Standing jump without weights. Attic r.-f. krater, about 400 B.C. Louvre, G. 502, Dar.-Sag., Fig. 7451. The position of the feet suggests a standing jump, probably a long jump. From the figure of Victory bringing in her hands the fillet of victory, it seems probable that there was a competition for a standing jump without weights, of which we know nothing.

individual jumps were marked by pegs placed in the ground. Three such pegs marking the jumps of previous performers are clearly shown underneath the jumper in Fig. 106. They were formerly interpreted as sharp spikes placed in the ground to add zest and danger to the competition!

The Greeks always used jumping-weights, *halteres*, in the long jump.[1] These jumping-weights, which somewhat resemble and were probably the origin of our dumb-bells, were made of metal or stone and varied in weight from 2¼ to more than 10 lb. though the latter weight is exceptional. The simplest form is that of a

[1] See Jüthner, *Turngeräthe*, p. 3, and *Röm. Mitt.* xliii. 13.

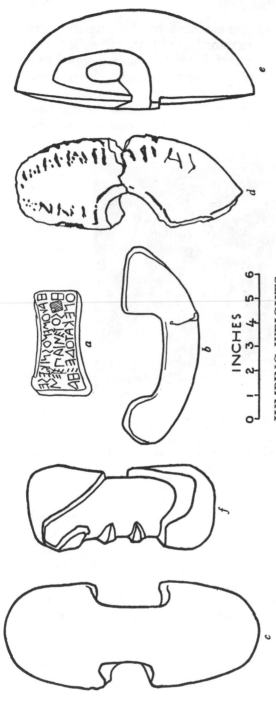

INCHES

0 1 2 3 4 5 6

100. HALTERES DRAWN TO SCALE.

JUMPING WEIGHTS

a. Leaden halter found at Eleusis. Athens, National Museum, 9075. 4¼ × 1½ in., weight 4 lb. 2 oz. 6th century. Inscription: ᾽Αλλόμενος νίκησεν ᾽Επαίνετος οὕνεκα τοῦδε: ά, 'Epainetos by means of this won the jump'.

b. Leaden halter, one of a pair. British Museum. The type is that usually depicted on fifth-century vases. Length 8½, width at grip 1¼ in. Much worn, about 2 lb. 3 oz. A similar pair found at Athens are shorter but weigh 3¼ and 3½ lb.

c. Stone halter found at Olympia, 11⅝ in. long. Weight more than 10 lb. (4.629 kg.). Olympia.

d. Marble halter found at Sparta. 9 in. long. About 3 lb. Inscription: τᾶι ᾽Αθαναίαι Παιτιάδας, 'Paitiadas to Athene'. 5th century. B.S.A. xxvii, p. 251.

e. Stone halter. One of a pair found at Corinth. Athens, National Museum. 10¾ × 4 × 3 in. About 4½ lb. c, d, e are of the type commonly shown on sixth-century vases.

f. Stone halter found at Rhodes. British Museum. 7½ in. long. Nearly 5 lb. This is the type represented in later art, e. g. Fig. 70.

For halteres see J.H.S. xxiv, p. 181; Gk. Athletics, p. 298; Jüthner, Ant. Turn. p. 3. The cylindrical halteres are fully discussed by Jüthner in Röm. Mitt. xliii, p. 13. He conclusively disproves the conjecture of Bruno Schröder that they were a sort of weapon used by boxers.

sixth-century halter from Eleusis. It is a rectangular slab of lead with slightly concave sides (Fig. 100 *a*). A more usual type is a semicircular piece of metal with a deep recess on the straight side serving as a grip for the hand (Fig. 100 *b*). The stone halteres are usually heavier than the metal. They are made of hemispherical blocks of stone, pointed or rounded at the ends, the upper side being pierced or cut away so as to provide a grip (Figs. 100 *c, d, e*).

101. Youth running with halteres. Attic r.-f. kylix. About 520 B.C. Klein, *Euphronius*, p. 306.

A later cylindrical type (Fig. 100*f*) seems to have been common in Roman times.

The modern long-jumper depends for his impetus on his pace, and tries to reach his maximum speed at the take-off. The jumper with weights depends for his impetus partly on the swing of the weights, partly on the run. The run is shorter and not so fast. He begins with a few short springy steps, holding the weights by his side or swinging them slightly as we see in Fig. 101. As he nears the take-off he checks his run and takes two or more long slow strides, swinging the weights once or twice vigorously forwards and backwards, taking off with his last forward swing.

This swing of the weights backwards and forwards is almost the same in a running jump and in a standing jump, but in the latter the feet are usually close together and the jumper takes off from both feet. In the running jump he takes off from one foot, and this is what we see constantly represented on vases. The position most commonly depicted is the top of the upward swing when the body is usually leaning slightly backwards and the front foot is slightly raised from the ground (Figs. 102, 104). The downward swing seems somewhat exaggerated for a running

102. Swinging the halteres upwards. Attic r.-f. kotyle. About 480 B. C. Boston. *Am. Journal of Arch.*, xix, p. 129, Figs. 1, 2; pl. VII, VIII. Youth practising in palaestra. Behind him a slave boy holds his stick, clothes, oil-flask and sponge. The position of the body inclined backwards suggests the final upward swing at the end of the run.

jump (Fig. 103). But our illustrations probably represent not the actual jump so much as practice for the jump. A long jump with weights involves most carefully timed movements, and we cannot doubt that the various movements were taught as a sort of drill. It is perhaps for this reason that the long jump was practised to the accompaniment of the flute (Fig. 104).

As the jumper takes off he swings the weights forward, so that in mid-air arms and legs are almost parallel, as we see in Fig. 105. Before landing he swings them backwards, a movement which shoots the legs to the front and so lengthens the jump (Figs. 106, 107). Some modern jumpers for the same purpose make two or more piston-like movements of the arms backwards and forwards in mid-air. These two drawings represent absolutely perfect style; they correspond exactly to the positions of a modern jumper as we see them in photographs (Figs. 108, 109).

At the moment of landing the weights must have been swung forward again to preserve the balance and prevent the jumper from falling backwards. The Greeks, according to Philostratus, did not allow the jump to be measured unless the impress of the feet was regular. From which we may conclude that if a jumper stumbled or fell, or landed with one foot in advance of the other,

103. Swinging the halteres downwards. R.-f. kylix. Bologna. Zannoni, *Scavi della Certosa*, lxxvii. 1. A similar scene occurs on other vases, e. g. New York, Met. Mus. No. 06.1133. Here we have clearly an exercise in swinging the halteres. For the swing before the actual jump the position is too low. About 480 B. C.

the jump did not count. Some such regulation would not be out of place to-day. We should then be spared the unedifying spectacle of a high jumper landing on all fours. The Greek paid more attention to style than to records.

The positions represented on the vases prove that the Greek long jump with weights was generally a running jump. But the vigorous little athlete shown in Fig. 22 seems to be an exception. He has raised the bells straight above his head, a position un-intelligible for a running jump, but quite natural in the swing for a standing jump. The size of the halteres and the position of the feet close together point to the same conclusion. The bronze belongs to the early part of the fifth century, and at this date the artist is not likely to have represented a mere dumb-bell exercise.

The standing jump without weights is clearly represented in Fig. 110 and on several other vases, where we see a youth standing with both feet together, knees bent, and hands straight forward

THE LONG JUMP

104. JUMPER AND FLUTE PLAYER. Attic r.-f. pelike. About 440 B.C. British Museum, E. 427. *J.H.S.* xxiv, p. 185. The position seems to follow that of Fig. 102. The jumper is swinging the halteres down. A further stage is depicted on a r.-f. column krater in the Villa Giulia, 1796. *Corpus Vasorum V. G.* III. i, pl. XVI 1.

◀ 105. JUMPER IN MID-AIR. Attic r.-f. kylix. About 500 B.C. Boston, 01.8020. Beazley, *Attic r.-f. Vases*, p. 83, Fig. 51. To the left a youth exercising with halteres in a way that has no connexion with the jump. For the position cp. Fig. 108.

106. THE FINISH OF THE JUMP. Attic b.-f. neck-
◀ amphora. Second quarter of the sixth century B.C. British Museum, B. 48. New photograph.

107. THE FINISH OF THE JUMP. Attic b.-f. lekythos.
◀ End of the sixth century. New York, Metropolitan Museum, 08.258.30. Photograph from Miss Richter. For the positions 106, 107 cp. Fig. 109.

◀ 108, 109 THE MODERN LONG JUMP

These two photographs are selected from the collection of the Sport and General Agency. It is seldom that we get a photograph representing the very top of the jump when both arms are parallel as in Fig. 108. Usually we see the jumper still rising with one arm higher than the other. Nor do we often catch the moment just before landing in Fig. 109.

preparing to jump. The pillar placed sometimes before him, sometimes behind, marks the take-off. That it is a standing jump is certain, but it is impossible to determine whether it is a high jump or a long jump: the position of the feet seems to me in favour of a long jump. In Fig. 99 we see a figure of Victory flying towards the jumper holding a fillet in her hands. This certainly suggests some form of competition different from that in the pentathlon, but of this we have no further evidence.

We do not know how the Greeks came to discover the use of weights for jumping. They are not of course used in any modern

110. Standing jump without weights. Attic r.-f. pelike, in Leipsig, T. 642, about 420 B.C. *Jahrb.* x (1895), p. 185.

competitions, but during the latter half of the last century they were frequently used by professionals in music-hall displays of trick jumping. They were used both for the high jump and the long jump, with a run and without. As a recent German writer has declared a running jump with weights to be incredible, it may be of interest if I quote a few records of jumping with weights which were given me by Mr. G. Rowdon, who once held the amateur championship for the high jump and afterwards gave displays as a professional.

In the running long jump J. Howard jumped 29 ft. 7 in. at Chester in 1854. He used 5-lb. dumb-bells and took off from a board 2 ft. long and 3 in. thick. Rowdon estimates that the use of the weights and the board, which can hardly be described as a spring-board, added at least 8 ft. to his jump. In the high jump R. H. Baker cleared 6 ft. 8¼ in. at Leeds, July 14, 1900, taking off with one leg. K. Darby jumped 6 ft. 5½ in. at Wolverhampton,

February 5, 1892. He used 8-lb. weights and took off with both feet after taking three hops, and threw the bells away in mid-air. He also did a standing long jump of 14 ft. 9 in., using 8-lb. weights at Liverpool, September 19, 1900. Rowdon, who never used weights himself, challenged Darby to jump 5 ft. 6 in. without weights, but the challenge was not accepted.

These figures are sufficient proof of the advantage obtained by the use of weights. The following quotation from Rowdon's account of the method of jumping with weights shows the close similarity between the style of the modern jumper and the Greek. Of the high jump he says: 'The jumper starts about 14 yards from the posts taking two thirds of the distance with short quick steps hardly swinging the weights at all, after which he takes one or two comparatively long slow strides, swinging the bells together twice and at the second swing taking off the ground as the bells come to the front.' The run for the long jump is very similar, the chief difference being that while in the high jump the weights are thrown away backwards at the moment of jumping, in the long jump they are retained.

The use of weights cannot explain however the extraordinary feats ascribed to the Greeks. Till recently it was asserted and perhaps believed that the Greeks jumped more than 50 feet. Such a jump, which is twice the record distance of the modern athlete, is a physical impossibility. Two explanations are possible. Either the Greek jump was not a single jump or the record is pure fiction.

It has been suggested that the Greek jump was a hop, skip, and jump, and on the strength of this suggestion this event was introduced into the revived Olympic Games. Another conjecture is that the Greek jump was a triple jump, an exercise known to-day in parts of northern Greece. But apart from the fact that there is not a particle of ancient evidence to support these guesses, it is hard to understand how the Greek jumper could after landing in the soft sand of the skamma take two more jumps, or a skip and jump.

It is much more probable that the record is pure fiction. It rests almost entirely on an epigram on one Phayllus which states that he jumped five and fifty feet and threw the diskos ninety-five feet. This Phayllus was a noted athlete of Croton who early in the fifth century won two victories in the pentathlon and one in the foot-race at Delphi. Herodotus, Aristophanes, Plutarch, and Pausanias all mention him but know nothing of his fabulous jump. The epigram is said to have been inscribed on his statue at Delphi. But though the base of this statue has been found there is no trace on it of the epigram. Nor is there any evidence that the epigram was contemporary with the event. Indeed we cannot trace it further back than the second century A.D. But whatever its date there is no reason for taking it seriously. The sporting story is notorious: still more so is the sporting epigram; and this epigram is merely an alliterative jingle. The pages of the *Anthology* are full of epigrams on famous athletes such as Milo and Ladas. Milo, we are told, picked up a four-year-old heifer at Olympia and after carrying it round the Altis killed it and ate it at a single meal! This extraordinary gastronomic feat rests on quite as good evidence as the 55-foot jump of Phayllus.[1]

The halteres were the origin of our dumb-bells. We have seen that swinging the halteres for the jump was probably practised in classes to the accompaniment of the flute. Here we have at once a familiar dumb-bell exercise, though in the fifth century it was probably regarded merely as an exercise for jumping. But we have many pictures of athletes swinging the halteres sideways in a style which can have no connexion with the jump (Fig. 105). In fact their value for training the muscles for other exercises must have been recognized at an early period. In the medical writings of the second century A.D. this 'halter-throwing' (ἀλτηροβολία) has developed into a regular system of dumb-bell exercises.[2] Antyllos describes three kinds of halter-throwing. The first consists in bending and straightening the arms, an exercise which strengthens the arms and shoulders. In the other two exercises the athlete with his arms extended lunges as in boxing, or alternately bends and straightens the trunk. These exercises strengthen the legs and trunk. Galen describes another exercise for strengthening the side muscles of the body. The performer places the halteres six feet apart, and taking his stand between them picks up first the left-hand halter with his right hand, next the right-hand halter with his left hand, and then replaces them, repeating the movement.

[1] I have collected and discussed all the evidence in *J.H.S.* xxiv, pp. 70 ff.
[2] Oribasius, vi. 14, 34.

XI

THROWING THE DISKOS

WE have seen that the word *diskos* [1] meant originally nothing more than a 'thing for throwing', and a thing for throwing might be any convenient object near at hand. A stone, a lump of metal, a tree trunk offered to early man a natural weapon or a means of testing his strength. From such simple objects are derived our modern sports of putting the weight or the shot, throwing the hammer or the caber. The diskos that Odysseus threw at the Phaeacian Games was a stone, the weight that Polypoetes flung at the funeral games of Patroclus was an unwrought *solos*, or pig of iron. The word '*solos*', which is sometimes used by late poets as a synonym for *diskos*, means merely a boulder, a mass of stone or metal. Such was the stone that Bybon threw over his head (p. 54). The little bronze statuette in Fig. 23 represents an athlete 'putting' the stone in modern style, but the Greek did not put the diskos, he threw it, as we shall see, with an underhand swing.

The popular translation of 'diskos' by 'quoit' is singularly unfortunate. And still more so is the myth preserved in Liddell and Scott's *Lexicon*, though deleted in the edition now appearing, that the diskos 'had a hole in the centre for a wooden helve or leathern strap to swing it by'. For nothing is more certain than that the diskos, whether of stone or of metal, was solid and had nothing to do with a strap. The blunder preserved by generations of lexicographers probably had its origin in some game in which a round object was bowled along by means of a cord wound round it. A game of this sort called 'ruzzola' is still played on the roads in parts of Italy.

The diskos was a circular plate of stone or metal somewhat thicker in the centre than at the circumference. On the sixth-century black-figure vases it is usually shown as a thick white object (Figs. 131, 139), but the handier metal diskos must have come into use before the end of the century and seems to have been universal in the fifth century. Few stone diskoi have survived; the only specimens of which I have been able to obtain details (Figs. 112, 113) measure more than 11 inches in diameter and must have weighed when whole over 15 lb., approximately

[1] See *Gk. Athletics*, p. 313; *J.H.S.* xxvii, pp. 1–36; Jüthner, *Turngeräthe*, p. 18.

the weight of the stone or shot used in 'putting' to-day. Metal diskoi are far more numerous and vary considerably in size and weight. The only diskos that approaches in weight and size the stone diskoi is one dedicated at Olympia by one Publius Asclepiades in the year A.D. 241. It weighs above 12½ lb. The rest vary in diameter from 6½ to 9 inches, and in weight from 3 to 9 lb.

The difference in weight is remarkable. It is partly due to the fact that lighter weights were used by boys than by men, and partly to different practices at different festivals. The inscriptions on the sixth-century stone diskoi prove that they were used in actual competition; while the lightest specimen that we possess was also used in competition, for its sixth-century inscription tells us 'Exoïdas dedicated me to the twin sons of Great Zeus, the bronze diskos wherewith he conquered the high-souled Kephallenians' (Fig. 111).

With such differences in the weight of the diskos it is obvious that we have no means of estimating the standard attained by the Greek diskos-throwers. Phayllus, of jumping renown, according to the epigram, threw the diskos 95 feet; and Philostratus[1] speaks of Protesilaus as throwing beyond a hundred cubits, and that with a diskos twice the size of those used at Olympia. Statius, again, describes Phlegyas as throwing a diskos across the Alpheius.[2] But such statements are worthless as we do not know the weights used. In the modern Olympic Games the diskos used weighs 2 kilos. The record throw in the free style is nearly 160 feet. In 1908 J. Sheridan, throwing in the cramped Hellenic style, succeeded in throwing 124 ft. 8 in.

The place from which the diskos was thrown was called the *Balbis*. It is described by Philostratus[3] in a passage narrating the death of Hyacinthus who was accidentally killed by a diskos thrown by Apollo. 'The balbis', he says, 'is small and sufficient for one man, marked off except behind, and it supports the right leg, the front part of the body leaning forward, while it takes the weight off the other leg which is to be swung forward and follows through with the right hand.' The description is evidently based on Myron's diskobolos. He continues: 'The thrower is to bend his head to the right and stoop so as to catch a glimpse of his (right) side and to throw the diskos with a rope-like pull, putting all the force of his right side into the throw.'

From this passage we learn that the balbis was marked off by

[1] *Heroic.* p. 291.   [2] *Theb.* vi. 675.
[3] *Im.* i. 24.

THE DISKOS

METAL DISKOI

111. Bronze Diskos in the British Museum. Inscribed:

'Εχσοίδας μ' ἀνέθηκε ΔιϜὸς ϙο(ύ)ροις μεγάλοιο χάλκεον ᾧ νίκασε Κεφαλ(λ)ᾶ-νας μεγαθύμους.

6th century. The details of this (no. 15) and other diskoi are given in the following list.

Finding-place	Museum	Weight in kilos	Diameter in cm.	Thickness in mm.
1. Olympia	Olympia, *Inv.* 7567	5·707	34	5–13
2. Corfu	B.M. 2691	3·992	23	6–13
3. Gela	Vienna	3·800	28	7
4. Amyclae	Athens, De Ridder, *Cat.* 530	3·349	19	
5. Olympia	Olympia, *Inv.* 4257	2·945 (?)	22	6–12
6. Olympia	Olympia, *Inv.* 12892	2·775	18	11–12
7.	Rome, Museo Kircheriano	2·378	21, 21·5	
8. Olympia	Olympia, *Inv.* 2859	2·083	19, 22·5	3 at edge
9. Sicily	B.M. 248	2·075	21	5
10. Olympia	Berlin	2·023	17·5	9–10
11. Aegina	Berlin	1·984	21	
12. Olympia	Berlin	1·721	20	7
13. Olympia	Berlin, *Inv.* 2286	1·353 (?)	20·5	4
14. Olympia	Olympia, *Inv.* 12,891	1·268	17	4–12
15. Cephallenia	B.M. 3207	1·245	16·5	5

They are all of bronze except no. 3 which is of lead. Nos. 8 and 10 are engraved with the figure of a jumper on one side, javelin-thrower on the other. Both belong to the 5th century B. C., but their flatness and the sharpness of their edges makes it probable that they were votive offerings not intended for use. This was certainly the case with no. 1, which is dated from the inscription Ol. 255 (A. D. 241). See Jüthner, *Ant. Turn.*, p. 18; *J.H.S.* xxvii, p. 5.

◄ STONE DISKOI

112, 113. Two stone diskoi in the Collection of the late E. P. Warren. Sotheby's *Sale Catalogue*, May 1929, nos. 89, 90. Photographs by Professor B. Ashmole.

112. Diameter 11¼ in., weight 14 lb. 10 oz., originally at least 15 lb. In the centre remains of painted decoration. Inscribed *EK ΤΩΝ ΑΘΛΩΝ*, 'From the Games'. 6th century.

113. Diameter 11½ in., weight 13 lb. 12 oz., originally at least 15 lb. Inscribed: *ΤΕΛΕ(ΣΑΡ)ΧΟ(Y) ΕΚ ΤΟ(Y) ΗΡΙΟ(Y)*, 'Belonging to Telesarchos from the barrow'. The barrow was presumably the tomb of the hero in whose honour the games were held. 6th century.
A third stone diskos is figured by Schröder, *Sport im Altertum*, Fig. 56. It was exhibited in Berlin, but I have failed to find particulars of it.

a line in front and by lines on either side but not behind, so that the thrower could take as many steps as he pleased. It is natural to suppose that in the stadium the diskos and spear were thrown from the line of stone slabs already described which were called *balbides*, but for this we have no direct evidence.

The throw was measured from the balbis to the place where the diskos or spear fell, and it is obvious that competitors might not overstep the line. The direction was limited by the breadth of the stadium, and a throw that fell outside did not count. The place where the diskos fell was marked by a peg; in Fig. 115 we see a diskobolos in the act of marking the spot.

115. Marking the throw of the diskos. Attic r.-f. kylix, About 525 B.C. Würzburg, 357 A. Jüthner, *Ant. Turn.* Fig. 27. Drawn from a photograph. The youth is either placing or pulling up the mark.

Throwing the diskos has acquired a practical interest owing to the modern revival of this event; but the modern method of throwing is very different from the ancient method. We can reconstruct the latter from numerous representations on vases, gems, coins, in statuettes, and in two life-size statues, the so-called Standing Diskobolos attributed to Naucydes and the Diskobolos of Myron (Figs. 116, 117). In interpreting the lesser monuments, such as vases and coins, it is important to remember that the artist is often influenced by laws of composition and the shape of the space that he has to fill, and that apparent divergences are often due to differences of space and material. Further, there were as many differences in style in throwing the diskos as there are in swinging a golf club. But though it is impossible to force all the representations of a diskos-thrower into a single series, there was only one principle, and it is embodied in the Diskobolos of Myron. The motive of this statue is reproduced on gems, coins, and reliefs. On it are based the scanty descriptions of this

116. THE STANDING DISKOBOLOS. Marble copy of bronze statue about 400 B. C., found near Rome. In the Vatican. The head is ancient but does not belong to the statue. The true head is preserved in a replica in the Museo Mussolini in Rome. The right elbow and most of the fingers are modern. The tree-trunk support is an addition of the copyist. For a discussion of the many replicas of this statue, see Sieveking in Text to Brunn-Brückmann's *Denkmäler* nos. 682–5.

117. MYRON'S DISKOBOLOS. Marble copy of bronze statue by Myron, about 450 B. C. Photograph from composite cast which combines a body in the Terme Museum at Rome and the head in the Lancelotti Collection, Brunn-Brückmann, 566. For illustrations of various replicas see Brunn-Brückmann, nos. 256, 631, 632, 681, and for the latest literature on the subject see Sieveking in Text to no. 681; B. Schröder, *Arch. Anz.*, xxxvii. 614; xxxv. 61; Jüthner, *Jahreshefte des Oesterr. Arch. Inst.*, xxiv, p. 123.

THE DISKOBOLOS

118, 119. These two drawings illustrate the attempts of the vase painters in the generation before Myron to represent the actual throw of the diskos. In Fig. 133 we see a yet earlier attempt to grapple with the same problem. The coins of Cos (Fig. 35) also belong to the first half of the fifth century. The Panathenaic amphora (Fig. 132) is not much earlier than 400 B. C. To attempt to arrange these more or less impressionist attempts in a consecutive series is obviously impossible.

118. DISKOS-THROWER, THE THROW. Attic r.-f. kylix. About 480 B.C. Louvre. Hartwig, *Meisterschalen*, lxiii, *n. 2.* In this and in Fig. 119 the left foot rests on the extreme point of the toe as in Myron's statue. It is difficult to feel certain as to the exact moment represented. Formerly I held that it was the moment in the swing back preceding that of the statue. But from the position of the head I am inclined to think that Jüthner is right and that these figures belong to the forward swing when the left foot is just leaving the ground. Jüthner, *l.c.*

119. DISKOS-THROWER, THE THROW. Drawing from r.-f. kylix. About 480 B.C. Villa Giulia, Rome. *Dedalo*, iv, pp. 735, 736. For the scene on the other side see Fig. 46.

event in Lucian and Philostratus, and the latter significantly adds in the passage quoted above which describes the death of Hyacinthus, 'This was how Apollo threw the diskos. Indeed he could not have thrown it any other way.'

Myron's statue was of bronze: it is known to us only in marble copies, and some of these, including that in the British Museum, are wrongly restored with the head facing the direction of the throw. As we know from the only copy where the head is preserved, the head was turned backwards to the right. This turn of the head actually helps the swing of the body, whereas if the head is kept stationary the turn of the shoulder is slightly checked.

Another point to be noticed is the peculiar position of the left foot resting on the tip of the toes which are even turned back and dragging. This position seems to some modern critics so unnatural and indeed impossible that they have argued that our existing replicas are all wrong, and have tried to reconstruct the statue with a flatter foot.[1] In support of this they point to certain late reliefs and gems where the foot is in its natural position. But we must remember that the Greek athlete, who was usually barefooted, had not lost the use of his toes as we have owing to the crippling effect of boots, and that his toes were probably as strong as his fingers. Moreover, in this particular instance the weight rests entirely on the right foot and there is little or no strain on the left. Further, this position with the left foot on tiptoe is also represented on fifth-century vases (Figs. 118, 119, 132, 133) and on the coins of Cos (Fig. 35). Finally, no reason can be shown why a late copyist should have introduced a less natural and more difficult position of the foot, if in Myron's original statue the foot had been in what seems to us the more natural position.

Myron has chosen to represent a moment between the backward swing and the forward swing where there is an apparent pause. I say 'apparent' because, as Jüthner has recently shown,[2] there is really no check in the movement which is continuous, the right arm continuing to move backwards even while the left foot is lifted off the ground, and this is skilfully indicated by the dragging of the toes which shows that the forward movement of the left leg is actually beginning. The thrower, raising the diskos level with his head in both hands, has swung it vigorously downwards and backwards in his right hand, at the same time turning his whole body and his head to the right. The right leg, which

[1] Schröder, *Arch. Anz.* xxxv. 58.
[2] *Jahreshefte*, xxiv. 123.

is advanced, is the pivot on which the whole body turns, the left foot and left arm merely helping to preserve the balance. We may note, too, the rope-like pull of the right arm. This turn of the body round a fixed point is the essence of the swing of the diskos. The force comes not from the arm, which serves only to connect the body and the weight, but from the lift of the thighs and the swing of the body. The thrower gets his weight into the throw.

Such was the principle of the throw; but in the preliminary movements there was considerable variety. There were at least two positions for the stance. One of them is represented in the 'Standing Diskobolos', a statue which in spite of other interpretations does, I am still convinced, represent a diskobolos taking his stance. The weight is still on the left leg, but he has carefully planted his right foot in front and is looking downwards at the balbis line, measuring the distance so as not to overstep it. It is not, as has been asserted, the attitude of prayer, but of preparation for action. The thrower then, after rubbing the diskos with sand to prevent it from slipping, takes his stance holding the diskos by his side in his left hand, and swings it up in his left hand or possibly in both hands till it is level with his head. Then, if he has not already done so, he grasps it with his right hand. This position with the diskos held to the front in both hands is the beginning of the backward swing and is constantly represented on vases (Figs. 21, 122, 129). From this position, if the right foot is in front he swings the diskos downwards in his right hand till he reaches the position of Myron's statue without any change of foot. Frequently, however, the diskobolos is represented holding the diskos in both hands with the left foot forward. Either he has taken up his stance with the left foot forward (Figs. 120, 121) or he has advanced it as he swings the diskos upwards. How, then, does he reach the position of Myron's statue? Two solutions are possible. Either he takes a step forward with the right foot, or he draws back the left foot. The former was the method adopted by the competitors in the first Olympic Games held at Athens in 1896. Starting with the left foot forward the thrower raised the diskos in both hands to a level with his head and at the moment of swinging it back advanced the right foot, taking another step forward with the left in making the throw. This method requires room for two or, if the thrower starts with right leg forward, for three steps, the impetus being helped by the forward movement. The other method requires room only for one step, and the pendulum-like 'swing' of the left leg, first forward, then back,

THE STANCE AND PRELIMINARY MOVEMENTS

A. DISKOS SWUNG FORWARD IN LEFT HAND.

120. Figure from Attic r.-f. kylix. Berlin, 2284. About 500 B.C. Pfuhl, *Malerei*, 450.
121, 122. Figures from r.-f. kylix. Munich, 2637. *Arch. Zeit.* 1878, pl. XI.

In all three figures the left leg is advanced, but the same motive occurs with the right leg forward. Thus with 120 cp. the standing Diskobolos (Fig. 116); the position of 121 is well shown on a r.-f. kylix in the Louvre, G. 292; with 122 cp. 129, left leg forward, 21, right leg forward.

B. DISKOS RAISED LEVEL WITH THE HEAD IN LEFT HAND.

123. Attic r.-f. amphora by Phintias, late 6th century. Louvre. F.R. 112.

124. Attic r.-f. amphora by Euthymides, late 6th century. Munich, 2308. F.R. 81; Pfuhl, *Masterpieces*, p. 40. The diskos-thrower here is called Phayllos, and probably represents the famous pentathlete of that name (p. 152). Notice the thumb on the inside of the diskos, and compare Figs. 126, 130, 129.

and finally forward again, is at least equally effective, as helping the swing of the body like the preliminary waggle of a golf club. From the vases it seems possible that both methods were practised.

An alternative stance is represented in some bronze statuettes (Figs. 125–7) and on many vases (Figs. 123, 124, 130). The thrower holds the diskos in his left hand level with the head. He then grasps it with his right hand and raises it in both hands above his head. It will be observed that in this position the thumb of the left hand is on the inside, the fingers outside, while in the first style the position of the hand is reversed. A bronze in the British Museum (Fig. 127) carries the movement a little further and shows the transition to the downward swing. The diskos instead of being upright lies flat on the right hand. In this stance sometimes the left, sometimes the right foot is in front, and there is the same evidence of change of feet as in the first style.

The position of the diskos flat in the right hand and resting against the forearm is the characteristic of the backward swing, another movement frequently depicted. There are many varieties of this motive. Some of them are due to artistic considerations, to the shape of the space that the artist wishes to fill. Others are due to the different movements in the swing represented. At the beginning of the swing the body is upright or even inclined backwards (Fig. 122), then it assumes a stooping position (Figs. 114, 128). But all these variations belong to the same movement, the backward swing. In all of them the diskos is held flat against the forearm, remaining in this position till the arm has passed the leg, while the left arm is extended sideways or raised over the head to help the balance of the body, for on the balance the success of the throw depends. Here, too, there is evidence of change of foot. In the forward position the left foot is usually in front, and it may continue so momentarily at the beginning of the backward swing. Usually, however, the right foot is advanced forming the pivot on which the body turns, as in Myron's statue. This is clearly shown in the bronze illustrated in Fig. 128 where the heel of the left foot is already raised.

Most of the representations of the top of the backward swing are evidently based on Myron's statue, but there is an interesting variation on the fifth-century coins of Cos (Fig. 35), where a diskobolos is represented beside a prize tripod. An examination of a series of these coins proves that the artist has attempted the difficult task of representing this position from the front. But the amount of foreshortening required is too much for him and

THE STANCE AND PRELIMINARY
MOVEMENTS

Figs. 125–7. Bronze Statuettes of Diskobolos showing three
consecutive positions starting from stance B.

125. THE STANCE. Bronze statuette found in Peloponnese. Height 9¼ in. 480–470 B.C. New York, Metropolitan
Museum, 07.286.87.

**126. DISKOS RAISED ABOVE HEAD IN BOTH
HANDS.** Bronze statuette found in Boeotia. Height about
7½ in. About 480 B.C. Athens, National Museum, no. 7412.
Stais, i, p. 270.

127. BEGINNING OF DOWNWARD SWING. Bronze
statuette. Height 6¼ in. About 500 B.C. British Museum,
675. *J.H.S.* xxvii, p. 22.

128. THE DOWNWARD SWING. Bronze statuette.
Height a little more than 3 in. About 500 B.C. Formerly
in Wyndham Cook Collection. *Burlington Fine Arts Club
Catalogue*, 1903, pl. 50. This bronze represents the backward
swing.

129. DISKOS HELD TO FRONT IN BOTH HANDS.
Attic r.-f. neck-amphora. About 480 B.C. Madrid. Drawing
by Professor Beazley. The fingering of the left hand shows
that the diskos has been swung up from stance A.

130. DISKOS HELD HIGH IN LEFT HAND. Attic r.-f.
column-krater. About 500 B.C. Oxford, Ashmolean Museum,
561. The same position as Figs. 123, 125, but the thrower
seems about to step forward with the left foot. New photograph.

131. THE DOWNWARD SWING. Attic b.-f. neck-
amphora. Late 6th century. British Museum, B. 271.
J.H.S. xxvii, pl. I. For the position with diskos flat in the
right hand cp. Figs. 114, 128. In this as in many b.-f. vases
a large white stone diskos is represented.

he is cramped by want of space. So instead of showing the body stooping forward he turns it sideways. Further, as the diskos if shown sideways would be hardly intelligible, he gives a full view of it. The position of the left arm raised above the head may be due to a difference in style, or to exigencies of space.

'The diskobolos', says Lucian, speaking of the statue, 'seems as if he would straighten himself up at the throw.'[1] At the begin-

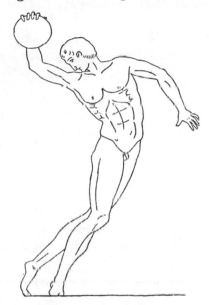

132. The throw of the diskos. B.-f. Panathenaic amphora. Late 5th century. Naples. *J.H.S.* xxvii, p. 32; *Jahreshefte*, xxiv, p. 140, Fig. 128. An impressionist view of the moment when the left foot leaves the ground, cp. coins of Cos, Fig. 35 d, and Fig. 133. This position must precede that shown in Figs. 118, 119, where the head has been turned forward. In all these attempts to represent the actual throw it is extremely difficult to co-ordinate rightly the movements of arms, legs, body, head. The Greek had no camera to help him.

ning of the forward swing the extensor-muscles come into play and by a vigorous lift from the right thigh the whole body is straightened. This momentary but most important movement is clearly depicted on a Panathenaic vase in Naples (Fig. 132), and a slightly later position on a vase in the British Museum (Fig. 133). The attitude shown is unique in Greek athletic art which prefers positions of comparative rest and equilibrium. But here we have a sort of snapshot, an impressionist picture of a position almost too momentary to be seen, certainly too unstable

[1] *Philopseud.* 18.

to maintain. On the Panathenaic vase especially the thrower seems to be flying from the ground in a way that suggests the figure of winged victory. But the diskobolos has no wings, and unless he promptly recovers his equilibrium by advancing the left foot he must fall to the ground. As Philostratos says in the passage quoted above, 'The left foot must be swung forward and follow through with the right hand', and it is off the left foot that the actual throw takes place (Figs. 134, 135).

133. Diskobolos and flute-player, trainer, youth seated fastening the amentum. Attic r.-f. hydria. Late 6th century. British Museum, E. 164. *B.C.H.* xxiii (1899), p. 164; *J.H.S.* xxvii, p. 32. The position is similar to that of 132, but later; the diskos is already swinging down.

On the Panathenaic vase we notice that the hand holding the diskos is turned outwards, and the same peculiarity is found on the coins of Cos and on a few other vases. Here again we have a variation of style, and it is interesting to note that the same variation occurs in the modern method of throwing the diskos. For while most throwers swing the diskos back with the hand turned inwards, some, as on our vase, turn the hand outwards.

A summary of the movements described may be useful:

   1. The Stance:
     (*a*) position of Standing Diskobolos with diskos in left hand;
     (*b*) diskos held in both hands level with waist; or
     (*c*) diskos raised in left hand level with the head.
The thrower may take up his stance with either foot forward. From these positions, with or without change of foot, the diskos is raised to:

2. Position with diskos held in both hands:
    (*a*) extended horizontally to the front;
    (*b*) raised above the head.
    The left foot is usually forward.
3. The diskos is swung downwards, resting on the right fore-arm. If the left foot is forward, either before or in the course of the swing
    (*a*) the left foot is drawn back, or
    (*b*) the right foot is advanced.

134. Diskos thrower, javelin thrower. Attic r.-f. kylix. Late 6th century. Bou-logne, Musée Communal. *Le Musée*, ii, p. 281. The diskos thrower has here advanced his left leg, but his head is still turned backwards.

4. Position of Myron's diskobolos:
5. At the beginning of the swing forward the body is straightened.
6. As the diskos swings down the left foot is vigorously ad-vanced.
7. After the diskos has left the hand, the right foot is again advanced.

We see, then, that while the principle implied in Myron's statue remained fixed, there was considerable diversity in style and in detail. It was essentially a 'free style'. When diskos-throwing was revived at the end of the last century various styles were tried. The Greeks, regarding many of these as unorthodox, devised what they considered to be the true 'Hellenic style'. First the

throw was to be made from a small platform 80 cm. long by
70 cm. wide with a height of 15 cm. behind and 5 cm. in front.
The only authority for this form of 'balbis' was a misinterpreta-
tion of an old corrupt text of Philostratus. Again, because
Myron's diskobolos had his right foot forward it was ordained
that the thrower must keep his right foot forward till the com-
pletion of the throw, and further that the diskos must be kept in
the same plane, swung straight backwards and forwards and not
round the body. For none of these restrictions was there any
justification, and the 'Hellenic style' has now died a natural death.

135. The throw of the diskos. Etruscan b.-f. hydria.
Early 5th century. Vienna Oest. Mus., 318. Masner,
p. 38. A position a little later than 134.

The modern free style unfortunately has abandoned the principle of the Greek throw and is based on experience gained in
throwing the hammer or the shot. The diskos is thrown from
a circle and the throw is measured to the inner edge of the circle
along a line drawn from the place where the diskos falls to the
centre. No throw is allowed to count unless the diskos falls
within a sector of 90 degrees marked on the ground. Direction,
therefore, is of little importance. The thrower takes his stand
with the feet well apart and body well balanced, and gripping the
diskos firmly in the right hand swings it a few times to and fro
from left to right. He then pivots quickly on the left foot, and
directly the right foot touches the ground makes the throw, the
left foot swinging round and striking the ground so as to keep
the body from going out of the ring. At the moment before the
heave the thrower is sometimes almost in the position of Myron's
diskobolos, as can be seen from Tait McKenzie's diskos-thrower
(Fig. 31). Indeed a partial turn of the body is by no means
incompatible with the position of the statue. But the complete
turn of the body is fatal to the accuracy required by Greek conditions. Some modern athletes make two complete turns, but it
is doubtful if any advantage is gained thereby.

XII

THROWING THE JAVELIN

THROWING the javelin [1] is another event that has been revived in modern times. It had long been practised in Germany, Finland, and Scandinavia, and since the revival of the Olympic Games has become popular in America. But to-day it is merely a form of athletic exercise; to the Greeks and Romans the javelin was the ordinary weapon of war and of the chase, and

136. Fastening the amentum. Attic r.-f. kylix. About 525 B.C. Würzburg, 432. Jüthner, *Ant. Turn.* Fig. 37, cp. Fig. 133.

every boy learnt to use it. It was the special weapon of the Athenian *ephebos*, who is generally represented with a pair of javelins in his hand. From the time of the Peloponnesian war, when the value of light-armed troops and cavalry began to be realized, competitions in javelin-throwing multiplied and special trainers in javelin-throwing were employed by the state at Athens and elsewhere. At the great festivals it was only one of the events in the pentathlon.

Javelins are among the commonest objects represented on the vases. They are straight poles nearly equal to the height of a man and almost the thickness of a finger. They are usually pointless and often provided with a blunt ferule. Xenophon recommends cavalry soldiers to use in practice javelins furnished with a rounded cap or ball.[2] Such ferules and caps served not only for protection against accidents but to give the head of the javelin

[1] See *Greek Athletics*, p. 338: Jüthner, *Turngeräthe*, p. 37; *J.H.S.* xxvii, pp. 249–73.
[2] *De re equestri*, xiii. 10.

137. WARRIOR THROWING JAVELIN UNDERHAND.
Attic b.-f. kylix. 2nd quarter of 6th century. British Museum,
B. 380. *J.H.S.* xxvii, p. 252.

138. HUNTERS THROWING JAVELINS. Detail from François vase, b.-f.
volute-krater. About 560 B.C. Florence. *J.H.S.* xxvii, p. 253. F.R. 13.

139. PENTATHLON. B.-f. Panathenaic amphora. About 525 B.C. British
Museum, B. 134. Jumper, diskos-thrower, two javelin throwers. The foremost
javelin thrower has his javelin at the carry, the other poises it in the position of
aiming. The fingering of the amentum is very clearly shown, cp. Fig. 148.

140. CAVALRY THROWING JAVELINS WITH AMENTUM. Attic b.-f.
dinos. About 560 B.C. Athens, Acropolis Museum. The javelins are just being
thrown and are held only by the amentum. Graef. pl. XXXI.

the necessary weight without which it would not fly properly. Blunt javelins could only be used for distance-throwing, and the competition in the pentathlon was for distance only. For target practice pointed javelins were necessary, and their use in the gymnasium is shown by the speech of Antiphon[1] in defence of a youth who accidentally killed a boy who crossed the range as he was throwing. On vases which represent throwing on horseback at a target pointed javelins are always used.

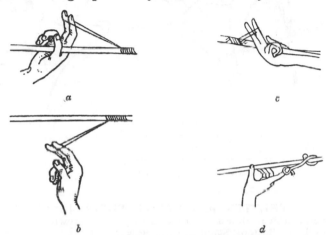

141. Illustrations of the use of the throwing thong. *a, b*. The amentum. Jüthner, *Ant. Turn.* 47, 48. *c.* Detail from B.M. vase, B. 134. *d.* The ounep of New Caledonia.

The athletic javelin was a light weapon and was thrown by means of a throwing-thong, called *amentum* (ἀγκύλη). It was a leather thong a foot or eighteen inches in length, and before use was firmly bound round the centre of the shaft in such a way as to leave a loop three or four inches long in which the thrower inserted his first, or his first and middle fingers. The point of attachment was near the centre of gravity, in the light-headed athletic javelins almost in the centre of the shaft, in the heavier javelins of war or the chase nearer to the head. Possibly its place varied according as the javelin was to be thrown for distance or at a mark. By putting the amentum behind the centre of gravity it is possible to increase the distance thrown but at a sacrifice of accuracy. In Fig. 136 we see an athlete winding the amentum tight round the shaft.

The amentum was no invention of the gymnasium but was

[1] *Tetralogia*, ii. 4.

142. JAVELIN THROWERS. Attic r.-f. kylix. About 500 B. C. Munich, 2667. Jüthner, *Ant. Turn.* Fig. 41. The position of the youth to the right is a moment later than that of the youth on the left. The fingering of the centre figure is difficult. Unless it is a mistake of drawing, he must reverse the javelin completely before throwing.

143. ATHLETES ADJUSTING THEIR JAVELINS: perhaps in readiness for a lesson in javelin throwing. R.-f. psykter. Boston. Same vase as Fig. 51.

144. JAVELIN THROWER. Attic r.-f. stemless cup. About 420 B. C. Berlin, 2728. Photograph from Museum. The pillar probably marks the place from which the throw is to be made.

145. JAVELIN THROWER. Attic r.-f. kylix. About 525 B. C. Cambridge. Photograph from Professor Beazley.

adopted from war and the chase. In Fig. 137 we see a fully armed warrior preparing to throw a javelin with a sort of underhand throw, a throw in which certain savages are said to be extraordinary skilful. The more usual overhand throw is shown in a hunting scene on the François vase (Fig. 138). The hunters advance with arms drawn back and fingers inserted in the thongs precisely in the manner which Xenophon recommends.

The use of a throwing-thong of this type seems to have been widely distributed throughout Europe.[1] It was known at an early date in Italy and was used by Etruscans, Samnites, and Messapians, but does not appear to have been used in the Roman army till after the Punic Wars. The tragula, the weapon of the Spanish, was thrown by means of an amentum; in Caesar's time it was the weapon of the Gallic cavalry. There is reason to believe that the light javelins found at La Tène were similarly thrown. The amentum was certainly known in Denmark in the early Iron Age. On the shafts of spears found at Nydam there were rivets for fastening the cord, and in some cases portions of the cord were found between the rivets. Lastly, we find it frequently mentioned in old Irish stories, and it is said to have been introduced into Ireland by Gallic mercenaries in the fourth century B.C.

This fixed amentum does not seem to have been used outside Europe, but somewhat similar contrivances survive to-day among uncivilized tribes. Such is the Ounep used by the people of New Hebrides and New Caledonia. It is a thickish cord, 6–8 inches long, with a loop for the finger at one end and a knot at the other. There is a projection about the centre of the shaft behind which the cord is placed and twisted over the knot in such a way as to unwind as the spear is thrown, remaining in the thrower's hand. In New Zealand is found a combination of the throwing-thong and the throwing-stick. The latter is the commonest and probably the oldest contrivance for increasing the carry of the spear.

A drawing in the Ethnographical department of the British Museum (Fig. 141) clearly shows the working of the throwing-thong. As the javelin leaves the hand the pull on the amentum gives the javelin a half-turn, and like the rifling of the gun imparts to it a rotatory motion which not only helps it to maintain its direction but increases its carry and penetrating power. The carry is still further increased by the increased leverage given to the thrower's arm. It is obvious that, as Philostratus tells us, length of finger was a great advantage to a javelin-thrower.[2]

[1] *J.H.S.* xxvii, p. 255. [2] *Gym.* 31.

The effect of the amentum on a light javelin was demonstrated by experiments conducted by the Emperor Napoleon. It was found that an unpractised thrower who could only throw 25 metres unaided increased his throw to 65 metres by using the amentum. The meaning of this can be realized from the fact that the record throw in the revived Olympic games is less than 60 metres. It must be noted, however, that the javelin used in these games is a heavy one, weighing about 3 lb.

Two styles of javelin-throwing can be distinguished, one in which the javelin is held horizontally, the other in which it is

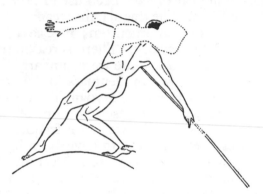

146. Javelin thrower. Attic r.-f. kylix. About 480 B.C. Torlonia Museum, 270 (148). Jüthner, *Ant. Turn.* Fig. 49. This represents a moment later than that shown in Fig. 144. Note the outward turn of the hand.

pointed more or less upwards. The former is the practical style of war, of the chase, and for throwing at a target. The soldier or hunter must have his weapon ready for use at a moment's notice. He therefore carries it with his fingers passed through the loop (διηγκυλισμένος), usually sloped over his shoulder and pointing downwards (Fig. 139). From this position he raises his elbow so that the javelin is level with his head, the natural position for taking aim. He then draws his arm back to the full extent as shown in Fig. 140. In the actual throw the movement is reversed, arm and javelin travelling through the same positions, except that as the amentum unwinds the hand releases the shaft of the javelin which for the moment is held merely by the amentum.

In this practical style everything depends on accuracy of aim and rapidity of action. In an athletic competition the thrower may take his time. It is the difference between throwing in a cricket-ball from the long field and throwing it in a competition. The purely athletic character of this style is obvious from the fact that till the moment of the throw the head is always turned backwards, the eyes fixed on the hand holding the amentum, a position absurd for war or the chase or for taking aim (Figs. 142, 144, 146).

After carefully adjusting and testing the amentum (Fig. 143) and inserting his fingers in the loop, the thrower extends his right arm backwards to the full extent, while with his left hand he holds

147. Javelin thrower. The reverse. Attic r.-f. kylix. About 480 B. C. Formerly on the Roman market. From a drawing made by Jüthner, *Ant. Turn.* Fig. 43.

the end of the javelin and presses it backwards so as to draw the thong tight. As he starts to run, he draws his right arm still farther backwards, turning his head to the right, and extends his left arm to the front. The movement is clearly shown in Fig. 142 where we have three consecutive positions. From the position of the head it is clear that the run, as in throwing the cricket-ball, consists only of a few short steps. Immediately before the throw a still further turn of the body takes place, the right leg being bent and the right shoulder dropped, while the hand is turned outwards so that the shaft rests on the palm of the hand (Fig. 146). This turn of the body is followed by what modern athletes call 'the reverse'. The right foot is placed in front of the left and the whole position of the body is reversed, the throw taking place off the right leg. The beginning of this movement is seen in Fig. 147.

A comparison of these illustrations with photographs of modern competitors in this event shows how closely the ancient and modern styles resemble one another. The chief difference is in the use of the amentum. The modern athlete having no amentum has no need to turn his head to the right to watch his hand, and consequently can make more use of his run.

We have seen that from an early date the javelin was used on horseback both for war and for the chase. Plato [1] tells us that Themistocles taught his son to throw the javelin standing on horseback, and he recommends javelin-throwing on horseback as a useful accomplishment. Xenophon in his treatise on the duties of a cavalry officer urges the latter to encourage his men in javelin-throwing, and in his treatise on horsemanship he gives full instructions in the art.[2] At Athens there were competitions in this event as early as the fifth century. At the Panathenaic Games five amphorae of oil were given for the first prize and one for the second prize. There were similar competitions in Thessaly and other parts of Greece. In Fig. 12 we have a picture of the competition. A shield is set up as a target, with a wreath in the centre which perhaps served as a bull's-eye, and the epheboi, fully dressed, gallop past, hurling their javelins at it as they pass. We do not know the method of scoring, nor have we any knowledge of target competitions on foot.

[1] *Meno*, 93 D; *Leg.* 834 D.   [2] *Hipparch.* i. d; *de re equestri*, viii. 10.

XIII

THE PENTATHLON

THE pentathlon[1] was a combined competition in five events: running, jumping, throwing the diskos, throwing the javelin, and wrestling. This is one of the facts that may be regarded as absolutely certain, though the antiquated idea disproved long ago that boxing was originally one of the events in the pentathlon still finds a place in Liddell and Scott's *Lexicon*. These five events were representative of the whole physical training of the Greeks, and the pentathlete was the typical product of that training. Inferior to the specialized athlete in his special events, he was superior to him in general development, in that harmonious union of strength and activity which produces perfect physical beauty, and this beauty of the pentathlete won for him the special admiration of thinkers like Aristotle,[2] who condemned all exaggerated or one-sided development.

A combined competition is evidently later than the events of which it is composed. The pentathlon was unknown to Homer; but the fact that it was introduced into the programme of the Olympic Games as early as 708 B.C. is a striking proof of the fact already noted of the high state of development that Greek athletics had attained even in the eighth century. We need not of course suppose that the idea of such a competition originated in any abstract theory of physical training in which light and heavy exercises, quick and slow, were carefully balanced. It is more probable that the pentathlon began not as a separate competition but as a sort of athletic championship, a means of deciding who was the best all-round athlete among the victors at a meeting.

The order of events and the method of deciding the competition have produced endless controversy. As to the order, the one fact that we know is that wrestling was the last of the five events. A comparison of the various passages in which the events are enumerated makes it probable that the foot-race was the first, and after it came the three events which were peculiar to the pentathlon: the jump, the diskos, and the javelin. One or more of these three events are always represented on the prize vases for the pentathlon given at the Panathenaea.

[1] *Greek Athletics*, p. 358; *J.H.S.* xxiii, p. 54, where the previous theories are fully discussed; *J.H.S.* xlv, p. 132.
[2] Aristot. *Rhetoric*, i. 5; Plato, *Amatores*, 135 D, E.

It is unnecessary here to discuss the numerous theories suggested as to the method of deciding the pentathlon. Many of them are quite unpractical. The explanation that I am offering is a modification of the views put forward in my *Greek Athletic Sports and Festivals*, a modification suggested by a Finnish athlete, Captain Pihkala.

The antiquated view that the pentathlete could not receive the prize unless he was victorious in all five events may be dismissed at once. It is unpractical, for the prize would have been hardly ever awarded. It is also contrary to the evidence which proves beyond dispute that victory in three events was sufficient.

This is clear from a passage of Herodotus,[1] where he says of one Tisamenus, 'he came within a single contest or fall (πάλαισμα) of victory, being matched against Hieronymus of Andros'. Pausanias supplies the explanation (iii. 11. 6): 'In two events he was first, for he was superior to Hieronymus in running and jumping, but he was defeated by him in wrestling and so failed to win the victory.' The interpretation is obvious. Tisamenus won two events but lost the odd; or perhaps we can go further and give to πάλαισμα its literal meaning, 'a fall in wrestling'. He came 'within a single fall' of winning. Each had won two events, each had scored two falls in wrestling, and the whole contest was decided by the last fall, just as we talk of winning a golf match by a putt.

Victory in three events was thus sufficient, and there is some evidence that the victor in the pentathlon was generally regarded as a triple victor (τριακτήρ). But it is clear that it must often have happened that no single competitor was absolutely first in three of the events. And of this we have proof in a passage of Philostratus giving the mythical origin of the pentathlon.[2]

'Before the time of Jason, there were separate crowns for the jump, the diskos, and the javelin. At the time of the Argo's voyage Telamon was best at throwing the diskos, Lynceus with the javelin, the sons of Boreas were best at running and jumping, and Peleus was second in these events but was superior to all in wrestling. Accordingly, when they were holding sports in Lemnos, Jason, they say, wishing to please Peleus combined the five events, and thus Peleus secured the victory on the whole.'

Peleus was only first in wrestling, but he was awarded the prize for the whole because he was second in the four other events. He had, in fact, defeated each of his opponents in three, or rather

[1] ix. 33   [2] *Gym.* 3.

in four events, and as compared with each individually was actually 'a triple victor'. Here in the comparison of each competitor's performance with those of each of his fellow competitors we have evidently the clue.

It is an easy matter by means of a simple marking-sheet to compare the performances of each competitor individually with each of his fellows. But there are two objections. In the first

148. Pentathlon. B.-f. Panathenaic amphora. Leyden. About 525 B.C. *Arch. Zeit.* 1881, pl. IX. This vase is by the same hand as the B.M. vase, B. 134 (Fig. 189). The same three events are shown, the jump, the diskos, and the javelin—the three events typical of the pentathlon. But whereas in B. 134 the artist has represented the athletes walking in a sort of procession, here to give life to the scene he makes them run, and the result is somewhat grotesque. It is clearly useless to draw any inferences from such a scene as to the style of throwing the diskos or javelin, or jumping.

place the result would often be inconclusive. It might happen, for example, that A beat B in three events, B beat C; and yet C beat A. Secondly, it is extremely difficult to place a number of wrestlers in order of merit.

There is, however, reason to think that only those who had qualified in the first four events were allowed to compete in the final wrestling. Xenophon, in describing the fighting at the Olympic Games in 364 B.C. when the Eleans were attacking the Arcadians who had usurped the presidency of the games, says: [1] 'They had already finished the horse-race and the track events in the pentathlon (τὰ δρομικά), and *those who had reached the*

[1] *Hellenica*, vii. 4. 29.

wrestling were no longer in the dromos but were wrestling between the dromos and the altar.' It is generally agreed that the
events that took place in the *dromos* or stadium were the first four
events, the foot-race, jump, diskos, and javelin. And from the
words 'those who had reached the wrestling' the only possible
conclusion is that some of the competitors had been eliminated.

Such an elimination is easily effected if the performances of
each competitor in the first four events are compared as a whole
with those of each of the others, and any competitor who is
defeated by any other in three events is cut out. If one competitor is actually first in three of the four events, he alone is left
in and must be the winner. Similarly, any competitor who is
actually first in two events must be left in. It will generally happen that the events are divided between three or four competitors.
The usual result is that from two to four competitors are left in,
each of them having defeated each of the others in two, not
necessarily the same, events; a larger number is possible but very
improbable. These then compete in wrestling, and the winner in
the wrestling is the winner of the pentathlon; he is indeed a triple
victor, for he has defeated each of his rivals in three events. The
working of this scheme is clear from the following table, giving
the imaginary performances of 6 competitors A B C D E F placed
in order of merit in the four events I II III IV:

	I.	II.	III.	IV.
1	A	B	C	D
2	E	A	B	F
3	B	D	E	C
4	C	E	A	A
5	F	C	D	B
6	D	F	F	E

Comparing A with each of the other five, his score is A 2, B 2—
A 2, C 2—A 3, D 1—A 3, E 1—A 3, F 1. D E F therefore drop
out. Similarly B has defeated C in two events, lost in two events.
No one has defeated A B C in more than two events. These
three all tie and qualify for the wrestling match.

That this was the actual method of deciding the pentathlon
cannot be proved, but it so completely satisfies all the conditions
imposed by such evidence as we possess that we may safely accept
it as approximately correct.

XIV

WRESTLING

WRESTLING is the oldest and most widely distributed of all sports.[1] The very name palaestra, 'the wrestling-school', indicates its importance in Greek life. Metaphors from wrestling abound in Greek literature, and scenes from the wrestling-ring occur not only in athletic art but also in mythological subjects. Heracles is represented as employing the regular holds of the palaestra not only against the giant Antaeus but against monsters like Achelous and the Triton and even against the Nemean lion. The fight between Theseus and the robber Cercyon is represented as a wrestling match in which Theseus, the reputed founder of scientific wrestling, displays his skill. Even on coins we find wrestling scenes; we find them on the fifth-century coins of Aspendus, and they survive even into imperial times (Fig. 35).

To the Greek, wrestling was a science and an art. The greatest importance was attached to grace and style. It was not sufficient to throw an opponent: it had to be done gracefully and in good style. So even when athletics had become corrupted by professionalism, wrestling remained for the most part free from the brutality that has so often brought discredit on one of the noblest of sports. Pausanias records the case of a certain Sicilian wrestler who defeated his opponents by breaking their fingers, and he expresses his disapproval of such tactics by the significant comment that he did not know how to throw his opponent.[2]

Competitions in wrestling, boxing, and the pankration were conducted in the same way as a modern tournament. Lots marked in pairs with letters of the alphabet were thrown into a helmet and each competitor drew one.[3] If there was an odd number of competitors one of them drew a bye. This gave him a natural advantage over his less fortunate competitors, and it was regarded as an additional distinction to win a competition without drawing a bye.[4]

The Greeks distinguished two styles of wrestling—one which they called 'upright wrestling' or wrestling proper (ὀρθὴ πάλη or σταδαία πάλη or simply πάλη), in which the object was to throw

---

[1] See *Greek Athletics*, p. 372; *J.H.S.* xxv, pp. 14, 263; xxvi. 4.
[2] Paus. vi. 4, 2.   [3] Lucian, *Hermotim.* 39.
[4] The drawer of the bye was called ἔφεδρος. The term ἀνέφεδρος is frequently used in inscriptions of a victory won without drawing a bye; see *J.H.S.* xxv, p. 17.

your opponent to the ground (καταβλητική); the other ground wrestling (κύλισις or ἀλίνδησις), in which the struggle was continued on the ground till one or other of the combatants acknowledged defeat. The former was the only wrestling admitted in the pentathlon or in wrestling competitions: the latter did not exist as a competition except in the pankration, in which hitting and kicking were also allowed.

In the palaestra both forms of wrestling were practised and separate places were assigned to them. Ground wrestling took place usually in some place under cover, and the ground was watered till it became muddy.[1] The mud rendered the body slippery and difficult to hold, while wallowing in the mud was regarded as beneficial to the skin. Wrestling proper took place on sandy ground carefully dug out and levelled, and the ring was therefore called *skamma*, the same word that is used for the jumping-pit.

In discussing Greek wrestling we must not be misled, as many modern writers are, by the misuse of the term Graeco-Roman to describe a style of wrestling in vogue among professional wrestlers to-day. There is nothing in Greek wrestling or even in the pankration that has any resemblance to, or can offer any justification for, this most useless and artificial of all systems which, as one of our greatest modern authorities on wrestling remarks, might have been invented for the express purpose of bringing a grand and useful exercise into disrepute.

We have no definite information as to the rules of Greek wrestling and can only infer them from the somewhat fragmentary evidence of literature and art. The two essential points which distinguish one system of wrestling from another are the definition of a fair throw and the nature of the holds allowed.

In most modern systems a man is considered thrown only when both shoulders, or one shoulder and one hip, touch the ground at the same time; in the Cumberland and Westmorland style he is thrown if he touches the ground with any part of his body or even with his knee. A throw may be a clean throw or the result of a struggle on the ground. In Greek wrestling it is certain, as implied in the name 'upright wrestling', that only clean throws counted, and there is no evidence at all that the bout was ever continued on the ground. Further it is certain that a fall on the back, on the shoulders, or on the hip counted as a fair throw. Whether a fall on the knee counted is a question difficult to

[1] See Jüthner, *Philostratus*, pp. 206, 297; Lucian, *Anacharsis*, 2. 28, 29.

decide. The literary evidence is of uncertain interpretation.[1] We have, however, a group of vases representing 'the flying mare', and on some of these a wrestler as he throws his opponent over his head sinks on his knee. Certainty is impossible, but on the whole I am inclined to believe that a fall on the knee did not count. If both wrestlers fell together, it seems probable from the description of wrestling in Homer that no fall was counted.

Three clean throws were necessary to secure victory. Hence

149. Heracles and Antaeus wrestling. B.-f. amphora. Late 6th century. British Museum, B. 222. Antaeus grabs at the foot of Heracles, and thereby puts himself at his mercy.

the technical term for winning a victory in wrestling was τριάσσειν, 'to treble', and the victor himself was a τριακτήρ, or 'trebler'.

We pass on to the means employed by the Greek wrestler to throw his opponent. In particular was tripping allowed, and were leg-holds employed? In the artificial Graeco-Roman wrestling of to-day neither tripping nor leg-holds are allowed, but this need not trouble us. Tripping is rarely represented in Greek art except as a means of defence (Figs. 154, 164), but the frequent references to it in literature from the time of Homer to that of Lucian leave no doubt that it played as important a part in Greek wrestling as it has in every rational system of wrestling. On the other hand, it seems certain that leg-holds were seldom used even if they were not absolutely forbidden. Plato in the *Laws*[2] contrasts the

[1] For a full discussion see *J.H.S.* xxv, p. 20, and *Greek Athletics*, 377.
[2] 796 A, B.; see *J.H.S.* xxv, p. 27.

methods of the pankration, in which leg-holds and kicking were allowed, with the methods of upright wrestling. The latter is the only form of wrestling that he will allow in his ideal state, and he defines it as 'the disentangling of neck and hands and sides', a masterly definition showing a true understanding of the art of wrestling. The vases show that the omission of 'leg-holds' in

150. Wrestlers engaging. R.-f. kotyle. Ashmolean Museum, Oxford, 288. About 440 B. C. The vase is a good deal restored.

Plato's definition is no accident. In the pankration one combatant is frequently represented as seizing his opponent's foot or leg (Fig. 149), but in wrestling proper, though arm-, neck-, and body-holds occur frequently, we never see a leg-hold. It is probable that this is the result not so much of a direct prohibition as of the riskiness of such a method of attack under the conditions of upright wrestling. A wrestler who stoops low enough to catch an opponent's foot is certain to be thrown himself if he misses his grip. On the other hand, there is no practical objection when the wrestlers are engaged to catching hold of an opponent's thigh whether for offence or defence.

The conditions of Greek wrestling may be summed up as follows:

1. If a wrestler fell on *any* part of the body, hip, back, or shoulder, it was a fair fall.
2. If both wrestlers fell together, nothing was counted.
3. Three falls were necessary to secure victory.

151. Theseus and Cercyon wrestling. Attic r.-f. kylix. About 430 B. C. British Museum, E. 84. Cercyon rushes in to obtain a body hold. Theseus steps aside, and passing his left arm round his body is in a position to throw him over his thigh. The same motive in Fig. 172.

4. Tripping was allowed.
5. Leg-holds, if not actually prohibited, were rarely used.

Wrestling is a very complicated subject, and it is impossible here to give more than a selection of the principal grips and throws represented in Greek art. Nor can we here discuss the various technical terms employed, many of them very difficult of interpretation.[1]

The attitude adopted by the Greek wrestler before taking hold was very similar to that of the modern wrestler. Taking a firm stand with his feet somewhat apart and knees slightly bent,

[1] The student will find full discussion of these in *J.H.S.* xxv, pp. 14, 263 ff.

152. WRESTLERS PREPARING TO ENGAGE. Attic
r.-f. oenochoe. About 430 B.C. Cracow, 1260. Beazley,
Vases in Poland, pl. XXIX. 1. It is impossible to determine
whether these are wrestlers or pankratiasts. The preliminary
positions must have been the same.

153. BRONZE WRESTLING BOY. One of a pair of
statues at Naples. Free copy of Greek work of about
300 B.C. *Photo. Brogi.*

154. THE WRESTLING SCHOOL. Attic r.-f. amphora.
About 530 B.C. Berlin, 2159. F.R. 133. The figure to the
left seems to be a youthful trainer. In the centre a bearded
athlete has tried to obtain the hold for the 'flying mare',
p. 187, but his opponent frustrates the attack by moving
to his right and grasping his right arm below the elbow. To
the right a youth has obtained a body hold and lifted his
opponent, who tries to break his grip and clicks his left knee
with his right foot. Cp. Fig. 164.

rounding (γυρίσας) his back and shoulders, his neck advanced but pressed down into the shoulder-blades, he tried to avoid giving an opening himself, while his outstretched hands were ready to seize any opportunities offered by his opponent.[1] It is the position represented frequently in art, especially in the well-known pair of wrestling boys in the Naples Museum (Figs. 152, 153).

Generally the wrestlers stand square to one another (σύστασις) and prepare to take hold somewhat in the style of Westmorland and Cumberland wrestlers, 'leaning against one another like gable rafters of a house', or 'butting against each other like rams', or 'resting their heads on each other's shoulders' (Figs. 8, 150). Sometimes instead of taking hold from the front they try to obtain a hold from the side, turning their bodies sideways to one another (παράθεσις) (Fig. 151).

In endeavouring to obtain a hold wrestlers frequently grasp their opponents by the wrist (Figs. 155, 164, &c.). This is often a purely defensive movement to prevent an opponent from obtaining a neck- or body-hold. There is, however, one arm-hold constantly represented and evidently very popular. It is the hold that leads to the throw known in modern wrestling as the 'flying mare', which is probably what Lucian describes as 'hoisting on high' (ἀναβαστάσαι εἰς ὕψος).

To execute this throw the wrestler seizes one of his opponent's arms with both hands, one hand gripping the wrist, the other the forearm just below the elbow (Figs. 53, 155 a). He then rapidly turns his back on him, draws his arm over his own shoulder, and using it as a lever hoists him clean over his head, while at the same time he stoops forward, or even sinks on one knee. The result is a heavy fall as can be seen in Figs. 156, 157. On a vase in the British Museum we see Heracles hoisting the Nemean lion over his head in this way. For in his struggle with the lion Heracles is often represented as the skilled athlete employing all the tricks of the wrestling school.

Not only does Greek art illustrate this throw from beginning to end, but it also shows us the various methods of countering this attack. The wrestler whose arm has been seized at once with his free hand grasps his opponent's arm under the arm-pit or close to the wrist, thus preventing him from turning round. Another mode of defence is seen in Fig. 154, where we have scenes from the wrestling school, perhaps a lesson. Here the bearded wrestler has seized his opponent's left wrist, but the latter

---

[1] Heliodorus, *Aethiop.* x. 31.

◀WRESTLERS AND BOXERS

155. Attic b.-f. neck-amphora by Nicosthenes. 3rd quarter of 6th century. British Museum, B. 295. New photograph.

a. On neck. Wrestlers. The wrestler to the right has seized with both hands his opponent's right arm, the hold for the flying mare (p. 187). The other counters the attack by placing his left hand under his left armpit, thus preventing him from turning round. *J.H.S.* xxv, p. 270. Cp. Peleus and Hippalcimus in Fig. 8.
On body. Boxers. A very symmetrical group, with the left arms extended, and the right arms drawn back for a blow.

b. On neck. Boxers sparring in a very open position. The guard of the right hand boxer has a very modern look.
On body. Wrestlers engaging, cp. Figs. 150, 164.

◀THE FLYING MARE

156. R.-f. kylix. About 430 B. C. British Museum, E. 94. The drawing is careless. The position of the wrestler with both knees bent is hardly possible, unless he is represented as falling himself. Possibly the bend of the knees is exaggerated from want of space. New photograph.

157. Interior of r.-f. kylix. About 500 B. C. Paris, Bibliothèque Nationale, 523. Hartwig, *Meisterschalen*, pl. XVI. *Photo. Giraudon.* The exterior of this vase shows hoplitodromoi, boxers, and wrestlers. Unfortunately the lines of the figures have been so much obscured by modern paint and restoration that it is impossible to interpret some of them.

by a quick movement forward has rendered useless the left arm which should have grasped his upper arm, and passing his own right arm behind his back grasps his right arm just below the elbow. In all these cases the object is to prevent the opponent from turning round or to weaken his grip by pinching the arm.

The neck is an obvious and effective place by which to secure a hold, and strength of neck was essential to a wrestler. Pindar speaks of the wrestler's 'strength and neck invincible',[1] and in the *Knights* of Aristophanes Demos advises the sausage-seller to grease his neck in order to escape from Kleon's grip.[2] The technical word for obtaining a neck-hold is τραχηλίζειν. Many varieties of neck-hold are represented. Often a wrestler seizes his opponent's neck with one hand and grasps his wrist with the other (Figs. 150, 160), or passing it under his arm links his two hands together (Figs. 159, 161). Both of these grips are used by Heracles in wrestling with the Nemean lion. We may notice that the interlocking of the hands is the same as that employed by Cumberland and Westmorland wrestlers, the hands being turned so that the palms face one another and the fingers hooked together. In Fig. 159 we have an excellent illustration of a throw from a neck-hold. Theseus has secured a powerful hold on Cercyon with one arm passed over his left shoulder and the other under his right arm-pit and is swinging him off his feet.

A fall from a neck- or body-hold is often secured by the movement known to the Greeks as ἕδραν στρέφειν,[3] 'turning one's buttocks towards an opponent'. The commencement of the movement is shown in Fig. 160, further stages in Figs. 162, 163. It is a throw very similar to our cross-buttock and was evidently as familiar to the Greeks as it is to the modern wrestler. Theocritus tells us that Heracles learnt from Harpalycus 'all the tricks wherewith the nimble Argive cross-buttockers (ἀπὸ σκελέων ἑδροστρόφοι) give each other the throw'. Theophrastus in his character of the Late Learner who wishes to be thought thoroughly accomplished and up to date describes him as strutting about in the bath, pretending to give the cross-buttock like a wrestler.[4]

A most effective hold is obtained by seizing an opponent with both hands round the waist; he can then be lifted off his feet and thrown to the ground. 'To hold round the waist' (μέσον ἔχειν) was, like our phrase 'to catch upon the hip', a proverbial expression for having any one at one's mercy. The body-hold can be obtained from the front, from behind, or from the side.

[1] *Nem.* vii. 73.   [2] *Eq.* 491.   [3] xxiv. 111.   [4] *Char.* xxvii.

158. PELEUS AND ATALANTA WRESTLING. Attic b.-f. neck-amphora. Late 6th century. Munich, 1541. Gerh. *A.V.* 177; *J.H.S.* xxv, p. 275.

159. THESEUS SWINGING CERCYON OFF HIS FEET. Attic r.-f. psykter by Euthymides. End of 6th century Turin. *J.H.S.* xxxv, pl. V.

160. WRESTLING HOLD FOR THE CROSS-BUT-TOCK. Attic r.-f. kylix. About 420 B.C. Villa Giulia, Rome. *Mon. Ant.* xxiv. 894. The left-hand wrestler has obtained a hold that enables him to throw his opponent across his buttock.

161. THESEUS AND CERCYON. Attic r.-f. kylix. About 500 B.C. Louvre, G. 104. *F.R.* 141. Notice the interlocking of the hands.

162. B.-f. Panathenaic amphora. Late 6th century. Boulogne, Musée Communal, 441. *Gk. Athletics*, p. 390. Photograph from Mrs. Beazley.

163. Attic b.-f. stamnos. Rome, Vatican. *J.H.S.* xxv, p. 288. This is one of a small group of vases belonging to the end of the 6th century, where all the athletes wear white loincloths, cp. Fig. 182. Thucydides (i. 6) states that the use of the loincloth had only been abandoned even at Olympia shortly before his own time. Yet the vase-paintings and art prove that absolute nudity had been the rule in Greek sport. Is it possible that an attempt was made at the close of the sixth century to introduce the loincloth, and that this temporary fashion is the reason for Thucydides' statement?

The body-hold from the front is very difficult to obtain, but very effective when obtained (Fig. 154). Clumsiness and slowness are fatal, for as the wrestler stoops to obtain the undergrip, his opponent may by a sideways movement obtain a hold for the heave, or falling on him may force him to the ground. This danger is well illustrated in Fig. 165.

164. Body-holds. Attic b.-f. amphora. 2nd half of 6th century. Munich, 1461. *J.H.S.* xxv, pl. XII. The left-hand group is an excellent illustration of the body hold from behind. The man who is lifted defends himself in correct style by hooking his right leg inside his opponent's right leg.

More commonly the body-hold is obtained from behind, as shown in Figs. 164 and 171. We may notice in the former that the wrestler who has been lifted employs the very means of defence that the modern wrestler does, hooking his right foot behind his opponent's knee. The hands, too, are interlocked in the modern fashion. This hold is particularly connected with Heracles and Antaeus. The lifting of Antaeus is represented on fourth-century coins of Tarentum, and from this time the type is constantly repeated, especially on gems and coins (Fig. 33). Roman poets said that Antaeus being the son of Earth derived fresh force from his mother each time that he touched the earth,

and that Heracles therefore lifted him off the earth and crushed
him to death. But this version of the story is unknown to the
literature and art of the Greeks. With a few doubtful exceptions
Heracles is always represented as lifting Antaeus not to crush
him but to swing him to the ground.

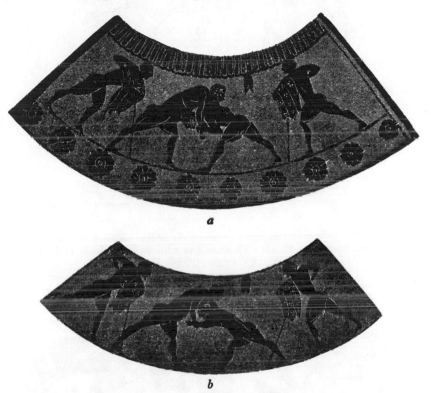

a

b

165 *a, b*. Body-holds. Attic b.-f. amphora. 2nd half of 6th century. Munich,
1468. *J.H.S.* xxv, pl. XII. Good examples of the danger of trying to obtain a
body hold from the front.

For no throw have we such abundant evidence as 'the heave',
the hold for which is obtained from the side by passing one arm
across and round the opponent's back and the other underneath
him. This is the hold represented in the illustration of a wrestling
lesson in Fig. 51. It is a throw particularly associated by the
Greek artist with Theseus and Cercyon. In Fig. 166 Theseus is
just in the act of lifting Cercyon off his feet. The latter with one
foot just touching the ground has tried to apply a similar hold on
Theseus, but too late. In Fig. 167 he has already been lifted off

166. Theseus and Cercyon. Attic r.-f. kylix. About 490 B.C.
British Museum, E. 48. Theseus has obtained the hold and is
swinging Cercyon off his feet.

167. Theseus and Cercyon. Attic r.-f. kylix. Late 6th century B.C. British
Museum, E. 36. A later stage in the same movement.

the ground and tries to save himself by grabbing at Theseus's foot. The well-known metope from the Theseum (Fig. 170) shows a slightly later stage; Theseus is in the act of turning Cercyon over, while in a bronze statuette in Paris he has turned him completely over and, standing upright, prepares to dash him to the ground. The fall itself is shown in Fig. 168, and here we note that as in the 'flying mare' the victor sinks on one knee.

Many of the holds described were combined with various turns of the body and with tripping. For both of these we have

168. Throw from a body-hold. B.-f. cup. 2nd quarter of 6th century. Florence, Museo Archeologico 3893. Drawing by Prof. Zahn. The victor sinks on one knee, as in Fig. 157.

numerous technical terms which we cannot discuss here. Tripping, as I have already remarked, is seldom represented in Greek art. The best illustration of its use in attack is a group from the Theatre at Delphi where one wrestler pulls his opponent backwards across his thigh (Fig. 170). Tripping seems also to be represented in a group of bronzes to be discussed later (Figs. 197, 198). These I formerly classed as wrestling groups. But Mr. Percy Longhurst, one of our greatest authorities on wrestling, has pointed out to me that the position shown in some of the bronzes can hardly have been reached from upright wrestling, and that the object of the arm-lock represented is not to obtain a fall but to cause pain and so force the victim to acknowledge defeat. These groups therefore must belong not to wrestling proper but to the pankration.

169. THESEUS AND CERCYON. Metope from the Treasury of the Athenians, Delphi. About 500 B. C. *Fouilles de Delphes*, iv, pl. 46. Theseus has seized Cercyon round the waist and tries to lift him while Cercyon strains forward with bent head. This group is quite misinterpreted by Poulsen (*Delphi*, p. 184) who connects it with the flying mare.

170. THESEUS AND CERCYON. Metope of the Theseum, Athens. About 440 B. C. A good illustration of the heave, Figs. 166, 167.

171. BRONZE WRESTLING GROUP. Several photos of this group were in the possession of the late Mr. E. P. Warren, but no indication where he saw the group. Several similar groups exist. *Collection Gréau*, pl. XXXIII; *A.Z.* 1890, p. 138, no. 14; *Collection Borelli Bey*, 257, pl. XXIX. They seem mostly to come from Alexandria. They bear a striking resemblance to the group of Heracles and Antaeus on Alexandrian coins of Antoninus Pius, Fig. 35, m.

172. HERACLES AND ANTAEUS. Frieze of the theatre at Delphi. 3rd century B. C. *Fouilles de Delphes*, pl. 76. The motive is almost the same as that of Fig. 151. Heracles is about to throw Antaeus across his thigh.

XV

BOXING

THE story of Greek boxing [1] is full of interest and instruction. It is, as we have seen, difficult to establish any connexion between Greek boxing and Crete; but apart from this we can trace its history continuously in literature and art from the times of Homer to the Roman Empire. In Homer boxing was already a highly specialized art, and the competitors at the games of Patroclus had their hands covered with well-cut thongs of ox-hide. The use of some sort of covering or protection for the hand necessarily determines the whole style of fighting. It will be convenient therefore before we consider the style of Greek boxing to trace the history and development of what for convenience we may call the Greek gloves.

Simple thongs of ox-hide, raw or dressed with fat to make them supple, were the only protection that the Greek boxer wore from the time of Homer to the close of the fifth century. Later writers described them as 'soft gloves' (ἱμάντες μαλακώτεροι or μείλιχαι) in contrast with the more formidable implements that succeeded them. In reality they must have been far from soft, and served, like the light modern gloves, to protect the knuckles rather than to soften the blow.

These thongs are among the commonest objects represented on sixth- and fifth-century vases. They appear to have been ten to twelve feet long. On the interior of the cup shown in Fig. 173 is a youth standing before an altar with the thongs gathered up into a bundle. On the exterior we have a series of boxing scenes. A youth with a pair of thongs in his hands is holding out one of them to his fellow. The latter holds a thong in his outstretched hands and gathers one end of it into a loop. This loop is clearly connected with the method of fastening the thongs. Philostratus, [2] in describing these soft gloves, says that the four fingers were inserted into a loop in such a way as to allow the hand to be clenched. The thumb is always uncovered, though occasionally the thong is wound round it separately. As a rule the thong is wound several times round the four fingers and knuckles, passed diagonally across the palm and back of the hand, and wound

---

[1] In *Greek Athletics*, p. 402; *J.H.S.* xxvi, p. 213; Jüthner, *Turngeräthe*, p. 66.
[2] *Gym.* 10.

round the wrist, the binding being sometimes carried some distance up the forearm (Fig. 174).

These soft thongs seem to have been superseded early in the
fourth century by the more formidable gloves described by Plato [1]
as σφαῖραι or balls, which he recommends for use in his ideal
state as more closely reproducing the conditions of actual warfare.
This type is shown in Fig. 175. The glove seems to be formed
of thick bands of some soft substance stretching along the forearm and bound round with stout, stiff, leather thongs fastened
apparently between the fingers and the thumb. In Fig. 175 *a*
a youth is drawing the fastening tight with his teeth.

To bind on the hand these complicated thongs must have been
a troublesome and tedious process, and the introduction of the
sphairai was followed almost immediately by the invention of
gloves that could be drawn on more readily. These gloves, which
are appropriately described as 'sharp thongs', are familiar to us
from the statue of the Seated Boxer in the Terme at Rome
(Fig. 72) and the Sorrento boxer at Naples (Fig. 176). They con-
sist of two parts, a glove and a hard leather ring encircling the
knuckles. The glove extends almost to the elbow and ends in
a thick strip of fleece which served to protect the arm which
might easily be broken by a blow from so formidable a weapon.
The glove itself appears to have been padded, the ends of the
fingers are cut off, and there is an opening on the inside. On the
knuckles is a thick pad which prevents the ring from slipping.
This ring is formed of three to five strips of hard, stiff leather,
bound together by small straps and held in its place by thongs
fastened round the wrist. It is about an inch wide and half an
inch thick, and its sharp, projecting edges must have rendered it
a weapon of offence as effective as the modern knuckle-duster.

These 'sharp gloves' remained in use till the second century
A.D. at least. Indeed it is doubtful if any other gloves were ever
used in Greek festivals. No Greek writers mention the masses of
lead and iron with which, according to Roman poets, the caestus
was loaded. The use of metal to make the caestus heavier and
more dangerous was a purely Roman invention, utterly barbarous
and fatal to scientific boxing. In the representations of the caestus
the hand seems to be encased in a hard ball or cylinder, from the
back of which over the knuckles is a toothed projection which
sometimes takes the form of two or three spikes. At the same
time the arm is protected by a padded sleeve extending almost

[1] *Leg.* 830 B.

up to the shoulder. This sleeve is usually made of a skin or fleece with the rough side turned inwards and secured by straps (Figs. 74, 177, 178).

We can distinguish, then, three periods in the history of ancient

173. Boxing scenes. Attic r.-f. kylix by Duris. About 490 B.C. British Museum, E. 39. *J.H.S.* xxvi, pl. XII. In upper half to r. fallen boxer acknowledges defeat by holding up his right hand. Below, boxers getting ready the *himantes*.

boxing. The first is the period of the soft thongs, and extends from Homer to the close of the fifth century; the second is that of the sphairai and 'sharp thongs', lasting from the fourth century into late Roman times; the third is that of the Roman caestus. We shall see how the change in the form of the glove completely altered the style of boxing, how, as the glove became a more formidable weapon, boxing became less scientific and more brutal.

◄174. BOXER FASTENING BOXING THONG. Interior of Attic r.-f. kylix. About 480 B.C. British Museum, E. 78. For exterior see Fig. 188. New photograph.

◄175. BOXERS WEARING σφαῖραι. B.-f. Panathenaic amphora. Archonship of Pythodelos, 336 B.C. British Museum, B. 607. New photograph.

175 *a*. BOXER FASTENING THONG WITH HIS TEETH. Detail from figure of boxer awaiting his turn on Fig. 175.

To understand Greek boxing we must realize the conditions under which it took place. Those conditions are chiefly responsible for the differences between Greek boxing and modern. In the first place there was no regular ring. Greek boxers had ample

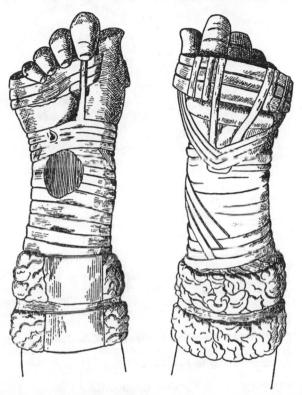

176. THE SHARP THONGS. Drawing of right hand of marble statue of boxer from Sorrento. Naples Museum. For the statue see Brunn-Brückmann 614, 615. This form of glove is similar to that worn by the Seated Boxer (Fig. 72). The British Museum possesses a small terra-cotta hand wearing a similar glove, *B.M. Guide to Greek and Roman Life*[2], Fig. 52.

space, and there was therefore no opportunity for cornering an opponent and fighting at the ropes. This tended to discourage close fighting and to encourage defensive and waiting tactics.

Secondly, there were no rounds in Greek boxing. The competitors fought to a finish. It might happen that both were exhausted and by mutual consent paused to take breath. But usually the fight went on till one or other acknowledged defeat

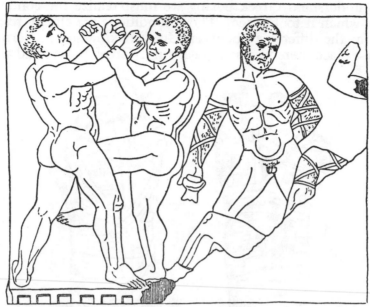

177. BOXERS AND PANKRATIASTS. Relief in the Lateran, Rome. 2nd or 3rd century A. D. *Röm. Mitt.* x, p. 120; Jüthner, *Ant. Turn.* Fig. 71. The caestus is here clearly shown as a semi-cylindrical case into which the hand is inserted with sharp projections over the knuckles. Cp. boxers in Mosaics, Figs. 70, 74. The pankratiasts too are very instructive with the brutal knee stroke.

178. BRONZE HALF FIGURE OF BOXER. National Museum, Athens, 7574. Photo from the Archaeological Institute, Athens. The caestus is similar to that in Fig. 177.

179. RELIEF IN THE LATERAN, ROME. Helbig, 1145. The right arm of the elderly boxer is restored. Helbig assigns the relief to the time of Trajan. It is popularly supposed to represent Dares and Entellus. If so it is an appropriate rendering of this fight, see p. 210. The gloves are a development of those shown in Fig. 176. See Jüthner, *Ant. Turn.* p. 85, n. 77. New photograph obtained for me by Dr. A. H. Smith.

180. ATHLETE ACKNOWLEDGING DEFEAT. Attic b.-f. neck-amphora. End of 6th century. British Museum, B. 271. New photograph. Here, as in Fig. 173, the victor is about to strike his fallen opponent who raises his left hand with open finger.

181. LAPITH GIVING CENTAUR A STRAIGHT LEFT ON THE JAW. Attic r.-f. column-krater. About 470 B. C. Florence, F.R. 166. The vase shows scenes from the marriage-feast of Peirithous. The Lapiths represent the trained Greek athletes in combat with their barbarous foes. The wrestling group is excellent: the young Lapith is almost lifted off his feet by the effort of swinging the ponderous monster who defends himself with a table. Equally good is the boxer's straight left.

182. IN-FIGHTING. Attic b.-f. stamnos. Late 6th century. Paris, Bibliothèque Nationale, 252. Vase of the same type as Fig. 163.

by holding up his hand as we see in Figs. 173 and 180. Nor was any grace allowed if a boxer fell: there was no rule against hitting a man when down (Figs. 173, 180). In such a fight forcing tactics do not pay: it is usually the clumsy or untrained boxer who forces the pace with consequences disastrous to himself. Caution was therefore the rule of the Greek boxer, and the fighting therefore tended to become slow.

Lastly, classification by weights was unknown to the Greeks. Competitions were open to all comers, and under the conditions described weight had perhaps a greater advantage than it has to-day. Consequently boxing tended to become the monopoly of the heavy-weight and therefore slower and less scientific. These conditions determined the whole history of Greek boxing.

The best period of Greek boxing is undoubtedly that of the sixth and fifth centuries as we see it depicted on the vases (Fig. 173). The boxer's position as he first 'puts up his hands' is excellent, his body upright, head erect, and left foot advanced. The left leg is usually slightly bent, the foot pointing forward while the right foot is sometimes at right angles to it, the correct position for a lunge. The left arm, which is used for guarding, is extended almost straight, the hand sometimes clenched, more often open (Figs. 182, 183, 184). The right arm is drawn back for striking, the elbow sometimes dropped, but usually raised level with the shoulder.

This sideways position with the left arm extended was an effective guard for the head, but left the body exposed in a manner that would be fatal in the modern ring. This brings us to one of the chief peculiarities of the Greek boxer. He confined his attention to his adversary's head and made no use of body blows, whether it was that he did not understand their value, or thought them bad form, or that they were actually prohibited. Philostratus, indeed, tells us that boxing was invented by the Spartans because they did not wear helmets, considering the shield the only manly form of protection.[1] They practised boxing in order to learn to ward off blows from the head and to harden the face. Further, in describing the physical qualities of the boxer he regards a prominent stomach as an advantage because it renders it less easy to reach the head! Without attaching too much value to such statements we may certainly infer from them that body blows were practically unknown in Greek boxing. Certainly they are never represented on the vases ; and even when in-fighting is

[1] *Gym.* 10, 23.

depicted (Fig. 182) the boxers are hammering at each other's heads, not at the body.

It would appear at first sight from the vases that the left hand was used almost exclusively for guarding, and the right hand for attack. For though the actual blow with the right is never represented, the right hand is almost invariably clenched and drawn back to strike. But this is certainly not the case. For it would seem that as long as the boxer kept his left arm extended it was only possible to reach his head with the right hand by stepping to the right so as to get outside his guard or by breaking down his guard. In the first place it was possible to deliver a swinging blow on the left side of the chin, the knock-out blow described by Homer and Theocritus. But as the opponent naturally met the movement by stepping himself to the right, the result was that the two circled round one another ineffectively. It can indeed seldom have been possible to bring off such a blow as a lead. Consequently an opening had to be made by sparring with the left hand. In this sparring the left hand was usually open (Figs. 184, 185). In Fig. 183 the boxer on the right has exposed his face and his opponent has shot out his left hand without even closing it. Indeed, whenever the actual blow is represented or one boxer is being knocked down or has been knocked down, the blow is delivered with the left (Figs. 186, 187). We may conclude, then, that the Greek was a two-handed boxer, and this conclusion is borne out by the descriptions of fights in Homer, Theocritus, and other writers.

The position of the right arm indicates that it was employed chiefly for round or hook hits, upper cuts, and chopping blows. Sometimes the right hand is swung back in preparation for a knock-out blow (Fig. 183). Sometimes it is raised as if for a chopping blow (Fig. 182). More rarely it is level with the shoulder, in which case a straight hit may be intended. On the other hand, with the left straight hits appear to be the rule, and as the left foot is advanced and the right foot is usually lifted from the ground, it appears that the force of the blow was obtained from a lunge. In Fig. 186 we have an illustration of a straight left on the temple, in Fig. 187 a boxer is knocking his opponent down with a straight left on the point of the chin. Fig. 181 is an excellent example of the way in which the Greek artists introduced motives from the palaestra into mythological subjects. The Lapiths in their fight with the Centaurs are always represented as trained athletes. Here we see one Lapith with his arms round

183. BOXER DELIVERING BLOW WITH OPEN
HAND. B.-f. Panathenaic amphora. Late 6th century.
Petrograd, Hermitage, Stephani, 76. *Compte Rendu*, 1876,
109.

184. BOXERS AND PRIZE TRIPOD. Fragment of b.-f.
situla. Middle of 6th century. Found at Naucratis. British
Museum, B. 124. New photograph.

185. BOXERS SPARRING WITH OPEN HANDS
ἀκροχειρίζεσθαι). B.-f. amphora of Panathenaic shape. Castle
Ashby. About 500 B.C. Photograph by Mrs. Beazley.

a Centaur's neck trying to heave him off the ground, another delivering a straight left at a Centaur's chin.

On the foot-work of the Greek boxers the vases naturally throw little light. But as they knew how to give force to a blow by lunging, it is probable that they understood the importance of not changing feet. Further, in all descriptions of boxing the value of quick foot-work is clearly recognized. Bacchylides describes the youthful Argeios of Ceos, a victor in the boys' boxing at the Isthmian Games, as 'stout of hand, with the spirit of a lion and

186. Boxer knocking opponent down. Attic r.-f. kylix; *Mon.* xi–xii, pl. XXIV. Tarquinia.

light of foot'.[1] In Philostratus we read: 'I do not approve of men with big calves in any branch of athletics, and especially in boxing. They are slow in advancing and easily caught by an opponent's advance.'[2]

Such appear to be the general characteristics of the Greek boxer of the fifth century. He used both hands freely, was active on his feet, and had a considerable variety of attack. His style resembled the freer modern style of boxing rather than the somewhat conventional, almost one-handed style that was traditional in England. From later literature we learn that he was an adept at dodging, ducking, and slipping. The defect of this style was the stiff high guard with the left hand, which cramped the attack and encouraged the use of downward chopping blows. As boxing

[1] Bacchylides, i.　　　　　　　　[2] *Gym.* 34.

became the monopoly of heavy-weights, the style became more cramped and the fighting slower. How hard it was to get within the guard of a big boxer we can see from Fig. 175, which gives a picture of two fourth-century heavy-weights. This was perhaps the reason for the introduction at the beginning of the fourth century of the sphairai and the 'sharp thongs'. But the remedy only made matters worse. A single blow with those sharp, cutting gloves would often decide the issue of the fight. The forearm, as we have seen, was protected by padding, and a thoroughly vicious style of boxing arose. The heavy-weight, instead of relying on his activity and skill, relied more and more on his stiff defence. He even practised holding up his guard for long periods so as to tire out his opponent. The absurdity of this style reaches its climax in the highly rhetorical tales of Dion Chrysostom. De-scribing Melancomas, the favourite of the Emperor Titus, he says that he could keep up his guard for two whole days and so forced his opponents to yield without even striking them.[1] The story is sufficiently remarkable, but Eustathius, writing many centuries later, succeeds in improving on it, and asserts that Melancomas 'killed his opponents' by these tactics, an illustration of the growth of the sporting story which may well make us distrustful of the statements of late commentators. Dion, however, was writing of his own contemporary, and his story is certainly evidence as to the style of boxing in his time. Such a defence explains the employment of those slogging blows which figure so largely in the descriptions of late Greek and Roman poets. In these descrip-tions we see the decay of scientific boxing; but the faults that developed in Hellenistic and Roman times should not be ascribed to Greek boxers of the fifth century.

Incomparably the best description of a fight which we possess is of that between Amycus and Polydeuces in the 22nd Idyll of Theocritus. It is a fight between a boxer of the old school who relies on science and activity and the coarse, braggart prize-fighter with whom the poet was perhaps familiar in Alexandria. The bully is sitting in the sunshine beside the spring, the muscles on his arms standing out 'like rounded rocks' just as we see them in the Farnese Heracles. His ears are bruised and crushed from many a fight. There he sits sullenly guarding the spring, and when Polydeuces approaches and with courtly grace craves hos-pitality, he challenges him to fight. The boxing thongs are ready to hand, not soft but 'hard' thongs. Straightway 'they made their

[1] *Orat.* xxix; Eustathius, ψ. 1322, 1324.

hands strong with cords of ox-hide and wound long thongs round
their arms'. A keen struggle ensued for position—which should
have the sun's rays at his back—and the more active Polydeuces
naturally outwitted his clumsy opponent. Exasperated at this
Amycus made a wild rush at Polydeuces, attacking with both
hands, but was promptly stopped by a blow on the chin. Again
he rushed in head down, and the Greeks feared that he would
crush Polydeuces by sheer weight in the narrow space; but each
time Polydeuces stopped his rushes with blows right and left on
mouth and jaw till his eyes were swollen and he could not see,
and finally knocked him down with a blow on the bridge of the

187. Boxing: a knock-out. B.-f. Panathenaic amphora. Late
6th century. Paris, Louvre, F. 278. *J.H.S.* xxvi, p. 222.

nose. He managed, however, to pick himself up, and the fight
began again; but his blows were short and wild, falling on his
opponent's chest or outside his neck, while the latter kept punish-
ing his face. At last in desperation he seized Polydeuces' left
hand with his left and tried to knock him out with a swinging
right-hander, 'driving a huge fist up from his right haunch'. It
is an admirable description of a knock-out blow, but he was too
slow; the very act of seizing his opponent's hand—an obvious
breach of the rules—spoilt his effort. Polydeuces slipped his head
aside and with his right hand struck him on the temple, 'putting
his shoulder into the blow', and he followed it up with a left-
hander on the mouth 'so that his teeth rattled'. After this he
continued to punish his face with quick blows till 'Amycus sank
fainting on the ground and begged for mercy'.

It is a truly masterly description, and shows us that Theocritus
thoroughly understood boxing and that at the beginning of the
third century the science of boxing still survived. It is a fight
between science and brute force. Amycus has the advantage of
height and weight, but he has no science and blunders hopelessly.

He rushes in head down, hits wildly with both hands, and neglects his guard. Polydeuces acts on the defensive, allowing the bully to exhaust himself, avoids his rushes by dodging or ducking, or stops them by well-aimed blows on the face. There can be little doubt that he used a straight left.

About a century later we have another description of the same fight in the *Argonautica* of Apollonius Rhodius,[1] a vivid description, for he, like Theocritus, understands what he is describing, but we notice in it a decided increase in brutality. The gloves are not the *sphairai* of Theocritus but the 'sharp thongs' of the boxer of the Terme. Amycus has manufactured them himself, 'rough and dry with hard ridges round them'. Amycus makes the fighting, Polydeuces retreating and dodging; but at last he stands his ground and a fight ensues so fast and furious that both men, utterly exhausted, break away and pause by mutual consent. After a moment they spring at one another again, and Amycus 'rising on tiptoe to his full height' aims a swinging blow at Polydeuces 'like one who slays an ox'. Polydeuces slips aside and, before his opponent can recover his balance, steps past him and deals him a swinging blow above the ear which not only knocks him out but kills him. The conclusion is an obvious imitation of Homer; an imitation, not an improvement. Apollonius has introduced a detail of his own when he makes the bully 'rise on tiptoe', but he knows that this is not boxing, it is 'like one that slays an ox'. Virgil imitates him, but he does not understand, and thinks it is heroic boxing.

The character of the fight between Entellus and Dares in the *Aeneid* is clear from the description of the caestus. Entellus throws into the ring the caestus of the hero Eryx, made of seven ox-hides stiff with iron and lead, and still stained with blood and brains, and at their sight Dares and all the host tremble. 'What!' cries Entellus, 'do these frighten you? What if you had seen the weapons of Heracles?' By the advice of Aeneas these murderous and clumsy weapons are rejected, but the point of interest is that the poet's Roman ideas have led him to reverse the whole history of boxing. We have seen how the caestus developed from the soft thongs of Homer. But, to the Roman, murder and bloodshed are the very essence of a fight. Therefore as the heroes of the past excelled the men of to-day in physical strength, they must have excelled them in the bloodiness of their fights and the murderous brutality of their weapons.

[1] ii. 25–97.

Both men rise on tiptoe and hammer each other as hard as they can. Entellus, who is the bigger man, for a time acts on the defensive, keeping his more active opponent at a distance. At last, tired of such tactics, he makes a big effort: rising on tiptoe he ostentatiously lifts his arm on high, thus giving Dares full notice of what is coming. Dares, of course, dodges the ponderous blow, and Entellus, unable to recover his balance, falls to the ground. Exasperated by his fall he picks himself up and chases Dares all round the ring till Aeneas in mercy stops the fight. Thereupon, baulked of his vengeance, he vents his rage and exhibits his strength by killing with a single blow the ox which is the prize. What a contrast to the finish in the *Iliad*, where the great-hearted Epeius picks up his fallen opponent and courteously sets him on his feet! What a contrast even to Theocritus and Apollonius! There the fight is between science and brute strength. Here both men are as devoid of science as Virgil is ignorant of boxing; if either of the two has any claim to science it is the defeated Dares. The relief in Fig. 179 is popularly supposed to represent Dares and Entellus. If so, it is a fitting counterpart to the poet's description!

A still more absurd result occurs in Statius. The lighter and more skilful boxer is declared the victor, but is only saved from the fury and vengeance of his opponent by the intervention of Adrastus, who separates them. But the brutalities and absurdities of these later fights need no discussion. Caestus-fighting may have appealed to the Roman crowd, but it was not boxing.

THE PANKRATION

THE pankration was a development from the primitive rough-and-tumble fight. The object was, as in boxing, to force the opponent to acknowledge defeat, and to this end almost any means were allowed. Such a contest may appear at first sight barbarous and brutal. But we must remember that it was conducted under strict rules, and these rules were enforced by the trainers or officials with the rod. Further, we know that the Greeks regarded it as a contest requiring not only endurance but the highest skill. No fewer than eight of Pindar's Odes are in honour of pankratiasts. Indeed the pankration finds its modern counterpart in jiu-jitzu, which is beyond doubt the most highly scientific of all systems of self-defence. Hardly anything was allowed in the pankration which is not allowed in jiu-jitzu. There was, of course, an element of danger, but as Pindar says, 'deeds of no risk are honourless'.[1] Serious injuries and indeed fatal accidents did sometimes occur, but they were rare, rarer probably than in boxing, or in football, or in the hunting-field to-day.

The best account of the pankration is given by Philostratus [2] in his description of the death of Arrhichion, the famous pankratiast who expired at the very moment when his opponent acknowledged himself beaten, and though dead was awarded the crown. 'Pankratiasts', he says, 'practise a hazardous style of wrestling. They must employ falls backward which are not safe for the wrestler and grips in which victory must be obtained by falling. They must have skill in various methods of strangling; they also wrestle with an opponent's ankle, and twist his arm, besides hitting and jumping on him, for all these practises belong to the pankration, only biting and gouging (ὀρύττειν) being prohibited. The Spartans allow even these practices, but the Eleans and the laws of the games exclude them, though they approve of strangling.'

The prohibition of biting and gouging is evidently a quotation from the rules. It is twice quoted by Aristophanes.[3] Biting needs no comment. The meaning of 'gouging' or 'digging' is clear from Aristophanes. It means digging the hands or fingers into an

---

[1] *Greek Athletics*, p. 435; *J.H.S.* xxvi, pp. 4–22.
[2] *Im.* ii. 6. [3] *Aves* 442; *Pax* 899.

opponent's eyes, nose, mouth, or other tender parts of the body. It is vividly illustrated in Fig. 188, where a pankratiast has inserted his thumb and finger into his opponent's eye, and the official is hastening up with rod uplifted to punish this infraction

188. Boxers, pankratiasts, hoplitodromos. Attic r.-f. kylix. About 480 B.C. British Museum, E. 78. *J.H.S.* xxvi, pl. XIII. For interior see Fig. 174. Two pankratiasts struggling on the ground. Trainer interferes to stop 'gouging'.

of the rules. In Fig. 189 we have a similar scene, where a pankratiast forces his hand into the mouth of his fallen opponent. Facing one another, much in the position of a pair of wrestlers, the combatants try to bring one another heavily to the ground by wrestling, hitting, or kicking. There is much preliminary sparring (ἀκροχειρισμός). The hands are uncovered and, as is natural in such a competition, generally open, though the clenched fist is also used for hitting. Both are represented in a most realistic scene reproduced in Fig. 190. The fallen competitor bleeds freely from the nose, while the marks of his opponent's blood-stained hand is visible on his back. His opponent, springing on him, grasps one hand with his left hand and prepares to finish him off with his right. As in boxing, there was no rule against hitting a man when down. But as a general rule the contest was decided on the ground, and, when both competitors were down, hitting was usually ineffective.

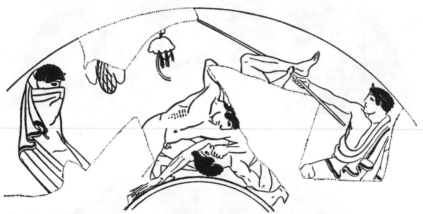

189. Pankratiast gouging. Attic r.-f. kylix. About 480 B.C. Baltimore. Hartwig, *Meisterschalen*, lxiv; *J.H.S.* xxvi, p. 9.

The relative importance of hitting and wrestling depended largely on the individual. The tall man with a long reach natu-rally relied most on hitting, the short, thick-set man on wrestling. In Figs. 191, 192 we see boxing and wrestling combined. One pankratiast has got his opponent's head in chancery and is pummelling him. In Fig. 193 a tall athlete is springing on his opponent to strike him, and the latter, a shorter man, seems to be catching his uplifted leg.

The last motive is clearly shown in Fig. 196. Here the athlete on the right seems to have been kicking the other, who, having caught his foot, passes his hand under his leg and is about to tilt him backwards. Kicking was an essential part of the pankration. In Theocritus[1] Polydeuces, challenged to fight by Amycus, inquires if it is to be a boxing match or whether kicking is to be allowed; and Galen,[2] in his skit on the Olympic Games,

[1] xxii. 66.   [2] Προτρεπτ. 36.

awards the prize for the pankration to Brayer, the donkey, as
the best of all animals at kicking. Kicking[1] in the stomach
(τὸ γαστρίζειν) was as favourite a trick in the pankration as it is
in the *savate*. The epithet 'hazardous', by which Philostratus
characterizes the wrestling of the pankration, appropriately describes such throws as 'the flying mare' and various foot- and leg-
holds which, though too risky for proper wrestling, were freely
employed in the pankration, where it was not sufficient to throw
an opponent, but he must be thrown heavily.

190. Pankratiast hitting fallen opponent. Fragment
of Attic r.-f. kylix. Late 6th century. Berlin, 2276.
Hartwig, *Meisterschalen*, Fig. 12. *J.H.S.* xxvi, p. 8.

A wrestler who was thrown on his back was defeated, but
a pankratiast might intentionally throw himself on his back in
order to throw his opponent more heavily or to throw him in
a worse position. A manœuvre of this sort, called the heel-
trick (τὸ ἀποπτερνίζειν), was invented, we are told, by a Cilician
athlete, nicknamed 'the Dumb-bell'.[2] On his way to compete at
Delphi he visited the shrine of the hero Protesilaus and asked
how he was to secure victory in the pankration. The hero replied, 'By being trampled on'. At first he was puzzled, but after
a little he realized that the hero's advice meant that 'he was not
to let go his opponent's foot: for the man who wrestles with the
opponent's foot must be constantly trampled on and underneath
his opponent'. So he devised 'the heel-trick', by means of which
he won great renown. This is probably the trick which Philostratus describes as 'wrestling with the ankle'. Such a hold en-
sures a heavy fall; but the peculiarity of the Dumb-bell's method
was that instead of merely throwing his opponent he retained his
hold on his foot and by twisting or bending it forced him to yield.

[1] Lucian, *Anacharsis*, 9; Aristoph. *Eq.* 272, 454.
[2] Philostratus, *Heroic.* 53, 54.

This foot-lock is well-known in jiu-jitzu. Arrhichion, we are told, forced his opponent to yield by twisting his foot out of its socket.

191. PANKRATION. B.-f. Panathenaic amphora. Archonship of Niketes, 332 B.C. British Museum, B. 610. *J.H.S.* xxvi, pl. IV.

192. PANKRATION. B.-f. Panathenaic amphora. Signed by Kittos, 4th century B.C. British Museum, B. 604. *J.H.S.* xxvi, pl. III.

Another throw in which a wrestler throws himself on his back is the stomach-throw. Seizing his opponent by the shoulders or arms he throws himself backwards, at the same time planting his foot in his stomach, and thus throwing him heavily over his head.

This favourite throw of the Japanese is depicted in the tombs of Beni-Hassan. Pindar probably refers to it when he describes Melissus as in craft like to the fox that spreadeth out her feet

193. PANKRATION. Attic b.-f. amphora of Panathenaic shape. Late 6th century. Vienna. *J.H.S.* i, pl. VI.

194. Heracles and Antaeus. B.-f. hydria. Late 6th century. Munich, 1708. *A.Z.* 1878, x; *J.H.S.* xxvi, p. 21.

and preventeth the swoop of the eagle.[1] It is perhaps represented in Fig. 194. Here Antaeus lies on his back with his right hand grasping Heracles' foot, and his left foot kicking him in the stomach. Antaeus, it seems, has tried the stomach-throw, but, as usual, has failed.

[1] *I.* iii. 65.

195. PANKRATIAST KICKING. Bronze statuette, found at Autun. Gallo-Roman work. Louvre, 1067. de Ridder, *Bronzes du Louvre*, i, pl. 63.

196. KICKING AND LEG-HOLD. B.-f. Panathenaic amphora. Beginning of 5th century. New York, Metropolitan Museum, 16.71. Photograph from Met. Museum. Here and in a very similar scene on a lost Panathenaic vase, *Mon. d. I.* I. xxii, one of the pankratiasts seems to have kicked his opponent who has caught his leg and is tilting him backwards.

197, 198. ARM-LOCKS. Bronze wrestling groups in the British Museum. Hellenistic period. In both cases the standing pankratiast has applied an arm-lock which must force the other to yield. See *J.H.S.* xxv, p. 290; *Greek Athletics*, p. 395; Sieveking in *Bronzen der Sammlung Loeb*, p. 52, where a full list of replicas is given. New photographs.

199. PANKRATION ON THE GROUND. Marble group of wrestlers in Uffizi, Florence. *Photo. Brogi.* Copy in marble of bronze about 300 B.C. This group was much broken and it is difficult to be certain how much of it is correctly restored. Both heads are restored; the right arm of the upper figure, probably his left arm, and his left leg and knee; the left arm of the figure underneath. See Hans Lucas in *Jahrb.* xix (1904), p. 127; *J.H.S.* xxv, p. 30; xxvi, p. 19.

200. ON THE GROUND. Attic b.-f. skyphos. About 500 B.C. New York, Met. Museum, 06.1021.49. Photograph from Met. Museum. The close resemblance of this vase to the Florence group goes far to justify the restoration of the victor's upper arm.

Locks applied to an opponent's limbs or neck were as distinctive of the pankration as of jiu-jitzu, and for the same reason —that they forced him to acknowledge defeat. Opportunities for applying them were more frequent when one or both the combatants were on the ground, where the struggle was usually decided. The best examples of arm-locks (τὸ στρεβλοῦν) occur on a group of bronzes already noticed. In Fig. 197 we see a thick-set bearded man wrestling with a youth. Both are still on their feet. The man has turned his opponent round and with his right hand draws the other's right arm across his thigh, while he has slipped his left arm under his left arm-pit and gripped his neck, thus rendering his imprisoned arm useless and applying a leverage similar to that of our half-Nelson. Perhaps the grip was obtained in the following way. The man seizes the youth's right arm, and by a quick movement pulls him towards him and turns him round, at the same time stepping to the left so as to be behind him. He then slips his left hand under his armpit. The grip obtained he turns to the right so as to twist him off his balance. In this position he can throw him, and I formerly thought that the group represented upright wrestling. But the real object of this lock on the right arm seems to be to produce pain and force the opponent to give in. If he does not do so, his arm will be broken. Moreover, the position could be reached more easily if the youth had been first forced on his knees and the other was on the top of him. That this interpretation is correct is rendered certain by a second group of bronzes.

In Fig. 198 one of the wrestlers is resting on one knee, the other stands over him. He has hooked his left leg in a vine-lock round his opponent's left leg; with his right hand he forces down his head, while with his left hand he presses back his right arm in the same way as in our first group. Here the object can only be to inflict pain. Moreover, it would be hardly possible for the victor to fix the leg-lock unless they had both been on their knees and he on the top. In a variation of this group the victor forces the other's neck down with his left hand, while with his right hand he has twisted his arm and shoulder backwards.

The Eleans, we have seen, especially commended 'strangling' as a means of defeating an opponent. This seems to us especially brutal; yet after all it is no more brutal than a knock-out blow on the neck or jabbing an opponent in the solar plexus or over the heart. Here, too, we have the parallel of jiu-jitzu. The Japanese not only practice the throat-hold, but develop the muscles of the throat so as to resist it. Moreover, a trained pankratiast would realize when his opponent had secured a grip which might cause serious injury, and would at once give in before harm could come. A strangle-hold can be obtained by any neck-grip, but the favourite method employed was the so-called 'ladder-trick' (κλιμακισμός). The attacker jumped on his opponent's back, twined his legs round his body and his arms round his neck. This trick could be employed while both men were still on their feet or when they were struggling on the ground. Both forms are represented in the Tusculum Mosaic, Fig. 70. It was the hold commonly employed by Heracles against the Triton or Achelous, and is constantly mentioned in literature. The struggle on the ground was probably as long and as complicated as it is in modern wrestling, the combatants sometimes sprawling at full length, sometimes on the top of one another, sometimes on their knees. It was this part of the pankration that Plato objected to and that made him exclude it from his ideal state as useless for military training because it did not teach men to keep their feet. Perhaps the pankratiast, like the modern wrestler, was apt to take to the mat, or rather the mud, in order to avoid the heavy falls or blows that he might receive while on his feet. If so, it was a sign of the decay of the sport. Pindar specially emphasizes the importance of boxing in the pankration, and ground wrestling is very seldom represented on fifth-century vases. Indeed it is practically confined to the contest between Heracles and Antaeus (Figs. 201, 202). It occurs frequently on later gems, but the best illustration of it is the well-known group of wrestlers in the Uffizi Gallery at Florence (Fig. 199). Unfortunately this group is badly mutilated, yet a comparison with the very similar composition on a vase (Fig. 200) makes it probable that the restoration is mainly correct.[1] Both are on their knees; the uppermost wrestler, with his legs twined round his opponent's body, has bent back his right arm with his left hand, and with his right seems preparing to hit him. The other, supporting himself on his left arm, looks round eagerly watching to take advantage of any momentary carelessness on his part. We may illustrate this from the story of Arrhichion to which allusion has already been made. His opponent was on top of him with arms and legs twined round him and was strangling him. But Arrhichion, even as he breathed his last, took advantage of a momentary relaxation of the grip to kick his right leg free and, rolling

[1] See *J.H.S.* xxvi, p. 19.

over, seized his opponent's right foot and twisted it with such force that he acknowledged defeat.

Sports like wrestling and the pankration naturally lend themselves to variations of rules and of style. Though the great national festivals of Greece tended to produce uniformity, local rules undoubtedly existed. Of such rules we have an example in an inscription, probably of the second century A. D., found at the village of Fassiller in Pisidia, containing rules for some local sports. The pankratiasts are not to use sand (ἀφή) to dust themselves with like wrestlers, nor are they to use wrestling, but to contend with upright hitting (ὀρθοπαλίᾳ). In other words, there is to be no wrestling, no struggle on the ground, only fighting with bare hands and perhaps kicking. It is further laid down that a man who has won one prize must not compete again the same day, while if a slave is successful, he must give up a quarter of the prize-money to the other competitors.[1]

[1] *Papers of the American School of Classical Studies at Athens*, iii, no. 275; *C.R.* xliii, p. 210.

A GREEK ATHLETIC FESTIVAL

I HAVE described the various events that made up the athletic programme of a Greek festival. Now let me try to picture a typical festival. I will take the Olympic festival about the middle of the fifth century; it is the greatest of all Greek festivals, and the half-century that followed the Persian wars was its most splendid period. It is thus the festival and the period of which we know most. At the same time it must be remembered that our knowledge of it is very imperfect and often derived from late authors. Many of the details of the festival, the order of events for example, are uncertain, but the general outlines are clear. We shall see at least that though the actual competitions are in many respects similar to our own, the Olympic festival was something very different from any modern athletic meeting, even from the modern Olympic Games. It was much more than a mere athletic meeting. It was the national religious festival of the whole Greek race. Olympia was the meeting-place of the Greek world.

First let us look at Olympia itself. The situation is strangely beautiful, beautiful with a peaceful charm that we rarely feel in that land of rugged mountains. Some faint idea of its beauty may be formed from our illustration (Fig. 203), which shows a view of Olympia looking eastwards from the hill of Drouva on the right bank of the Cladeus. There we see the river Alpheus cutting its way in many shifting channels through the rich alluvial plain. Immediately below us is the valley where its northern tributary the Cladeus rushes to join it along a ravine—hardly visible in our picture—between banks once bordered with plane trees. In the angle between the two rivers the broken hills that form the northern side of the Alpheus valley end in a conical pine-clad hill, the hill of Cronus. The trees at its foot still mark the site of the ancient grove that gave to the precinct its name of the Altis. There was no wall round it in the fifth century, only perhaps a hedge marking its boundary. The space within was crowded with temples, shrines, altars, and statues. Immediately at the foot of the hill was the long low temple known as the temple of Hera, a joint temple probably of Zeus and Hera. But this was completely dwarfed by the newly erected temple of Zeus that stood a little to the south. Raised on a solid platform of masonry, it rose on massive Doric pillars to a height of over sixty feet, dominating the whole Altis. We have already seen something of the sculptures that adorned its pediments and metopes (Figs. 20, 35). It was here that, a few years later, the great gold and ivory statue of Zeus by Pheidias was placed. But more important than any temple was the great Altar of Zeus, built up of the ashes of the sacrifices, the fire of which was kept burning perpetually. It stood a little farther north. It was the centre of the worship of Olympia, the altar of the oracle of Zeus, the chief altar of sacrifice. The open space east of it was commanded by a terrace along the foot of the hill supported by a stepped wall that formed a sort of grand stand, and on this terrace stood a row of small temples, called Treasuries, raised by the piety of various Greek states. In this open space probably all the sports had of old taken place on an improvised race-course ending at the Altar. But since the Persian wars the authorities of Olympia had been busy making the Sanctuary worthy of the festival. At the east end of the Treasury terrace they had built a covered colonnade, and beyond it had laid out the permanent stadium already described, and to the south of it a hippodrome.

The festival took place every four years, on the second or third full moon alternately after the summer solstice, in the months of August or September. Some months before the three sacred 'truce bearers of Zeus' set out from Olympia wearing crowns of olive and bearing heralds' staves. They travelled through the length and breadth of the Greek world, and to every state they proclaimed the Sacred Truce and invited them to the festival. From that time all competitors or visitors travelling to or from Olympia were under the protection of the god.

Competitors, it seems, had to arrive at Elis a month at least before the festival; and there they underwent the last part of their training under the eyes of the Hellanodikai, the official judges of the games. The training at Elis was noted for its severity: the Hellanodikai exacted implicit obedience and enforced it unsparingly with the rod. During this month they could test the capabilities of the candidates, and satisfy themselves of their parentage, for only those of pure Greek birth were allowed to compete. Above all, they had an opportunity for judging the claims of boys and colts to compete as such. Philostratus tells us that at the close of the training they called together the competitors and addressed them in these words:

'If you have exercised yourselves in a manner worthy of Olympia, if you have been guilty of no slothful or ignoble act, go on with a good courage. You who have not so practised go whither you will.'[1]

Meanwhile, visitors of all classes and from every part were flocking to Olympia. The whole Greek world was represented, from Marseilles to the Black Sea, from Thrace to Africa. There were official embassies representing the various states, richly equipped; there were spectators from every part, men of every class. Men, I say: for the only people excluded from the festival were married women, and even if unmarried women were allowed to be present, few probably availed themselves of the right except those from the neighbourhood. Apart from this Olympia was open to all without distinction, to hardy peasants and fishermen of the Peloponnese and to nobles and tyrants from the rich states of Sicily or Italy. All had the same rights. There was no accommodation for them except such as they could provide or procure for themselves; there were no reserved seats at the games, indeed there were no seats at all. The plain outside the Altis was one great fair, full of tents and booths. There you might meet every one who wished to see or to be seen, to sell or to buy: politicians and soldiers, philosophers and men of letters, poets ready to write odes in honour of victors in the games, sculptors to provide them with statues, perhaps already made, horse-dealers from Elis, pedlars of votive offerings, charms, and amulets, peasants with their wine-skins and baskets of fruit and provisions, acrobats and conjurers, who were as dear to the Greek as to the modern crowd (Fig. 205).

The festival lasted five days, from the twelfth to the sixteenth of the month. The first day was occupied with preliminary business and sacrifices, there were no competitions. The principal ceremony was the solemn scrutiny of the competitors in the Council House. There stood a statue of Zeus Horkios, the God of Oaths, who was represented with a thunderbolt in either hand ready to blast any who broke his oath. Before this awe-inspiring statue the competitors, their trainers, their fathers, and their brothers took their stand, and, having sacrificed a pig, swore on its entrails that they would use no unfair means to secure victory. The competitors further swore that for ten months they had trained in a manner worthy of the festival. Then the judges who decided on the eligibility of boys and colts to compete as such

[1] Vit. Apollonii, v. 43.

swore to give their decisions honestly and not to reveal the reasons for their decisions.

Throughout the day there were many other sacrifices and rites, both public and private, of which we know nothing. Competitors would offer their vows at the altars of the various gods or heroes whom they regarded as their patrons. The superstitious would consult the soothsayers as to their chances of success. Others would go off to the Stadium for a final practice. The crowd of sightseers would wander round the Altis, following in the train of some celebrity, athletic or otherwise, admiring the sculptures of the new temple, or listening to some rhapsodist reciting Homer, some poet reading his verses, some orator displaying his eloquence or sophistries. There were friends, too, to be seen, friends from all parts of the Mediterranean, for all came back to Olympia as to their mother-country.

The games started on the second day with the chariot-race and the horse-race. The Hippodrome lay to the south of the Stadium, the embankment of which bounded it on the north. Like the Stadium, it was merely a long rectangle surrounded by embankments, but larger. The actual course was marked by a pillar at either end round which the chariots and horses turned, but there was no wall, like the spina of the Roman Circus, connecting them. Not a trace of the Hippodrome remains and its dimensions are very uncertain. According to a document found at Constantinople, of somewhat doubtful authority, the distance between the pillars was three stades or about 600 yards. Elsewhere the distance was two stades.

At the western entrance of the Hippodrome was a colonnade, the portico of Agnaptos, and in front of it was a most elaborate starting-gate. Pausanius describes it as shaped like the prow of a ship, the sharp end pointing down the course. Its sides were 400 feet long and along them were arranged parallel pairs of stalls in front of each of which a rope was stretched. Here the competing chariots or horses were placed (Fig. 204). In the centre of the structure was an altar on which stood an eagle with outstretched wings; at the point was a bronze dolphin. When the official starter touched a piece of mechanism the eagle rose in the air and the dolphin dropped. This was the signal for starting, but we may suspect that it was not really given till the chariots were actually in line. The manner of starting was as follows. First the ropes in front of the pair nearest to the base were withdrawn, and the chariots started. As they drew level with the next pair, the ropes in front of these were withdrawn, and so on till when they reached the peak of the prow all were in line. The object of this elaborate arrangement must have been chiefly spectacular, and the racing did not actually start till all were in line. Whether this complicated starting-gate existed in the fifth century, we do not know. In the description of the chariot-race at Delphi in the *Electra* of Sophocles, there is no suggestion of any starting-gate. The chariots were drawn up in a line and started by the trumpet.

Early in the morning the crowds began to gather in the Hippodrome, occupying every place of vantage, especially at the ends where the chariots turned and accidents were most frequent. There were no seats except for the officials. The spectators sat or stood on the embankments, bareheaded under the scorching sun, often, as the day wore on, suffering severely from thirst and dust. There they waited till the official procession arrived. First came the Hellanodikai, or judges, robed in purple with garlands on their heads, the herald, trumpeter, and other officials, then the competitors, the chariots, and the horses. The judges took their seats and, as the chariots and horses passed before them, the herald proclaimed the name of each competitor, his father's name, and his city, and asked if any man had any charge to bring against him. Then he proclaimed the opening of the games and the chief Hellanodikas or some other distinguished person addressed the competitors.

The first event was the four-horse chariot race, the most brilliant and exciting of all the competitions, the sport of kings in the Greek world; for only the rich could afford the expense of a racing stable. The chariots were light cars mounted on two wheels, with a rail in front and at the sides, and room only for the charioteer to stand. The two middle horses who did the work were harnessed to the yoke attached to the chariot-pole, the outside horses were harnessed only by traces. The charioteer wore a long white robe, he carried a whip or goad, and held the reins in his left hand or in both (Fig. 35).

Once more the herald proclaimed the names of the competitors: lots were drawn for position, and the names perhaps were written on a white board. Then the chariots took their places at the start, the trumpet sounded, and the race began. The fields were large, sometimes as many as forty chariots competing. Alcibiades boasted that he himself had on one occasion entered seven chariots. Fortunately the course was long, twelve double laps,

72 stades or nearly 9 miles, and the pace must have been slow at first. But it must have been a thrilling sight to see a field of even ten chariots such as Sophocles describes in the *Electra*, all racing for the turning-post at the far end of the course. For to be first round the turn must have been a great advantage. It is no easy task to turn a team of four horses sharp round a post, but to do so in a field of ten chariots or more, all striving to be first, must have tasked nerve and skill to the utmost. No wonder that accidents were frequent. For it was not one turn only, but twenty-three turns, that the charioteer had to negotiate: and few must have been the chariots that reached the last lap safely. We

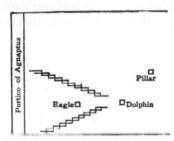

204. The Starting Gates of the Hippodrome at Olympia.

are not surprised that in the race where forty chariots competed the chariot of Arcesilaus of Cyrene alone survived.[1] When the last lap was reached the excitement of the spectators knew no bounds, they shouted, leapt from their seats waving their garments, wildly embracing one another.

When the race was over the owner of the victorious chariot advanced and bound a fillet round the head of his charioteer. For though in heroic times the heroes drove their own chariots, the rich nobles and princes of the fifth century, like rich owners to-day, employed professional charioteers and jockeys. The owner, however, as he does to-day, received the prize. Leading, perhaps, his chariot, he advanced to the place where the judges sat. Beside them was a table of gold and ivory on which were placed the crowns of olive leaves cut from the sacred wild olive tree behind the temple of Zeus. Then the herald proclaimed the name of the victor, his father, and his city (Fig. 207), and the chief Hellanodikas placed upon his head the crown[2] (Fig. 208),

[1] Pindar, *P.* v. 47.
[2] An imaginative writer has recently described the victor as 'ritually crowned upon a table'!

while the people shouted and pelted him with flowers and branches.

Next came the horse-race. It was started in the same way, but the distance was only one lap of six stades. The jockeys rode without shoes or stirrups (Fig. 206). The horse-race and the four-horse chariot-race were the only events in the Hippodrome at the beginning of the fifth century. Early in the century, a riding race for mares and a mule chariot-race were introduced, but these events were discontinued in 444 B.C. In 408 B.C. a two-horse chariot-race was added, and in the next century three races for colts.

When the horse-races were finished the crowd hurried over the embankment to the Stadium to witnesss the pentathlon. The first four events in this competition, the foot-race, the long jump, the diskos, and the javelin, took place in the Stadium, the last event, the wrestling-match, in the open space in front of the Altar. The details of these events have been described in the preceding chapters and need not be repeated.

The pentathlon occupied the rest of the day. Then in the evening, under the brightness of the mid-month moon, the precinct rang with revelry and song. The victors and their friends, with garlands on their heads, went in joyous procession round the Altis, chanting as they went the old triumphal hymn of Heracles, written by Archilochus, or some new hymn of victory composed by Pindar or Bacchylides. The procession was followed by banquets given by the victors to their friends. Sometimes a rich victor like Alcibiades would feast the whole assembly, and the revelry would last the whole night.

The third day, the day of the full moon, was the great day of the festival, when the official sacrifice was offered on the Altar of Zeus. The procession started from the Prytaneion. First came the Hellanodikai in their purple robes, the seers and priests, the attendants leading the victims for the sacrifice; then the Theoriai, the official deputations from the states of Greece, having in their hands costly vessels of silver and gold; after them the competitors, chariots, horsemen, athletes, trainers, and their friends. The procession moved along the boundary of the Altis, passed between the Council House and the Temple of Zeus, then made its way through the avenue of statues and monuments in front of the Temple to the Great Altar. The priests and seers mounted the ramp that led to the platform in front of the Altar, and there in the sight of all the people a hundred oxen were sacrificed. The thighs were taken to the top of the Altar and burnt, the rest of the flesh was removed to the Prytaneion to be cooked for the feast.

The sacrifice took place in the morning. In the afternoon the competitions for boys took place, the foot-race, wrestling, and boxing, and the evening was given up to revelry. The chief athletic events were reserved for the fourth day. The morning was occupied by the three foot-races in the Stadium, the afternoon by the three fighting events, wrestling, boxing, and the pankration. These last took place, not in the Stadium, but in the Altis, in front of the Altar. Here the ties were drawn in the presence of the Hellanodikai. Lots marked in pairs with the letters of the alphabet were put into a silver urn. Each competitor uttered a prayer to Zeus and drew a lot, holding it in his hand but not looking at it till all were drawn. Then the Hellanodikas went round and examined the lots, pairing off the competitors accordingly. The programme ended with the race in armour, and once more there was an evening of revelry.

The last day of the festival was spent in feasting and rejoicing. The victorious paid their vows at the altars of the gods. Of the other rites and sacrifices that occupied the day we know nothing, save that the victors were entertained at a banquet in the Prytaneion.

XVIII

BALL PLAY

BALL play [1] has been the recreation of the young of both sexes from time immemorial, and in its simpler forms is the same to-day as it was in ancient Greece or Egypt. The grace and rhythm of its movements appealed particularly to the Greeks. In Homer we find it combined with dance and song. Nausicaa and her maidens, having finished their washing, take to playing ball, and as they play they sing. The young Phaeacians, as they dance, toss to and fro a fair purple ball. Naturally, in the life of the palaestra and gymnasium, ball play occupied an important place. In contrast to athletic competitions it was suited to both sexes and to all ages. Sophocles in his youth was distinguished for his grace and skill at ball play. Alexander the Great and Dionysius the tyrant were fond of the game. There were special rooms (*sphairisteria*) for ball play in the palaestra, and there were teachers called *sphairistai*, who were often held in high honour. Among the Romans who disliked athletics ball play was very popular. The Roman gentleman played ball before bathing or to give him an appetite for the evening meal. Many of them had ball courts in their private villas. In the public baths there were professional ball players (*pilicrepi*) who picked up the balls and kept the score for players and also gave exhibitions of their skill.

Balls were usually made of strips of leather sewn together and were of various sizes. The smallest called *harpastum* (ἄρπαστον) was a hard ball stuffed with hair. The *pila* and *pila paganica* were larger balls stuffed with feathers, while the largest ball, the Roman *follis*, seems sometimes to have been filled with air, like the Italian 'pallone' or football.

Some of the games have been mentioned already. Many of them were merely variations of catch-ball and required no fixed number of players, indeed a player could play by himself (Fig. 214). Thus in the game called sky-ball (οὐρανία) a player threw a ball up in the air and the other players tried to catch it, or he might catch it himself. In Fig. 209 we see a variety of this game similar to one which we have also met with in Egypt (Fig. 1).

[1] For ball-games generally see Grasberger, *Erziehung und Unterricht*, i, p. 84; Krause, *Gymnastik*, p. 299; Dar.-Sagl. *s.v.* pila.

Three players are riding pick-a-back on three others while a trainer prepares to throw a ball to one of them. Possibly a player who missed it had to dismount and take the other on his back. A form of ball game very popular among the Romans was called the *Trigon* or triangle. The players were placed at the three angles of a triangle, and threw or struck the ball to one another. There is an endless variety of such games. Another important group consisted of games where the player bounced a ball against the floor or a wall and struck it back with his hand, counting the number of strokes. Out of this game developed modern games like fives and racquets. But in these games we miss the element of competition which is so marked a feature in modern ball games. There is nothing really athletic about them.

There were, however, other ball games of a more distinctly athletic character, and recent discoveries have revealed to us the existence even of team games and competitions among the Greeks. Ball games were particularly popular at Sparta and were so important that the name Ball players (σφαιρεῖς) was used to designate young Spartans in the first year of manhood. The excavations at Sparta conducted by the British School have brought to light a number of inscriptions dating from the time of the Antonines which record victories won by Spartan boys at some yearly competition.[1] The competition took place in the Dromos or race-course under the direction of a board of officials called Bideoi, who were responsible for the management of the Ephebic games. The teams represented the 'obes' or local districts of Sparta. Each team was under a Captain or Elder (πρέσβυς). We do not know the exact number of players in a team, but it cannot have been less than fifteen. The competition was conducted on the tournament system, for several inscriptions mention that the winning team had not drawn a bye. The prize seems to have been a sickle, which is represented at the head of the inscriptions; it probably had some religious significance. We do not know how the game was played, but there can be no doubt that it was sufficiently strenuous. The only Spartan game of which we have any details is that known as Platanistas. It was played on an island of the same name surrounded by ditches. Two teams of boys entered by bridges at opposite ends and each strove by fighting, hitting, kicking, even biting, to drive their opponents into the water. But for the absence of the ball the game bears no little resemblance to some of the primitive foot-

[1] See *Greek Athletics*, p. 184; *B.S.A.* x, p. 63, xiii, p. 212.

ball matches which were formerly played in the streets of some
of our towns.

Writers on the history of Rugby football are fond of finding
an ancient parallel to their game in the game of *harpastum*, a
game played with a small hard ball of the same name, and popular
alike among Greeks and Romans. In this they are probably
misled by an interesting paper by Mr. G. E. Marindin [1] in which
he tried to reconstruct *harpastum* as a game played between
teams on a ground marked out like a football ground with a centre
line and two goal lines. But for this reconstruction there is
absolutely no evidence. Our most valuable authority on ball
games is the Grammarian Julius Pollux [2] who lived about A.D. 180.
Now Pollux does describe a team game played on such a ground,
but he called it ἐπίσκυρος, and inasmuch as he says nothing of
the sort about *harpastum*, the probability is that it was not a team
game and was not played on a ground so marked at all. Further,
Mr. Marindin supposes that Galen's treatise on 'Exercise with
the Small Ball' refers to this game and to no other. Now Galen's
small ball may or may not be the *harpastum*, but there is no
reason to suppose that the small ball was used exclusively for one
game. A cricket ball may be used for games of catch, for throwing
competitions, for hockey: the uses of the tennis ball are number-
less. Moreover, Galen's work is not on *the Game* with the small
ball but on *Exercise* with the small ball, or, as he says in his first
chapter, *Exercises*.

This small ball, he argues, provides exercises suited to people
of all ages and conditions, from the most gentle exercise to the
most strenuous, according to the requirements of the player. A
player who wants the gentlest exercise plays standing still or with
quiet movements, and after a little play is massaged with oil and
has a hot bath. This is the form of play suitable to old men and
children. Some forms exercise the arms most, some the legs,
some all parts of the body a little. The most strenuous form of
play, and here Galen may be thinking of the game of *harpastum*,
is when the players form a scrimmage round the player in the
centre and try to prevent him from seizing the ball, tackling him
by the neck or the body and using all the holds of the wrestling
ring. In fact with the small ball a player can get just the sort of
exercise and the amount that he requires. This is excellent from
a medical point of view, but is quite incompatible with the description of any particular game. It would be a strange game

[1] *C. R.* 1890, p. 145.   [2] ix. 103.

indeed where every player could not only choose his own part in the game but also how much or how little he has to exert himself.

Let us see now what is the evidence that we possess about *harpastum*. The inquiry is an interesting illustration of the difficulty of forming any accurate idea of an ancient game. Our chief authority is Athenaeus,[1] a native of Naucratis, who in the beginning of the third century of our era wrote a book called the *Deipnosophistai*, or Professors of the Supper Table, an extraordinary medley of antiquarian knowledge. He tells us that *harpastum* is his favourite game, that it is a violent and exhausting game, involving a special strain on the neck owing to the tackling to which Galen also, as we have seen, refers. He also tells us that the game was originally called *phaininda*, a word of uncertain derivation which, it is agreed, denotes 'feinting', deceiving an opponent by pretending to throw the ball to one player and throwing it to another. The word *harpastum*, on the other hand, denotes 'snatching' or 'intercepting the ball'. These two ideas, 'feinting' and 'intercepting', give us the essential features of the game. As an illustration Athenaeus quotes a passage from the comic poet, Antiphanes, who lived in the fourth century before Christ. He is describing a player of *phaininda*.

'When he got the ball he delighted to give it to one player while dodging the other; he knocked it away from one and urged on another with noisy cries . . . "Outside, a long pass, beyond him, over his head, a short pass . . ."' The passage is unfortunately mutilated, there are some words wanting in the middle, and the last words are unintelligible and cannot be restored with any certainty. Without more knowledge of the game it is impossible to be sure of the translation, but the general meaning of the passage is clear; it describes two or more players passing the ball to one another so as to avoid a player between them. There is no suggestion of centre line, or goal lines, but such a game certainly suggests an enclosed space, possibly a circle formed, as in so many country games, by the players themselves, in the middle of which is one player who tries to intercept the ball as it is thrown across the circle, or perhaps the players are drawn up in two lines facing one another. There is some slight support for the view that the players stood in a circle from a passage in the dictionary of the grammarian, Isidorus,[2] who speaks of 'the circle of players standing by and waiting', but as the passage is quite unintelligible as it stands, little weight can be attached to it.

[1] i, p. 14. [2] xviii. 69.

This is all that we know for certain about the game of *harpa-stum*. The frequent mention of it by the poet Martial attests the popularity of this and other ball games in the first century A.D., but gives us no new information. It is usual, however, to refer to this game an interesting passage in a letter of Sidonius Apollinaris which has been used without the slightest justification to emend the passage from Antiphanes quoted above.[1] Sidonius was a wealthy Roman noble and landowner in Gaul who played a prominent part in the troubled history of the fifth century, retired from politics, became Bishop of Clermont, and was venerated as a saint. From his letters we learn that ball play and dice were the ordinary recreations of the well-to-do inhabitants of Gaul. In their luxurious country mansions they had special places for ball play. On his own estate at Avitacum he tells us of a grassy sward under two great lime trees where he and his friend Ecdicius used to play ball.[2] In describing a visit to the estates of two wealthy friends,[3] he tells us that as soon as you entered the house you would see pairs of ball players facing one another with the balls flying round and round, backwards and forwards. The letter with which we are concerned describes a festival at the church of St. Justus. In the long interval between the services, Sidonius and a party of his friends sat and talked in a vine-covered arbour. Growing tired of this, one party went off to play dice, another, led by Sidonius, to play ball. While the game was going on, an elderly man, Filimatius, who had been a great player in his youth, came and joined the ranks of the players, who were 'standing' waiting their turn. How they were standing, in a circle or in a line, we are not told. Anyhow, he was constantly being forced to leave this position and join in the active play by the 'mid-runner' (*impulsu medii currentis*). Did the mid-runner actually push him or throw the ball to him, or call him out? Anyhow when he came out into the field 'he could neither intercept or anticipate the course of the ball as it flew now past him, now over his head'. So in trying to turn sharply (*per catastropham*) he was constantly losing his balance and with difficulty recovering himself, and at last he retired from the game out of breath and very hot.' If this is the game of *harpastum*, the mid-runner must apparently be the player in the centre who intercepts the ball, and Filimatius, perhaps having dropped the ball or being tackled with it in his possession, has become the mid-runner. It is impossible to say. But one thing is certain. If this game is

[1] v. 17.   [2] ii. 2.   [3] ii. 9.

'harpastum', *harpastum* is not a team game. For it is impossible for a player to join in a team game and retire at his pleasure. Further, if it is the game of *harpastum*, we have an extraordinary example of the conservatism of games, for our scanty evidence begins with Antiphanes 380 B.C., and ends with Apollonius about A.D. 460!

It is not in *harpastum* but in a very different game, *episkyros*, that we really find anticipations of Rugby football, at least in the arrangements of the ground. Pollux evidently regards it as the most important of ball games and explains it carefully. The game, he says, is also known as *epikoinos*, or 'the team game', and as *ephebike* because it was the special game of the epheboi, youths, it will be remembered, between the ages of seventeen and eighteen, who were submitted to a severe physical and military training. It may well have been the game that the Spartan boys played, though we do not know. It was played, says Pollux, between teams of equal numbers. In the centre of the ground between the two teams they marked out a white line with chippings of gypsum or stone, from which the line was called *skyros* or *latype*. At some distance behind each team was another line, the goal line. The ball, says Pollux, was placed on the centre line. Then those who had secured it first—how they secured it he does not say—tried to throw it over and beyond their opponents, whose task it was to catch the ball and throw it back till at last one side was forced back over its goal line.

The description given by Pollux is clear as far as it goes. Fortunately we are able to illustrate it from a relief discovered at Athens in 1922 which from its style seems to belong to the end of the sixth century (Fig. 212). It is the earliest and indeed the only representation in Greek or Roman art of a true team game, and, like most works of that period, is extraordinarily vivid. We see six players, three on each side, between whom we must suppose is the *skyros*, or centre line. There is, of course, nothing to be inferred as to the numbers of the players, the artist had not room for more than six figures. But it is quite clear that the players are not drawn up in a line, but at intervals behind one another, like the forwards, half-backs, full-backs, in our own games. The team on the left has got possession of the ball; whether they have caught it, or whether the scene represents the beginning of the game, we cannot say; the latter seems to me more likely. At any rate they are attacking. The full-back, who possibly acts as skipper, is preparing to throw the ball. The other two are advancing to charge

211. Interior of r.-f. kylix. Late 6th century. Louvre, G. 36. Youth about to throw ball: cp. the position of the left-hand player in Fig. 213.

212, 213. Reliefs from the same wall at Athens as Figs. 53, 54.

212. BALL GAME BETWEEN TWO TEAMS, probably the game called *Episkyros*.

213. GAME WITH CLUB AND BALL RESEMBLING HOCKEY, the game known as κερατίζειν.

214. DRAWING OF A GAME LIKE HOCKEY IN FOURTEENTH-CENTURY MS. in the British Museum. B.M. Postcards, Set 58, *Medieval Sports and Pastimes*. An interesting parallel to the Greek relief, Fig. 213. The position of the sticks and ball is precisely similar.

down or hustle their opponents and prevent them from catching or throwing it back. The half-back, with his eye on the thrower, advances vigorously, the forward more cautiously. Perhaps they were not allowed to overstep the centre line till the ball was thrown. The team on the right stands ready to catch the ball. The centre player is on the alert with hands outstretched. The full-back or skipper, with a characteristic gesture, calls on the forward to fall back. The ball is somewhat larger than a cricket-ball and was presumably light, so that it could not be thrown too far. Of the details and rules of the game we know nothing, but we know enough to see that it was a really first-class team game and might, but for the predominance of field and track athletics, have developed like our own ball games, but we must remember that this development has only taken place in the last century.

The same wall at Athens provided yet another and still greater surprise. For another relief (Fig. 213) represents what seems at first sight to be no more or less than a hockey bully. Two players with curved sticks are hooking a ball, while four other players holding similar sticks look on. Yet we cannot feel certain that the game is a team game, for the other players seem to be merely looking on, or waiting their turn, and not to be taking part in the game. This however does not seem to me to be decisive. A curious parallel occurs in a drawing on a fourteenth-century manuscript in the British Museum, which is equally difficult of explanation (Fig. 214).

Previous to this discovery we were completely ignorant of the existence of such a game. The use of a stick, club, or bat to hit a ball is so natural and so widespread that it must have been known to the Greeks. The Irish played hockey or hucky in the second century A.D.; polo must have been known to the Persians at least as early. Yet in the whole of Greek and Roman literature there was, as far as we know, not a single allusion to the use of such an instrument before the twelfth century, when Cinnamon, the Byzantine historian, gives a vivid description of a kind of polo in which the players use a sort of racket strung with cords as in Lacrosse. Yet it appears that we might have known the name of the game all the time. For Plutarch describes a statue in a ball court at Athens representing the orator Isocrates as a boy κερητίζων, using a horn or horn-shaped implement. Editors, thinking the word unintelligible, inferred that the text was corrupt and altered the text to κελητίζων, riding. But when our relief came to light, it was pointed out at once, by a Greek archaeologist,[1] that the manuscript reading was undoubtedly correct and that the boy whose statue stood in a ball court was not riding but playing ball with the *keras*. It is a salutary warning against emending a manuscript because one does not understand a word.

Finds like these make us realize how very fragmentary is our knowledge of ancient games, and warn us against dogmatizing about them. They fill us, too, with expectations of further finds to lighten our darkness. Shall we one day discover a representation of Greek boys playing football? The Chinese certainly played football at an early date: the Italians in the Middle Ages had their game of Calzio. The Greeks and Romans had an air-filled ball, the 'follis', and they surely must have discovered how conveniently it could be propelled by the foot. For the present we do not know: we can only hope for future discoveries.

[1] M. Oikonomos in Ἀρχ. Δελτ. 1920–1.

SELECTED BIBLIOGRAPHY

ALEXANDER, CHRISTINE. Greek Athletics. New York, 1925.

BERGER, MARCEL, and ÉMILE MOUSSAT. Anthologie des textes sportifs de l'antiquité. Paris, 1927.

BRAUCHITSCH, GEORG VON. Die Panathenäischen Preisamphoren. Leipzig, 1919.

FORBES, CLARENCE A. Greek Physical Education. New York, 1929.

FÖRSTER, H. Sieger in den Olympischen Spielen. Zwickau, 1891, 1892.

FREEMAN, K. J. Schools of Hellas. London, 1917.

FROST, K. T. Greek Boxing. *J.H.S.* xxvi. 213.

FURTWÄNGLER, A. Die Bedeutung der Gymnastik in der Griechischen Kunst. Leipzig, 1905.

GARDINER, E. NORMAN. Greek Athletic Sports and Festivals. London, 1910. History and Remains of Olympia. Oxford, 1925.
The Method of deciding the Pentathlon. *J.H.S.* xxiii. 54; Notes on the Greek Foot-race, *ib.* xxiii. 263; Phayllus and his Record Jump, *ib.* xxiv. 70; Further Notes on the Greek Jump, *ib.* xxiv. 179; Wrestling, *ib.* xxv. 14, 263; The Pankration and Wrestling, *ib.* xxvi. 4; Throwing the Diskos, *ib.* xxvii. 1; Throwing the Javelin, *ib.* xxvii. 249; Panathenaic Amphorae, *ib.* xxxii. 179.
The Alleged Kingship of the Olympic Victor, *B.S.A.* xxii. 85.

GARDINER, E. NORMAN and LAURI PIHKALA. The System of the Pentathlon. *J.H.S.* xlv. 132.

GIRARD, P. L'Éducation athénienne. Paris, 1889.

GRASBERGER, L. Erziehung und Unterricht im Klassichen Altertum. Würzburg, 1864.

HYDE, W. W. Olympic Victor Monuments and Greek Athletic Art. Washington, 1921.

JÜTHNER, JULIUS. Antike Turngeräthe. Wien, 1896.
Philostratus über Gymnastik. Leipzig, 1909.
Körperkultur im Altertum. Jena, 1908.
Das Problem des Myronischen Diskobols. *Jahreshefte*, xxiv. 123; Die Zylindrischen Halteren, *Rom. Mitt.*, xliii. 13; Gymnastes, and Gymnastik in Pauly-Wissowa.

KRAUSE, J. H. Die Gymnastik und Agonistik der Hellenen. Leipzig, 1841.
Olympia. Vienna, 1838.
Die Pythien, Nemeen und Isthmien. Leipzig, 1841.

MEHL, ERWIN. Antike Schwimmkunst. Munich, 1927.

SCHRÖDER, BRUNO. Der Sport im Altertum. Berlin, 1927.

WILKINS, A. S. Roman Education. Cambridge, 1905.

For a fuller bibliography see *Greek Athletic Sports and Festivals*. For a fully illustrated account of Tait McKenzie's Athletic Sculpture see *Tait McKenzie*, by Christopher Hussey, London, 1930.

LIST OF COMMON ABBREVIATIONS

INDEX AND GLOSSARY

INDEX OF MUSEUMS AND COLLECTIONS

The references are to the numbers of the illustrations. Museum numbers are printed in italics

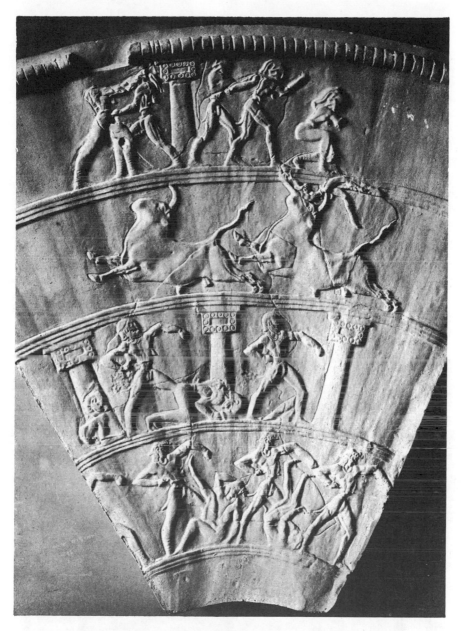

3. BOXER VASE FROM HAGIA TRIADA, ABOUT 1600 B.C.

Candia Museum. Photograph from facsimile in Berlin
from Professor G. Rodenwaldt

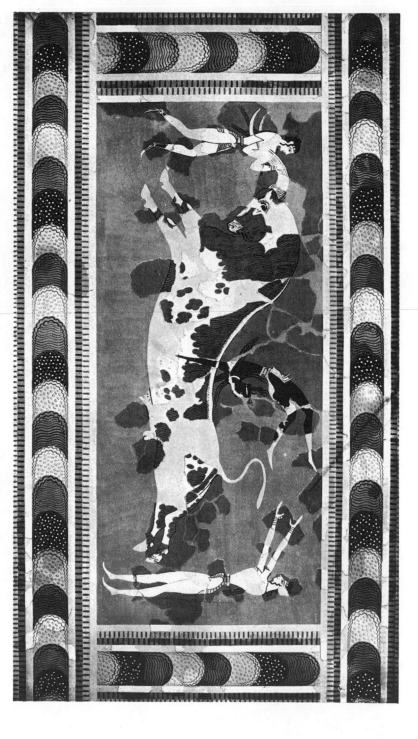

4. BULL-GRAPPLING FRESCO FROM PALACE OF CNOSSUS ABOUT 1600 B.C.

Photograph of facsimile of fresco, as restored, in the Ashmolean Museum, Oxford

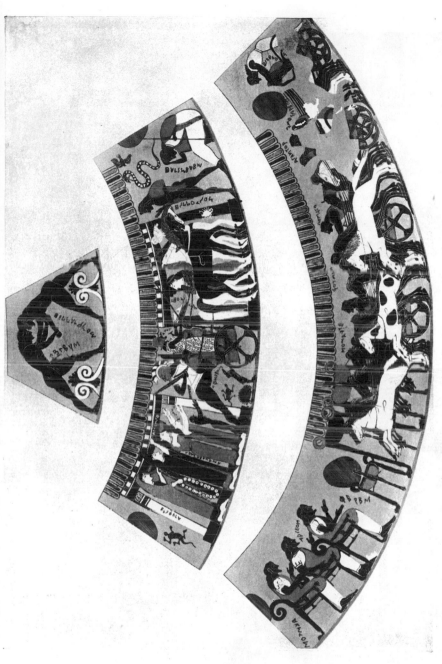

8. THE AMPHIARAUS VASE. B.-F. CORINTHIAN COLUMN-KRATER, EARLY 6th CENTURY

Berlin 1655, *F.R.* 121

Top. Wrestling match, Peleus and Hippalcimus, cp. Fig. 155, p. 188.   Middle. Departure of Amphiaraus.
Bottom. Chariot-race. To left three judges seated. In front of them three tripods, the prizes. Six chariots racing

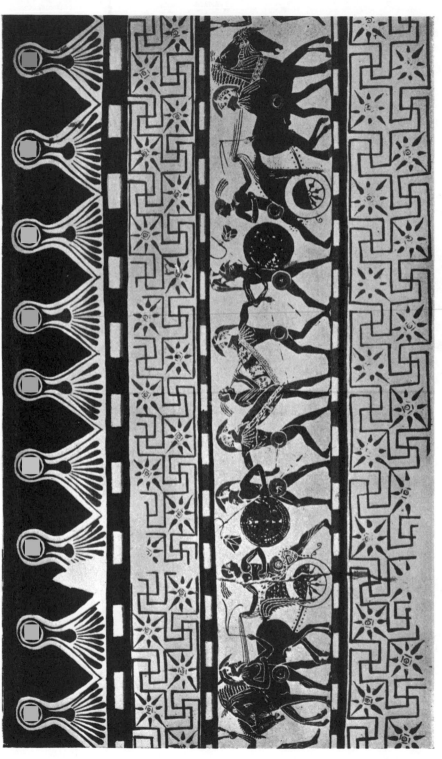

9. THE ARMED COMBAT. SCENE FROM CLAZOMENAE SARCOPHAGUS IN BRITISH MUSEUM. 6th CENTURY. Murray, *Sarcophagi in B.M.*, pls. II–VIII

On either side chariots preparing for the race. In centre two warriors fighting. They are armed with helmets, shields and swords. Between them a youth playing the double-pipe. The chariot-race itself is shown on the other side of the sarcophagus, also pillars bearing bowls for prizes

11

12

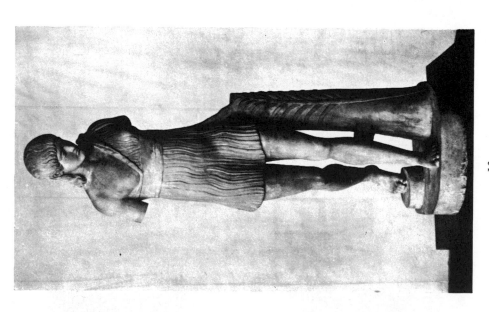

14

13

15

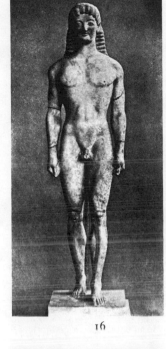

16

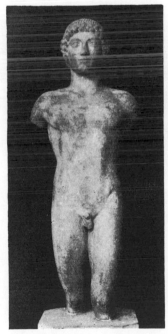

17

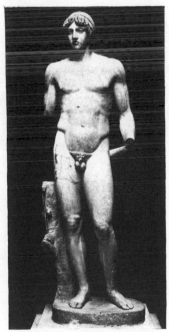

18

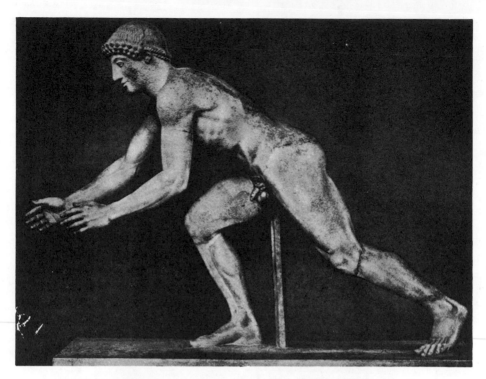

19

20

BRONZE HEAD OF BOY VICTOR

Either an original work of about 420 B.C. or a good copy. Munich. Sieveking &
Weickert, *Fünfzig Meisterwerke der Glyptothek*, XVIII

22

23

24

25

26

27

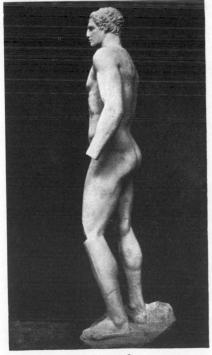

28

29

30

31

32

33. Figure from E. pediment of the Parthenon, generally known as Theseus. British Museum. 438–433 B.C.

34. Lapith from the W. pediment of the temple of Zeus at Olympia. About 460 B.C. Olympic Museum. Buschor and Hamann, *Die Skulpturen des Zeustempels zu Olympia*

THE ATHLETE AT REST AND IN ACTION

a   b   c

d   e   f

g   h   i

j   k   l

m   n

37

38

40

41

44

45

46

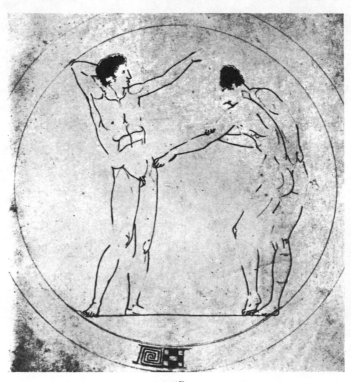

47

_a_

_b_

_c_

53

54

55

56

57

58

60 *a*

60 *b*

61

62

63

64

65

68

69

71

72

73

74

74. PROFESSIONAL ATHLETES OF THE EMPIRE. Mosaic found in the baths of Caracalla, Rome, Lateran, P. Secchi, *Musaico Antoniniano*. This huge mosaic contains portraits of famous athletes and trainers of the period. In our illustration we see full-length figures of a trainer and a boxer, and two busts. The form of the caestus with its two projecting spikes is clearly shown (cp. Figs. 177, 178). The cropped hair with its unsightly top-knot, *cirrus*, is typical of the professional athlete. *Photo. Anderson*

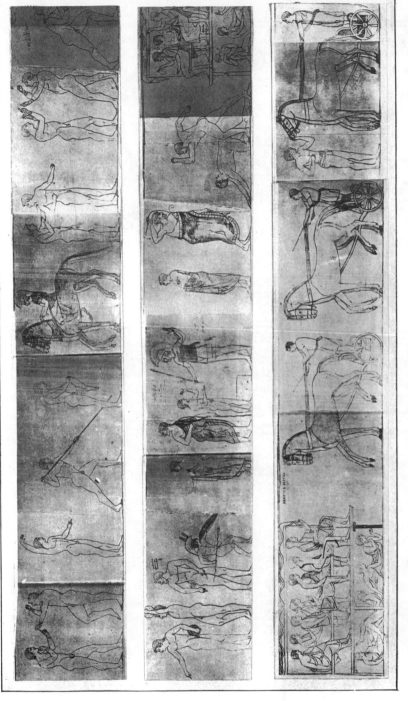

75. ETRUSCAN GAMES. Wall-painting from Tomba delle Bigne. Corneto. About 500 B.C. After a drawing by Stackelberg. *Jahrb.*, xxxi, pl. VIII. The athletic scenes in the two top lines are drawn directly from palaestra scenes on Greek vases.
Top line. From left to right—boxers, the oil pourer, cp. Fig. 44, youth mounting horse by means of pole, cp. Fig. 58, youth using strigil, cp. Fig. 60, boxers, wrestlers.
2nd line. Diskoboloi—boy with shield and spear dancing—spectators and warrior—pankratiasts and trainer using whip, cp. Fig. 188—part of grandstand—the upper classes sit on a raised stand under an awning—the lower classes sprawl below.
3rd line. Grandstand and parade of chariots.

77

78

82

83

85

86

89

88

90

92

93

94

95

105

106

107

108. PHOTOGRAPH OF THE WINNER OF THE LONG JUMP
in a match between Aldenham School and Mill Hill School

**109. PHOTOGRAPH OF L. G. D. CROFT (L.A.C.) WINNING
THE LONG JUMP**

112

113

114. DISKOS-THROWER; THE BACKWARD SWING

Interior of r.-f. kylix, Boston, of which the exterior is
given in Fig. 105

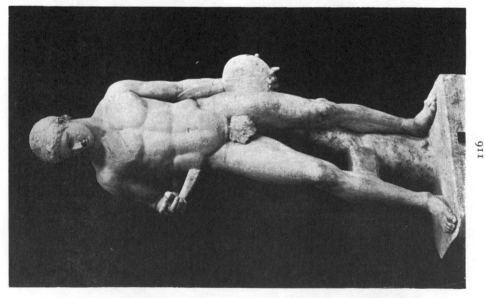

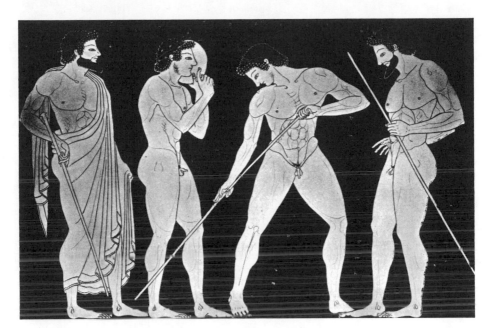

123

124

125

126

127

128

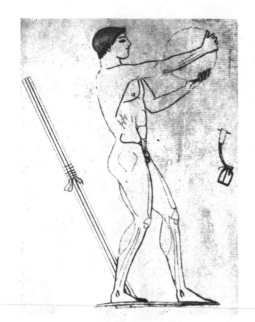

129

130

131

139

140

143

144

145

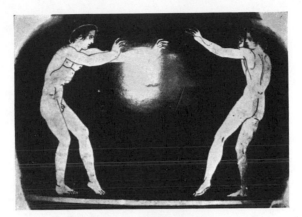

152

153

154

a

b

156

157

159

160

161

162

163

169

170

171

172

174

175

178

179

180

181

184

185

195

196

197

198

199

200

201. Attic r.-f. krater. About 520 B.C. Louvre. G. 103. *F.R.* 92

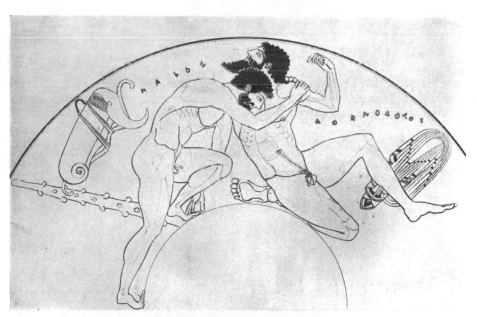

202. Attic r.-f. kylix. About 490 B.C. Athens. Nat. Mus. 1166. *J.H.S.*, x, pl. 1; xxvi, p. 10

HERACLES AS PANKRATIAST

203. View of Olympia. Photograph by Bernard Ashmole, *Olympia*, Fig. 1

205. ACROBATS AT A FESTIVAL. Attic B.-f. amphora of Panathenaic shape. Middle
of 6th century. Bibliothèque Nationale, 243. Salomann, *Nécropole de Camiros*, pl. LVII.
This scene with its stand of spectators has a very oriental appearance

206. HORSE-RACE. B.-f. Panathenaic amphora. About 470 B.C. Goluchow.
Photograph by Mrs. Beazley. See *Vases in Poland*, pl. II

A GREEK FESTIVAL

207. HERALD PROCLAIMS THE VICTOR IN THE HORSE-RACE.
ΔVΝΕΙΚΕΤV: ΗΙΓΟϚ: ΝΙΚΑΙ. 'The horse of Dysneiketos is victorious.' Behind the horseman youth carrying tripod, the prize for the race. Attic b.-f. amphora of Panathenaic shape. 3rd quarter of 6th century. British Museum, B. 144

208. VICTOR WREATHED IN FILLETS IS CROWNED BY JUDGE. Attic
b.-f. amphora of Panathenaic shape. Late 6th century. British Museum, B. 138

THE VICTOR IN THE GAMES

209. A BALL GAME. Attic b.-f. lekythos. Late 6th century. Oxford, Ashmolean Museum, 260. A bearded man prepares to throw a rather large ball. Three youths mounted pick-a-back are ready to catch it. Between two of them is inscribed κέλευσον, 'Give the order', the application of which is not clear. A similar scene occurs on a b.-f. amphora in the B.M. 182, where the man throwing the ball is seated. On the B.M. krater E. 467 satyrs are depicted playing the same game. See P. Gardner, *Gk. Vases in the Ashmolean*, 260

210. A BALL EXERCISE. Relief on sepulchral lekythos. 4th century B.C. Athens. Conze, *Die attischen Grabreliefs*, 1046, ii. 2, pl. CCIII. The motive is not easy to determine. It may be a mere exercise of balance: more probably the youth is bouncing the ball on each thigh alternately.
Photo. Alinari

212

213

214